POSTMODERN POLITICS IN GERMANY

Postmodern Politics in Germany

The Politics of Resentment

Hans-Georg Betz

St Martin's Press   New York

First published in the United States of America in 1991

Printed in Hong Kong

ISBN 0-312-04881-5

Library of Congress Cataloging-in-Publication Data
Betz, Hans-Georg, 1956–
Postmodern politics in Germany: the politics of resentment/Hans
-Georg Betz.
p.   cm.
Includes all bibliographical references.
ISBN 0-312-04881-5
1. Germany (West)—Politics and government—1982–   2. Grünen
(Political party)   3. Fascism—Germany (West)   4. Right and left
(Political science)   I. Title.
JN3971.A2B48   1991
320.5'0943—dc20   90–39843
                                                            CIP

For my parents

Contents

List of Tables   viii

Preface   ix

Introduction: The Postmodern Challenge   **1**

1 The Transformation of the New Left   **19**

2 From Green to Red   **42**

3 Postmodern Politics and the Greens   **63**

4 Postmodern Anti-Modernism   **89**

**5 The Politics of Discontent: Right-Wing Radicalism in West
   Germany**   **110**

6 The Dialectics of Postmodern Politics   **133**

Conclusion: The Future of Postmodern Politics   **158**

Notes   171

Bibliography   177

Index   193

List of Tables

3.1 New middle class value preferences 67
3.2 Distribution of materialist and postmaterialist value types within social groupings 68
3.3 Value priorities and political preferences by social groupings 72
3.4 Percentage Green preference by education, age and economic circumstances 76
5.1 Right-wing radical support: social and educational background 116
5.2 Individual perceptions of social location 117
5.3 Percentage value preferences 118
5.4 Support for immigrant groups 124
6.1 Attitudes towards German unification 141
6.2 Attitudes towards Western Alliance and the presence of American troops in Europe 145
6.3 Attitudes towards European integration 149
6.4 Attitudes towards foreigners in West Germany 152

Preface

The idea that modernity has run into serious problems and may have ground to a halt lies at the heart of a heated debate in contemporary Western intellectual circles over the notion of postmodernism. Most of the recent debate on postmodernism has focused on developments in architecture, literature, the arts, photography, cinema and social theory. Although a number of books have appeared explicitly dealing with the politics of postmodernism, little has been published on postmodern politics. This study seeks to fill some of that void. It challenges especially political scientists to think about the repercussions of the postmodern condition on the realm of politics. In particular it is concerned with the impact of the disintegration of advanced industrial societies on party politics.

A second purpose of this study is to come to terms with the recent developments in West German society. As I began my research on the evolution of postmodern politics in West Germany, I had little idea to what degree this would turn out to be an account of the hopes and frustrations of my own generation. This might help explain the emotions which I suspect might have found entrance into parts of this work. As of now, developments whose unfolding I only sensed rather vaguely when I started this project have begun to influence and shape German politics. The most important of these developments is of course unification. Promoted a few years ago only by fringe groups on both the left and the right, while the rest of the political establishment had abandoned its serious pursuit for all practical purposes, it has come close to being achieved at the time of writing. The rapid changes in Germany have made writing on German affairs both exciting as well as frustrating. However, I do suspect that once the last clouds of dust from the Berlin Wall have finally settled, the period covered in this study will help us understand the future course of a united Germany.

I have received support, criticism and encouragement from many people throughout this project. Its roots lie with the dissertation which I completed in the Department of Political Science at MIT. Suzanne Berger served as the chair of the thesis committee. Much of my thinking about political science has been influenced by her warm support, incisive criticism and steady encouragement. I owe particular gratitude to William E. Griffith, whose constant support, penetrating insights into the workings of West German politics and above all friendship have been invaluable to me. I have also greatly benefited from discussions with a number of my friends at MIT, particularly Carol Conway whose enthusiastic support was a constant source of inspiration.

I am pleased to acknowledge the research funding I received from the Bradley Institute for Democracy and Public Values of Marquette University in Milwaukee and from the Center for European Studies in Cambridge, Massachusetts. I am particularly grateful to Dieter Roth from the Forschungsgruppe Wahlen in Mannheim and Werner Harenberg from the Spiegel-Verlag in Hamburg for giving me the opportunity to use their surveys. I would also like to thank Karen Greenstreet at Marquette University for her helpful comments on an earlier draft and Sabina Bhatia for her patient support and encouragement. I have also greatly benefited from critical comments by Herbert Kitschelt and John McAdams. Finally I would like to thank my parents for their help and support. Their untiring willingness to track down various publications, their generous financial support and their patience and understanding have contributed immeasurably to this project. It is to them that I dedicate this book.

Earlier versions of parts of this book appeared in the following articles: '*Deutschlandpolitik* on the Margins: On the Evolution of Contemporary New Right Nationalism in the Federal Republic,' *New German Critique*, no.44 (Spring/Summer 1988); 'Strange Love? How the Greens Began to Love NATO,' *German Studies Review* 12, no.3 (October 1989); 'Value Change and Post-Materialist Politics: The Case of West Germany,' *Comparative Political Studies* 21, no. 2 (July 1990); and 'Politics of Resentment: Right-Wing Radicalism in West Germany,' *Comparative Politics* 22, no. 1 (October 1990).

HANS-GEORG BETZ

Introduction:
The Postmodern Challenge

We live in a time of transition. As yet it is uncertain whether the changes we see occurring all around us at an increasingly accelerated pace will lead to something completely new, transforming our way of understanding ourselves and the shape of our culture and politics, or whether they are a mere reflection of a wary, yet giddy excitement accompanying the approach of the *fin-de-millennium*. However, a growing number of critical observers of our age seem to expect something new and most probably would agree with the following statement:

> Our world, for good or ill, has begun to operate on principles different from those that have dominated much of the century and we tend to see ourselves as part of a culture that we may not altogether understand but which we can recognize as being 'after' what we have known. (Stevick, 1985, p. 136)

What is this new culture, still in formation, but already influencing the way we conceive of this world? Over the last decade this culture has come to be known as 'postmodernism.' Postmodernism has penetrated art collections, television, undergraduate curricula, politics, rock music, interior decorating, airline magazines, the list goes on. From the elegant neo-classicism of Rowes Wharf in Boston, the brassy Mediterranean flair of Washington Port in DC to Ricardo Boffill's monumental spatial structures imposing a vision of a world turned stage-set descending upon the *banlieues* of Paris, postmodern architecture has invaded the city, playful and exhilarating, shocking and more often than not just plain ugly. The same is true for the arts and literature. With Eric Fischl and David Salle the postmodern malaise has found its visual poets, their sets populated by the reflections of 'suicidal nihilism' wallowing in a mixture of 'excremental culture and hyper-aestheticism' (Kroker and Cook, 1986, p. 8) that reflects the daily banality and boredom of life in the suburbs, a search for 'desperate pleasures' in forbidden exposure (Storr, 1984) staged to forget for a while the sickening affluence that pervades the post-

1

industrial West. In the monumental myths/histories of Gabriel Garcia
Marquez, Carlos Fuentes and Isabel Allende, in the absurd world of
laughable loves and farcical lives created by Milan Kundera and
Botho Strauss, postmodernism has established its own pre-history
grounded in a self-generated past. More than anywhere else, however,
postmodernism has staked its ground in the mediascape, in the space
between 'TV or MTV,' C-SPAN, CNN, Home Shopping Network and
CBN, ranging from the nostalgic 1960s pastiche of the 'Wonder Years'
and the sociologically carefully balanced dramas of 'Family Ties' and
'Who's the Boss?' to the caricatures of TV redemption, Jim and
Tammy Bakker (Kroker and Kroker, 1987, p. 17) side by side with
Spuds McKenzie, Pee-wee Herman, ALF and David Letterman's
'stupid pet tricks.' Finally, on its most mundane level, postmodernism
celebrates its own triumph in the fake forests and fake marble halls of
the global shopping mall, where the self-appointed vanguard of the
société de consommation (where anything can be bought and everything is on sale, where 'to speak of intrinsic value is mere
sentimentality' [Gitlin, 1989, p. 56]) lives out its dream of commodi-
fied power.

Confronted with this invasion of distinctly postmodern styles it is
difficult not to come to the conclusion that postmodernism is
conquering virtually all fields of cultural production and reproduction.

After more than twenty years the Post-Modern Movement has
achieved a revolution in western culture without breaking anything
more than a few eggheads. It has successfully challenged the reign of
Modern art and architecture, it has put Positivism and other
twentieth-century philosophies in their rightfully narrow place,
brought back enjoyable modes in literature without becoming
populist and has slowed, if not halted altogether, the wanton
destruction of cities . . . This revolution has cut across film,
music, dance, religion, politics, fashion and nearly every activity
of contemporary life and, like all revolutions, including parliamentary ones, it entails a return to the past as much as movement
forward (Jencks, 1987, p. 11).

A growing number of critical observers maintain that the postmodern
turn (Hassan, 1987) is not only the most prominent symptom of the
fact that contemporary culture is in transition, but above all that the
underlying deep structure of contemporary culture is in a severe crisis.
If we can believe the prominent West German philosopher Jürgen

Habermas, then what is at stake today is nothing less than what he likes to call and defend as the project of modernity: the belief, advanced since the Enlightenment, in the liberating capacity and capability of reason, rationality and knowledge. Those who defend modernity against its new adversaries admit that today reason and rationality have become highly suspect: 'Today it would be an understatement to claim that the legacy of modernity has fallen under suspicion—in truth, it has fallen victim to a frontal assault from all quarters' (Wolin, 1984–85, p. 10).

This book deals with one aspect of the assault on the project of modernity which so far has been largely neglected in the growing literature on the subject of postmodernism, namely the political implications of the postmodern turn. It is an attempt to record a battle fought largely on the lowlands of politics, which the French new right has quite aptly called the realm of meta-politics: a protracted struggle for hegemony over ideas and ideology rather than straight, open politics. This struggle, it seems, is increasingly gaining importance in all major highly advanced industrial societies for reasons which are intricately connected to the emergence of postmodernism. If I restrict myself in the present text to an analysis of the emergence of postmodern politics in the Federal Republic of Germany, it is not only because this is the country with which I am most familiar; the rationale behind this choice is that in no other advanced industrial society has postmodernism been more intimately associated with lifestyle and political action than in West Germany: unlike France where the postmodern discourse originated with a new wave of philosophical thinking, or the United States where it manifested itself first in architecture and the art scene, in West Germany the postmodern turn emerged first as a 'diffuse feeling towards life' *(Lebensgefühl)* which quickly began to influence political action (Türk, 1988, p. 155).

In the Federal Republic of Germany this diffuse *Lebensgefühl* appeared for the first time by the end of the 1970s on the far left of the political spectrum. Its growing influence on politics and its political success in turn soon led to the revival of a reconstructed right-wing conservatism in the German new right. Of central importance for the spread of the postmodern turn was the transformation of the new left from orthodox Marxism to a 'new sensibility' which led to the recovery of individuality and a certain type of romanticism believed extinct for a long time. It found political expression in the rise of new social movements such as the ecology, anti-nuclear, women's, and alternative movements in the 1970s, and particularly of the Green party in the early 1980s, the first group of organized environmentalists to pose a serious political challenge to the traditional party system. But the influence of the postmodern turn has been hardly restricted to the left of the political spectrum. Since the electoral success of the Republikaner, a new right-wing party which rose from point zero in the Berlin elections in the spring of 1989, sent shock waves through the West German political establishment, a postmodern new right has emerged from its previous position of marginality on the lunatic fringes of West German society to be taken seriously as a threat and competitor to the established parties of the center right.

In the present text I argue that the emergence of the Greens as well as the new right are closely related. Both reflect a climate of political resentment on the two ends of the political spectrum fueled by the inability or unwillingness on the part of the established parties to confront new issues. Together they represent two diametrically opposed facets of a new politics (Hildebrandt and Dalton, 1977), whose impact on the established political forces has already been considerable and can be expected to grow. Together they have led to a fragmentation of West Germany's traditional two-and-a-half party system posing a serious challenge to the dominant catch-all parties of the center right and of the left. Expressing a new politics that is grounded less in the representation of interests than in the representation of a variety of new values, they articulate broadly what are rapidly becoming two of the most important emerging cultural priorities of Western Europe's postindustrial societies: on one hand the preservation of the natural environment, on the other the protection of national and cultural identity.

THE POSTMODERN CULTURE

The central proposition informing the discussion in this book is that Green and new right new politics represents a response to the process of postmodernization which increasingly characterizes all advanced capitalist countries in Western Europe, and, for a variety of reasons, especially West Germany. Among the participants in the debate on the postmodern turn there is hardly any agreement as to the exact nature and meaning of the term. It may no longer be true that postmodernism 'means all things to all people,' as Douglas Davis (1980, p. 13) charged a decade ago. Yet the term has remained so unspecific and often so arbitrary as to be open to a variety of divergent interpretations. As Linda Hutcheon (1989, pp. 23–29) recently reminded us, much of the confusion over the term postmodernism stems from 'the conflation of the cultural notion of postmodern*ism* (and its inherent relationship to modernism) and postmodern*ity* as the designation of a social and philosophical period or "condition".' The latter term has been variously defined as a new skepticism and 'incredulity' towards the grand narratives of enlightenment, emancipation and legitimation (Lyotard, 1984); the transformation of the structures of late capitalism into a postindustrial, information, and consumer society characterized by increasing automation of production and the manipulation of information (Poster, 1989); the realization that modernity has left us with a waste land of 'detritus, decomposition, and disaccumulation' against 'the background radiation of parody, kitch, and burnout,' a panic scene dominated by the simulated spectacle of the hyperreal (Kroker and Cook, 1986, p. 8; Baudrillard, 1983); or the spread of an 'eclectic and amorphous culture exhibiting plurality, mixed lifestyles and new attitudes based on immediate gratification, fantasy, novelty, play, hedonism, consumption and affluence' (Gibbins, 1989, p. 15).

What all of these characterizations of the postmodern condition have in common is the view that postmodernity must be understood in terms of both a transformation of the socioeconomic organization of highly advanced capitalist societies as well as a revolution in the philosophical interpretation of history and its meaning, both to be analyzed separately from the cultural notion of postmodernism. This approach to the postmodern turn is in stark contrast to those interpretations which insist on defining postmodernism merely as a reflection and reinforcement of the socioeconomic effects of postmodernity (see Hutcheon, 1989, pp. 25–26). Although these interpretations do provide some of the starkest accounts of the interrelationship between the transformation of the socioeconomic organization of late, multinational or consumer capitalism and postmodern culture, they turn out to be not very useful for the study of postmodern politics. Prominent among them have been the work of the American literary critic Fredric Jameson on the cultural logic of late capitalism and the work of the French philosopher Jean Baudrillard on the political economy of the sign (see Connor, 1989, ch. 2).

In Jameson's reading the essence of late capitalism is its complete penetration into the remotest areas of the globe, its increasing colonization of all aspects of human life, 'where even the unconscious can be said to have been penetrated and "colonized," with our plastic money cards, which seem to signify the apotheosis of the *interconnected* power of capitalism, the nightmarishly interwoven global network which has been feared and represented by artists since Kafka' (Gross, 1989, p. 107). This process of unbridled commodification and subjugation under the logic of capitalism of society (Hirsch, 1982, 1985) presumes the dissolution of all social fabric, of whatever mediating institutions there still might exist. Only under such conditions one could imagine an audience of atomized and utterly individualized masses receptive enough to the suggestive power of an all-encompassing capitalist world-system.

Late capitalism thus conceived corresponds to Baudrillard's phase three in his genealogy of exchange value, the age of simulation as the third-order simulacrum, whose essence he sees to be enclosed in the dominant of the exchange-sign value, a system of power 'more subtle and more totalitarian than that of exploitation' (Baudrillard, 1975, p. 121). In Baudrillard's hyperbolic and hyper-radicalized interpretation, consumer capitalism confronts us as a 'neo-capitalist cybernetic order that aims now at total control' (Baudrillard, 1983, p. 111). Continually colonizing new aspects of social and individual life, that had hitherto been spared by the unrelenting process of measuring, surveying, and coding in preparation for commodification, capitalism has finally succeeded in encroaching on areas progressively more removed from the domain of exchange value: from the elimination of the border between procreation and reproduction via gene manipulation, artificial insemination, and surrogate motherhood, to personal salvation via TV evangelism (see Baudrillard, 1981, pp. 92–93). It is at this moment that culture becomes accomplice to the extension and furthering of commodification, intensifying and reinforcing it. It is in this sense that postmodernism can be said to have become the dominant cultural logic of late capitalism. What characterizes the postmodern age is the dissolution of the cultural and economic as autonomous realms, a 'breakdown in the old structural opposition of the cultural and the economic in the simultaneous "commodification" of the former and the "symbolization" of the latter' (Foster, 1985, p. 145).

The most significant result of this implosion of the two once separate fields of social reproduction is the loss of distance necessary for both critique as well as resistance which the realm of culture formerly provided. With the aesthetization of capitalism and the commodification of aesthetics via advertising, design, styling, fashion, and above all television and the rest of the mediascape, adversary expressions of resistance and protest alike get almost immediately absorbed, commercialized, and quickly domesticated (for example graffiti and punk). In its own perverse way resistance thus feeds consumer capitalism's constant search for the new while contributing to the perfection of its logic of planned obsolescence (Jameson, 1984, pp. 87–8). In the dark world of mass-produced consumers of mass-produced products there is no place for resistance save for the specter of nihilism 'in the shadow of the silent majorities' (Baudrillard, 1983). The ascent of the masses without place or history cannot but mean the final triumph of commodification and the sign-value 'as people are reduced to a glutinous mass which refuses to stabilize in its absorption, reflection and cynical parody of media images' (Featherstone, 1989, p. 122), reflected off the TV screen.

It is hardly a coincidence that Jameson and Baudrillard figure prominently among those who theorize the postmodern condition. At least part of their appeal owes to the uncompromising and totalizing fashion in which they unravel the seemingly unrelenting inner logic of capital accumulation and technological innovation and expose their dark side while constructing the image of a brave new world without exit. However, this kind of analysis is both too reductionist, too narrowly focused on a Marxist critique of late capitalism, while at the same time too sweeping in its scope. Particularly Fredric Jameson's account relies on Marxism as a totalizing master narrative of theory and history to persuade the reader that postmodernism indeed is merely the cultural logic of late capitalism rather than 'an autonomous demi-urge which produces a new (post-capitalist?) social order' (Kellner, 1988, p. 262). Such a sweeping approach precludes any meaningful analysis of politics. As Mike Featherstone (1989, p. 120) has noted, those who interpret history 'as the outcome of a particular relentless logic' are forced to dismiss or at least diminish the role played by distinct social actors and their struggles for social, economic and political power instrumental in creating the very conditions that advance historical development. It is only by denying the continued relevance for social action of distinct social groupings with distinct social and political identities, that these theories can proclaim the death of the social, 'eclipsed by its own implosion into the density of the mass' (Kroker and Cook, 1986, p. 172).

One of the central points of this book is that in the postmodern age politics has not become irrelevant. The postmodern age, as any other, opens up new, hitherto unexplored opportunities for political discourse and action while precluding others. Postmodern political discourse, I will argue, responds to a large extent both to a revolution in the realm of what we usually call ideology (in the sense Clifford Geertz would assign to it) as well as to profound changes within the socioeconomic structure of highly advanced capitalist societies without the two developments being necessarily connected. In what follows I will first focus on ideology and in the next section on the socioeconomic structure.

THE END OF MODERNITY

Postmodern politics responds to a large extent to the widespread malaise engendered by what Gianni Vattimo has called 'the end of modernity': the sense that we have reached the end of 'a historical project of modernity, the project of European Enlightenment and, finally, also the project of Greco-occidental civilization' (Wellmer, 1985, p. 48). What has come to a close is an era which believed in the existence of objective, universal truth and science's ability to find and reveal it, in the expanding control over technology and, via technology, in man's ability to control nature, and, above all, in progress. There are many reasons why modernity has come under attack. Horkheimer and Adorno (1986, p. 3) undermined it some forty years ago analyzing the reasons why 'humanity instead of entering a truly human condition [was] sinking into a new type of barbarism.' It was further undermined by the new wedding of knowledge and the power of extinction symbolized by the nuclear bomb. However, it was not until the full realization of the extent to which man's attempt to gain control over nature had led to an ecological catastrophe (and the realization of the wisdom of Horkheimer and Adorno's dark observation that 'the fully enlightened world radiates disaster triumphant') that modernity lost its most dedicated advocates.

The main characteristic of the resulting condition is what Jean-François Lyotard has defined as a profound skepticism towards the grand narratives of modernity, those totalizing, monist theories of society and history which represented humanity as engaged in an attempt to reach universal moral and intellectual self-realization based on the gradual universalization of human reason which would allow for an assessment of social and political tendencies as progressive or otherwise: the Enlightenment's promise to emancipate humanity from ignorance through the spread of knowledge and education; the Hegelian notion of the emancipation of the mind from alienation through dialectics; the Marxist promise of emancipation of the working class from exploitation via the struggle of the working class; the liberal notion of the emancipation from want through the self-regulating forces of the market; the social democratic narrative of the emancipative power of technical progress, statist reformism, and administrative intervention; and finally the European notion that 'the "truth" of European culture is in the same measure the as-yet-hidden truth (and *telos*) of other cultures but that the time had not yet come for the latter to realize it' (Feher, 1987, p. 196).

In the 1980s, each one of the grand narratives of modernity has fallen into disrepute. Postmodern politics marks the exhaustion and collapse of the messianic ideologies of the eighteenth and nineteenth century and the social systems built upon them. In no other group has this been more obvious than among the Western European new left which in the 1980s largely abandoned the most ambitious and encompassing of all grand narratives, bidding farewell to the proletariat as the privileged and predestined subject of history and emancipation. The resulting vacuum has been bemoaned by some concerned observers as a loss of orientation, 'the shattering of the faith in a recognisable meaning in human life and of social evolution in general' (Löwenthal, 1977, p. 10). As one of the protagonists notes in the Canadian film *The Decline of the American Empire*: 'With the collapse of the Marxist–Leninist dream no model exists of which we can say "This is how we want to live." In our personal lives, unless one's a mystic or a saint, there are no models to live by. Our very existence is being eroded.'

However, as Chapters 1 and 2 will illustrate, this is not the only direction life and politics in the postmodern age can take. If, as Zygmunt Baumann (1987, p. 119) maintains, the postmodern condition is distinguished from modernity by giving up modernity's conviction of its superiority over alternative forms of organizing one's life and its pretension to universal validity, this does not necessarily entail the loss of all meaning. Instead a postmodern conceptualization of life can either maintain itself as a corrective force, looking back upon the past 'as a movement in a direction unlikely to be followed, as perhaps even an aberration, the pursuit of a false track, a historical error now to be rectified' (p. 117). As we will see, this is how the Green movement in West Germany sought to gain legitimacy for the radical alternative it proposed in order to rectify what it considered the disastrous path of modern German society. Or it can tune itself into the postmodern *Lebensgefühl*, not only accepting the emergence of a chaotic, fragmentized world, but enjoying the demise and loss of certainty and finite authority, rejoicing in the decentering impulses and indeterminacy characteristic of the postmodern age, 'a life in the presence of an unlimited quantity of competing forms of life, unable to prove their claims to be grounded in anything more solid and binding than their own historically shaped conventions' (p. 120). The latter, I would maintain, is becoming an increasingly important response with significant consequences for a postmodern politics.

In the wake of its erosion and collapse the modern consciousness has given way to a new, decentralized pluralism (cf. Hassan, 1987, ch. 8). Previously fixed identities have been replaced by 'a flux of contextualized identities: contextualized by gender, class, race, ethnicity, sexual preference, education, social role and so on' (Hutcheon, 1988, p. 59). This has furthered processes of social fragmentation and individualization, political dealignment and realignment. In terms of postmodern politics, the most important reflection of these processes has been the rise of new social movements (for example, ecology, women's rights, anti-nuclear, peace movements) whose 'conspicuous rejection of totalizing ideologies' is reflected in their basis of self-identification, which no longer derives from established political and socioeconomic codes (left/right, working class/capital and so on), but from a range of different issues 'such as gender, age, and locality, or even, in the case of environmental and pacifist movements, the human race as a whole' (Offe, 1987, pp. 72, 76). On the other hand, it has also led to the quite frantic attempt, on the part of the conservative right, to recover lost unity, identity, and community by redefining them in opposition to the new politics grounded in contextualized identities by emphasizing 'naturally' ascribed identities such as the nation or a national culture. This is the topic of Chapters 4 and 5.

It would be hard to deny that in the postmodern age culture has attained a privileged position in the construction of social and political reality. Through the entertainment and advertising industry, via the explosion in information technology and particularly the mass media, culture increasingly informs and shapes every aspect of daily life. In its most extreme case, the pervasive force of culture in the postmodern age erases the distinction between reality and fiction, creating a world of appearances, of imagination. This has been particularly noted and criticized in regard to TV news reporting, where 'the line between fact and fiction, news and entertainment is becoming blurred, and viewers do not quite know what to believe any more.'[1] It would therefore be quite intriguing to see in the spread of postmodern politics merely a reaction to, and reflection and manifestation of the broader dynamics and transformation that have become apparent within the realm of ideology. However, as I have noted above, even in the postmodern age, it is impossible to separate the cultural from the social and material realm. This is far from saying that the transformation of the cultural basis of the postmodern age represents a mere reflection of the profound changes within the social and material realms which have variously been described as the third technological revolution, the coming of postindustrial and/or consumer society, or the rise of the mode of information. The argument is, however, that the rise of postmodern politics is intimately connected to the material and social changes engendered by the reorganization of the basic structures of postindustrial society.

THE SOCIAL BASIS OF POSTMODERN POLITICS

The various theories on postindustrialism, information society, and the consumer society share four basic arguments: first, advanced capitalist societies have entered a new era dominated by the codification, processing, and control of information concomitant with a shift from standardized industrial mass manufacturing to flexible specialization characteristic of high-tech industries employing a polyvalent workforce and specializing in small-batch production which allows customization (see Piore and Sabel, 1984); second, the emerging social structure is characterized foremost by the expansion of new types of services in the growth sectors of social and health services, and in finance, research and development, and marketing; third, that these social changes have led to new social and cultural attitudes and their institutionalization within and via the emerging loci of potential social and political power; and fourth that these new social and cultural attitudes have led to new cleavages which in turn are expected to inform new lines of political conflict.

   This characterization of the postmodern age is still largely informed by the attempt to fit the structural changes associated with the shift to postindustrialism into a traditional model of economic and social evolution. According to this model 'the postindustrial is seen as a natural product of industrial development, as a next phase following the success of the preceding one' (Baumann, 1987, p. 119)—complete with the reorganization of its material, social and political basis. A central proposition of this book is that postmodern politics expresses largely the attitudes of a rising social stratum of symbolic specialists employed in the growing 'quaternary' and 'quinary' areas of the service sector (see Bell, 1989, p. 168).

One of the core features of the postmodern age has been the revolutionary growth of service sector employment, be it in the quinary area of human services including education, social and health services, or in the quartenary area of professional services such as research and development, information processing, analysis, marketing, programming, design and the like. What distinguishes these generally human oriented services from the more traditional production oriented and supporting services such as transportation, maintenance, or water and energy supply is the fact that compared to the latter the human oriented services are often difficult to quantify, their utility to the consumer is more often a matter of subjective rather than objective judgement, they are largely oriented towards the 'processing of symbols and/or symbolic objects' and especially to 'leisure and personal development based on the co-operative use of resources' (Jones, 1982, pp. 6, 48).

It is particularly for the latter two reasons that the new stratum of symbolic specialists, 'new cultural intermediaries' (Featherstone, 1989, 1989a) or what I will call the new service class, employed in the human oriented areas of the service sector, has increasingly come to be seen as the privileged audience and transmitters of postmodern culture. In an age characterized by the expansion of the sphere of culture throughout society (Jameson, 1984, p. 87) and the growing aestheticization of everyday life via symbols, signs, and images promoting the pleasure of consumption, those who manipulate symbols and handle images, those who are able to create and develop their life chances as well as their very lives (and, to make use of a worn out cliché, make them into a work of art) have 'the sensibilities and dispositions to attune themselves to postmodern cultural goods and experiences in the various roles of producers, transmitters, intermediaries, audiences, and consumers' and the opportunity to disseminate these goods and experiences among the wider population (Featherstone, 1989a, p. 131).

From this characterization emerge two diametrically opposed interpretations as to the role the new service class of symbolic specialists play in postmodern society. One interpretation focuses on their position as consumers, a second interpretation focuses on their privileged position as transmitters of an individualistic new lifestyle. The two interpretations lead to different conclusions as to the nature of postmodern politics and the direction it can be expected to take.

Following Pierre Bourdieu's influential analysis of social distinctions, a growing number of critics of the postmodern consumer society have stressed the importance of the sphere of culture as a central arena in the untiring struggle of various social groups to differentiate and distinguish themselves from each other. Consumption and taste are seen as an important instrument in the structuration of modern and postmodern, industrial and postindustrial societies as well as a means in the struggle between different classes and class fractions (Featherstone, 1987, p. 60). In this view the 'fetishism of commodities lies in their prestige value, in their ability as "signs" to command respect, authority, deference. In a world governed by symbols and sign-value, it suffices that one can *appear* powerful to be powerful and successful by acquiring the commodities that convey those human attributes' (Diggins, 1977, p. 365).

With the spread of mass affluence and the growth of the postmodern consumer society the shift to symbolic consumption has given the new stratum of symbolic specialists a privileged position of power and influence—not as the producers of postindustrial goods, but as the new heroes of consumer culture, the trendsetters of the postmodern age, who make lifestyle and the development of taste their life project (Featherstone, 1987, p. 59). The role of symbolic specialists thus is enhanced at a 'particular stage of economic development, that of industrial saturation, where the function of this new class is precisely to promote the consumption ethic' (Jager, 1986, p. 86). The trendy emerge as the vanguard of the spreading consumer society, the postindustrial 'change-masters' are replaced by the postmodern 'taste-makers' in a brave new world of commodities which has 'blossomed into a magical show where the material features of commodities are increasingly subordinated to their symbolic potential' (Mills, 1988, p. 170).

They are the foundation of postmodern capitalism promoting its ethos of planned obsolescence, production of waste, and restless search for the new via advertising, market research, and public relations. Their craving for distinction finds expression in the rediscovered interest in decoration and ornamentation characteristic of the 'new consumption landscape' of the gentrified inner city (Hasse, 1989;

Smith, 1987), in their conspicuous display of good taste in the form of French croissants instead of Wonder Bread, and pure cotton shirts to replace those made from polyester, in their craving for the sleek styling of Olivetti typewriters and Braun coffee machines. Profiting from the postindustrial turn to flexible specialization, which, by broadening access to customized products, set off the race towards differentiation (Harvey, 1987), they waver between critical taste and indulgence. A politics resulting from the celebration of consumer capitalism and the acceptance of the seductive dominance of the sign is by necessity affirmative. From this perspective postmodern discourse and politics easily turns into the cultural dominant of the conservative counter-attack of the past decade, and is thus pre-eminently consistent with the neo-liberal politics of Margaret Thatcher and the Reagan era (Lash and Urry, 1987, p. 299).

If this characterization of the new service class focuses primarily on its members' exposed position in the postmodern consumer society, other approaches have stressed a second aspect of their attraction to postmodernism. On this view, the demise of the great meta-narratives of modernity has set free a postmodern *citoyen* increasingly forced to take his or her life into his or her own hands. It has freed the individual from the modern quest for self-knowledge and replaced it with a postmodern quest for self-creation. Existence design and designer existence form the core of life in the postmodern age (see Kellner and Heuberger, 1988, p. 335). This increasingly spills over into the market, with a growing number of professions (for example, market researchers, advertising specialists, health and entertainment experts) creating rather than reproducing needs and with them new jobs and new markets (Lash and Urry, 1987, p. 295). However, it also affects particularly those professions closely connected to the growth of the welfare state (for example, education, social work) whose task it is to prepare and help individuals in their care to design their own existence (Martin, 1989).

What differentiates the new cultural intermediaries from employees in large organizations is the fact that they face the necessity, but also the luxury of making their own choices and decisions on the job and in their personal lives. This predisposes them on the one hand to place a high premium on individuality, to make their own decisions and follow their own rules, on the other to resist the spread of formal and functional rationality associated with large corporations or state bureaucracies which is 'all too likely to stamp out such enterprise before it raises its head.' What the new cultural intermediaries resist are 'the alienating and dehumanizing processes which result from bureaucratization and rationalization inherent in modernity' (Martin, 1989, pp. 31, 27).

A major part of this book is devoted to a discussion of the political response of segments of the new service class to the processes of rationalization and alienation inherent in advanced capitalist society. I shall argue first, that the growth of the new service class has given rise to an adversary politics or what Hal Foster (1987, p. xii) has referred to as a postmodern politics of resistance; second, that underlying the emergence of adversary politics in the new service class is the spread of new values that assign 'increasing priority to self-expression, equality, participation and the general quality of life' (Badham, 1984, p. 57), and which are best characterized as a mixture of left-libertarian and non-materialist values such as support for free speech, the expansion of political participation and the rights of minorities, a growing emphasis on self-realization and the reversal of humanity's relationship with nature (see Flanagan 1987; Kitschelt, 1989; Inglehart, 1990); and third that the resulting new politics has found its most vocal advocates in new social movements and the Greens.

The particular predisposition of the new cultural intermediaries to left-libertarian/non-materialist new politics is intimately connected to their rejection of rationalization and bureaucracy, or what Jürgen Habermas has called the 'colonization of the life world.' In his analysis of highly advanced capitalist societies Habermas differentiates between the monetary–administrative system dominated by economic and bureaucratic rationality and a communicatively structured life world centered on the reproduction of values and norms. During the past decades the imperatives of economic growth necessary for capitalism to survive have led to a substantial growth of what he calls 'the monetary–bureaucratic complex' resulting in the 'encroachment of forms of economic and administrative rationality into life-spheres that in fact obey the independent logic of moral–practical and aesthetic–practical rationality' (Habermas, 1986, p. 116; 1984, p. 20).

The rise and growth of new social movements, including the Greens, represent a response to this penetration of functional rationality into the life-world.

Once the steering media such as money and power penetrate these areas, for instance by redefining relations in terms of consumption, or by bureaucratizing the conditions of life, then it is more than an attack on traditions. The foundations of a life-world that is already rationalized are under assault. What is at stake is the symbolic reproduction of the life-world itself. (Habermas, 1986, p. 117)

What new social movements attempt to do is either to defend and reinstate endangered lifestyles or 'to put endangered lifestyles into practice' (Habermas, 1981, p. 33). As long as they do not go beyond a defense of the life-world by disavowing reason and rationality in its entirety, new social movements and the Greens thus represent a corrective force rather than implacable adversaries of rationality and the project of modernity (see Offe, 1987, p. 90). At the same time, as Chapter 3 will show, they share a predisposition towards a range of non-materialist values which are decidedly postmodern.

As Chapter 3 shows, it is particularly among the human oriented service sector workers that new social movements and the Greens have found a disproportionately large number of supporters. This can be explained by the fact that both the new social movements and the Greens focus on defending the life world against the encroachment of functional rationality. Studies on the composition of the British environmental movement (Cotgrove and Duff, 1980) and new social movements in the Netherlands (Kriesi, 1989), for example, have shown in both cases the main supporters of these movements to belong to social and cultural services including health services, education, social work, and creative arts and journalism. What differentiates the members of these services in particular from other occupations is their training in the social sciences and humanities—disciplines particularly suited to confront the student with the problems of the life world. As one observer succinctly notes:

> The pervasive importance of the social sciences in this is immedia-
> tely clear, not least the popularisation over the last two decades of
> interactionist, phenomenological and semiotic theories of everyday
> life. These revelatory but potentially ironising tools of understand-
> ing and self-understanding give the postmodern expert both a sense
> of privileged access to reality and, at the same time, a sense that
> 'reality' is not a unified, objective entity but a creation of
> 'discourse,' 'communication practices' and so forth. (Martin, 1989,
> p. 28)

The growth of the human oriented areas of the service sector and the rise of new values and new politics associated with it lend support to the contention that advanced capitalist societies are in a process of profound social and political change. In the most radical version of this proposition, some have argued that contemporary postindustrial/postmodern societies are going through a process of fragmentation, individualization and alienation. From this viewpoint, as a result of social and geographic mobility, heightened competition in the workplace, and a growing differention of career opportunities, the individual is increasingly released from those social forms which still inform modernity—the family, the community, classes and fixed gender roles (Beck, 1986, chs.3–5). At the same time, as a result of mass affluence 'subcultural class identities have dissipated, class distinctions based on "status" have lost their traditional support, the processes of "diversification" and "individualization" of lifestyles and ways of life have been set into motion' (Beck, 1987, p. 341). Or, as the British architecture critic Charles Jencks (1987, pp. 45–46) put it in deliberately exaggerated fashion, the postmodern world is populated by 'countless individuals in Tokyo, New York, Berlin, London, Milan and other world cities all communicating and competing with each other, just as they are in the banking world.'

If these processes of socioeconomic differentiation have created new opportunities for some social groups (such as service sector workers and particularly the new yuppie bourgeoisie), they have marginalized others. As Beck notes, reality in contemporary advanced capitalist societies is characterized by a peculiar transition phase, 'in which traditional and sharpening inequalities coincide with certain elements of a no longer traditional, individualized "post-class society"' (Beck, 1987, p. 351). The present acceleration of economic and social modernization has left considerable segments of the population of all advanced capitalist societies marginalized, others culturally and politically disoriented. The new socioeconomic reality, which demands flexibility, versatility and the ability to take responsibility for one's destiny, has created a climate of fear of failure and social decline and contributed to a loss of orientation particularly among young people, un- and semi-skilled workers, the structurally unemployed, but also among the traditional middle classes. What Jean-Marie Vincent (1985, p. 1773) has written about the Mitterand years applies as well to West Germany (see Glotz, 1989) and other West European countries: 'Among many social strata disillusionment, even desperation have replaced confidence in the future or the feeling that one lives at least in bearable conditions.'

This climate characterized by insecurity and a loss of orientation has contributed to the growth and success of right-wing radical and

extremist parties which have sprung up in most advanced capitalist
countries.[2] Appealing to widespread fears, anxiety, and resentment
they propose solutions supposed to provide security and a sense of
identity and worth at the expense of outsiders. Opposed to the new
values and lifestyle of postmodern society they represent a 'new
coalition of forces which see their common enemy in the postmaterialist oriented strata of the "new left", and their new political agenda'
(Minkenberg and Inglehart, 1989, p. 82). As Chapter 5 will show, they
might thus be characterized as the exact 'mirror image' of the new
social movements and the Greens. Although their electoral fate
appears to be more dependent on the direction of the prevailing
political wind and the mood swings that characterize the political
climate of postmodern society than the political fate of new social
movements and Greens, the rise of nationalism, nativism and
xenophobia not only in West Germany and Western Europe, but
also in Eastern Europe and the Soviet Union (ranging from the
national revolutionary movements in the Baltics and the Transcauca-
sus to the spread of Russian nationalism under the banner of Pamyat')
suggests that right-wing radicalism will remain a prominent feature of
the postmodern political discourse.

At the very least the rise of right-wing radicalism throughout
Western Europe has forced the postmodern left to re-examine a
variety of their political and philosophical positions. Chapter 6
focuses on Green politics towards three central issues of West
German foreign policy, NATO, German reunification and European
integration, to explore the extent to which the revival of nationalist
tendencies in West German politics during the past decades has had an
impact on the Green conceptualization of foreign policy. I will
contend that the core issues addressed by Green foreign policy are
informed by the very same left-libertarian values which already
informed their domestic political programs. The final chapter
summarizes some of the major points of this study and puts them in
the broader context of postmodern politics in general and its likely fate
in a future united Germany.

1 The Transformation of the New Left

The emergence and rise of postmodern politics in West Germany can be traced back to the turbulent mid-1970s. Postmodernism made in West Germany appeared first as a diffuse new way of looking at life and the natural and human-made environment surrounding the individual. The postmodern turn came at a point of transition in the self-understanding of West German society, at 'the tail end of a major thrust of modernization of German cultural and political life which seemed to have gone awry some time during the 1970s producing high levels of disillusionment both with the utopian hopes and the pragmatic promises of 1968–69' (Huyssen, 1984, p. 30). It made itself felt first in the generation which had fought hardest for these dreams and therefore was most affected by the ensuing malaise—the generation of 1968. It was segments within this generation which, disillusioned with the broken promises of the social-liberal welfare state and appalled by the banality of West German hyper-consumerism, became the protagonists of the turn towards a new conception of politics.

THE 68-GENERATION

When Willy Brandt became German chancellor in 1969, he proclaimed the famous slogan *Mehr Demokratie wagen!* (Let's dare more democracy). This promise of extended democracy and the resulting policy of domestic reforms encouraged many on the critical left to embark on a 'long march through the institutions' by joining the left wing of the SPD. Thus, between 1968 and 1974, the membership of the Young Socialists more than doubled from 150 000 to 350 000 making up more than one third of the total party membership (Dräger and Hülsberg, 1986, p. 47). New members under twenty-one increased from 10.4 per cent in 1969 to 21.1 per cent in 1971 (Paterson, 1986, p. 130).

However, the reform euphoria did not last long. The radical decree (*Radikalenerlass*), passed in 1972 with Willy Brandt still in power, was a first indication that the scope of extended democracy was rather limited. The radical decree was intended to prevent members of the left extremist DKP (German Communist Party) and of the right extremist NPD (National Democratic Party of Germany) from subverting democracy by keeping them out of the public service. Behind this intention, however, were political considerations, namely to draw a clear line between social democrats and communists and thus to counter any potential suggestion by the center right that, in the wake of *Ostpolitik*, the SPD's opening to the East, the SPD had become soft on communism (see Braunthal, 1983, pp. 247–250).

Brandt's resignation as chancellor in May 1974 was only an outward symbol of his political failure. In the eyes of his critics on the left, his successor Helmut Schmidt switched swiftly from reform politics to crisis management, that is, technocratic attempts to preserve the celebrated 'German Model' of a rather successful economy at a time of global economic turmoil following the oil crisis (Glaessner *et al.*, 1984, p. 93). The result was easy to predict. At a time when the West German economy gradually came under increasing pressure following the first oil price explosion of 1973, the social-liberal establishment came under growing pressure from the left. By the mid-1970s, the *Radikalenerlass* began to affect the left wing of the SPD (Braunthal, 1983, p. 248). In the wake of growing public concern over political terrorism, a further reversal of democratization occurred culminating in what the left would call the *Deutsche Herbst* (German Fall) of 1977. A new culmination of terrorist activity intensified the already prevailing climate of intolerance and suspicion fueled by the call for increasingly drastic measures to deal with politically motivated violence, and for ever greater surveillance (see Burns and van der Will, 1988, pp. 58–9). According to Peter Katzenstein (1982, p. 209),

the 1970s are noteworthy not for the courageous defense of liberal norms of privacy but for the speed with which traditional civil liberties were sacrificed in the interest of internal securities. This encroachment on West German democracy was inaugurated and supervised neither by authoritarian Junkers, nor aggressive generals, nor anti-Semitic Nazis. Well-intentioned Social Democratic reformers legitimized political practices that, under conservative auspices, would have elicited much sharper political protests at home and abroad.

The erosion of democratic liberties combined with internal pressure on the left wing of the SPD forced many left social democrats into open opposition (such as Karl Heinz Hansen), or to leave the party altogether (the prominent Jochen Steffen and later Hansen); others (for example, Manfred Coppick) were forced to resign from the party. The result was a growing polarization between a conservative, growth-oriented social-liberal majority which sought to preserve the welfare state at all costs[1]and a minority of left critical intellectuals to which Helmut Schmidt once referred as those 'environmental idiots who destroy everything' (cited in Bürklin, 1984, p. 104). Many of them would eventually join or at least support the Green party.

However, the disillusionment with social democracy was only one, albeit very important, reason why those of the 68-generation began to search for an alternative to the politics of the social-liberal coalition. Equally important was the growing disillusionment with Marxism, particularly among the orthodox and undogmatic Marxist groups and parties which had sprung up after the political and ideological collapse of the *Sozialistischer Deutscher Studentenbund* (Socialist League of German Students, SDS) in 1970.

For almost three years, between 1967 and 1970, the SDS considered itself not only the vanguard of the West German student movement, but was instrumental in organizing extra-parliamentary mass campaigns against the emergency legislation and the Vietnam war (see Burns and van der Will, 1988, ch.3). The student movement was primarily a response on the part of highly educated young people to the authoritarian climate on West German universities, the dominant anti-leftist consensus represented and perpetuated by the influential mass media, particularly the Springer press, and the lack of a viable political opposition in the wake of the grand coalition between SPD and the CDU/CSU (see Stamm, 1988, ch. 1). It was influenced by the critical theory of the Frankfurt School (Adorno, Horkheimer, Marcuse and Habermas), by anarchism, and the teachings of Rosa Luxemburg. The students promoted the idea of a cultural revolution to free the individual from all the repressive mechanisms of the system. Against the existing reality they held the vision of a *Reich der Freiheit* (Empire of Freedom). However, apart from vague dreams about the establishment of a council democracy, they put forward few concrete plans or visions for a future society. This may have been one of the reasons why the West German students, unlike their counterparts in France, never gained much support among the population at large and especially among the working class whose support they considered their primary political objective.

After the collapse of the SDS at the end of the 1960s, the new left focused primarily on what Rolf Peter Sieferle (1984, p. 236) has aptly described as 'the reanimation of the proletarian corpse.' In order to reach this goal, the new left 'interpreted itself to a large extent as "socialist", i.e. as a vanguard movement, that wanted to exhume the workers' movement which Nazism had "buried".' With a tinge of misplaced nostalgia they adopted the program and the symbols of the communist movements of the 1920s. What had already been outdated in the 1920s, was even more *déplacé* in the 1970s. 'The industrial workers were just enjoying the largest increase in prosperity and the most comprehensive gains of political power in German history. In this historically exceptional [period of] prosperity they were expected to take upon themselves the horrors and insecurities of a social revolution. Hardly has any program been less realistic than this' (p. 239). To make things worse, the new left failed even to agree on a common political strategy.

Two positions emerged. One side maintained that it was the students and intellectuals who had to wage the struggle for the proletariat because the proletariat, manipulated by the ruling class, could neither recognize nor represent its own interests. The other side bet on the proletariat as the decisive revolutionary subject arguing that, after all, it was ultimately the proletariat which was confronted daily with exploitation and oppression. These radically divergent views of the working class led to two different political strategies. Whereas the one faction organized in highly centralized Leninist cadre parties of Maoist persuasion, the other one left the universities to join the proletariat in the factories.

The short history of the Maoist parties was dominated by ideological infighting, sometimes erupting into physical violence, and by intrigues and frequent splits. Thus, at one point there existed up to five different splinter groups which had broken away from the Communist Party of Germany/Marxist–Leninist (KPD/ML) all of them calling themselves KPD/ML (Langguth, 1984, p. 67). Their ideology was characterized by dogmatism, hierarchical structures, discipline, and above all, a neo-Stalinist orientation. As one close observer noted:

These non-human parties, with their Stalinist organizational forms, turned young people into political automatons and failed totally to break out of their isolation. These organizations were not a continuation of the APO but a break with it. Self-organization, love of life, spontaneity and enlightenment were replaced by zombie-like obedience, discipline, asceticism, indoctrination and the regurgitation of the failed wisdoms of the Stalinist Comintern. (Hülsberg, 1988, p. 51)

For a generation of students who had organized to confront the authoritarianism of the West German universities, this was indeed a radical, and highly reactionary change of direction. What they shared was a common belief in the working class as *the* revolutionary subject, the belief that they worked for the creation of a communist party and the dictatorship of the proletariat, which they envisioned as the result of an armed rebellion and the overthrow of the bourgeois state, and a rejection of the Soviet Union as a model of socialist development and politics.

Whenever it was necessary to go beyond theory and to confront reality, the differences were profound. Especially in their view of post-Mao China the different Maoist parties diverged considerably. Whereas one side defended the Chinese regardless of what they did and turned against their former friends, the Albanians, others broke with China while strengthening its ties with the Albania Workers' Party, which eventually recognized the KPD/ML as a sister party.

Whereas the dogmatic Maoist parties saw themselves as the vanguard of the working class representing their objective interests, the undogmatic new left sought a direct contact with the working class. Most of the undogmatic leftists came from the anti-authoritarian wing of the Frankfurt SDS. There they organized the so-called *Betriebsprojektgruppe* (factory project group) consisting of a group of students (among them Daniel Cohn-Bendit and Joschka Fischer, both to become leading figures of the moderate wing of the Greens in the 1980s) who left university in order to join the 'proletariat' in the factories. Favorite targets were the car manufacturers Opel in Rüsselsheim, or BMW where 'they exchanged their normal political and intellectual activities for the assembly line.' But, besides discussions about 'the dimensions of the "proletarian family" and the "proletarian context of life"' the results were meager. When spontaneous strikes failed in the face of hostility from the official unions and from workers, the *Betriebsprojektgruppe* soon abandoned the project (Voigt, 1986, p. 485). As a result Joschka Fischer and some of his friends came to the conclusion that Marxism and the labor movement represented a dead end (Hülsberg, 1988, p. 52).

This pronounced turn towards the proletariat was one way the new left sought to create a new identity after the collapse of the SDS. The failure of the radical students to reach the working class had confronted them with 'their own social limitation' (Deutz *et al.*, 1979, p. 34). By trying to exhume the proletarian corpse, by substituting the interest of a mystified proletariat for their own specific interests, they sought to substitute an alien identity for their own. This tendency was even more pronounced in the new left's internationalism.

If the student protest against the Vietnam war in the late 1960s had included attacks on the West German government's support for the United States, after the collapse of the protest movement, many on the new left abandoned the Federal Republic. Instead they actively began to support the struggle for national liberation in the Third World. There, the world of violent revolution predicted by the theorists of the new left, seemed still intact. And if they represented only a tiny minority in West Germany without much hope of reaching the rest of the population, on a global scale they could still feel as if they represented the majority, namely the revolutionary world population. With this—at least for the time being—the question of identity seemed largely resolved.

However, this newly-found confidence did not last very long. In the late 1970s the new left plunged into a severe, and this time, decisive identity crisis. Again, one reason was frustration with the working class. But this time it was heightened by a widespread disillusionment with internationalism leading to a general disenchantment with Marxism and to a large-scale rejection of theory. The West German satirist Wolfgang Ebert (1985) has aptly characterized the new left's frustration with the working class:

> The revolution never materialized because the masses—not to speak of the working class as the so-called subject of the revolution—had failed. Actually, the masses always fail. Instead of following their true interests they had nothing better to do than to succumb to an unrestrained consumption frenzy. They either have not listened to their intellectual leaders—or have misunderstood them. Who would be so stupid to continue risking their necks for these dumb masses?

The ironic undertone in Ebert's account should not detract from the fact that it fairly accurately reflected the frustration and disillusionment of parts of the West German new left, a disillusionment which was hardly limited to West Germany. Thus, in 1981 the West German social scientists Jürgen Bacia and Klaus Dieter Scherer (1981, p. 41) complained that there was hardly a social scientist on the left still willing to put his or her faith in the world-historical role of the industrial working class. The prospects for a radical change were indeed rather bleak. Not even the economic crisis of the 1970s had advanced any of the highly advanced West European industrial societies closer to revolution. Instead large parts of the working class had acquired the consumption mentality of the middle class while imitating the latter's support for order and the Protestant work ethic. Instead of moving to the left they had become more conservative. Worst of all was that the social democrats were following them, projecting a conservatism that reflected the aversion of broad strata of society against radical political change (Bacia and Scherer, pp. 41–2).

It is unlikely, however, that the new left's frustration over the continued failure of the proletariat to meet their expectations alone would have destroyed their hopes as completely as did their disillusionment with internationalism. If in France the publication of Solzhenitsyn's *Gulag Archipelago* was the decisive event that marked the beginning of the end for Marxism, in West Germany the tide turned with Vietnam's invasion of Kampuchea, the ensuing border war between China and Vietnam, and above all the discovery of the atrocities committed by the Pol Pot regime in Kampuchea. After the invasion, Rudi Dutschke, the eminent leader of the West German student revolt, was one of the first to call upon the new left to put an end to their 'remote-controlled identity' with either Moscow or Beijing and to stand on their own feet in Europe.[2] Disillusionment soon turned into cynicism. In talking about the prospects for a post-revolutionary Iran, one member of the the unorthodox Socialist Bureau (a leading new left organization) went so far as to predict that even if there existed a Marxist movement in that country, 'after five years we would see the same outcome as in China, Vietnam, Cuba etc.'[3]

However, the impact of the armed conflict in Indochina was fairly mild compared to the shock of Kampuchea. According to Joschka Fischer, in the 1980s a leading figure in the Green party and at one time Green minister for the environment in the state of Hesse, for the new left Kampuchea represented two things: a 'moral immobility' *(Resignation)* in the face of what had happened in Kampuchea followed by immobility when confronted by 'one's own disaster of conviction.' And he concluded:

The good for which one fights turns into something much worse. For the left, Kampuchea was one of the turning points. We have turned away from the theories of salvation. Who still believes that he or she has to, ought to, or can save the world? What characterizes the international political system is oppression, exploitation, injustice, and a general instability. Now we have to come up with ideas of how we can secure survival, not how socialism can be built or democracy is secured. (*Die Zeit*, no.13, 1986, p. 46)

Kampuchea marked the endpoint of a process which had begun much earlier than when the news from the killing fields of Indochina reached Europe and had a chance to sink in. However, this news was particularly devastating for the West German left. A generation whose search for identity had at least partly been in reaction to their learning about the horrors of the German concentration camps found itself supporting a cause which ultimately would lead them back to the camps, even if they were thousands of miles away. The crimes of their fathers had revisited the sons' generation, and like their fathers they had—unwittingly or not—become accomplices. This discovery made them at least partly receptive to the charge of the French *nouveaux philosophes* that Marxism was deeply flawed. From then on many on the new left would turn to the question of how survival in an increasingly threatening world could be secured. From there it was only a short leap to the Greens.

FROM MARX . . .

The experience of many on the new left with the working class and particularly with internationalism contributed to a large degree to their disillusionment with Marxism. Its most immediate expression was a rejection of that 'new yearning for theory,' a theory which could 'open up and explain the *totality* of the social conditions' that had characterized the immediate post-1968 period (Sontheimer (1976, pp. 69, 75). Enthusiasm for theory turned into what many on the traditional left deplored as *Theoriemüdigkeit* (theory fatigue) or even *Theoriefeindlichkeit* (hostility towards theory). The renowned postmodern writer Botho Strauss (1982, p. 115) captured the new spirit in a short *bon mot* which soon became one of the most celebrated and most often analyzed dicta of the West German postmodern era: '(Without dialectics we immediately think more stupidly (*dümmer*); but it must be: Without them!)' (Brackets in the original). Marxism was under attack, and everyone wanted a piece of the action.

As early as 1978, Hans Magnus Enzensberger (1978, p. 7), the editor of the leading new left journal *Kursbuch*, charged leftist theoreticians with refusing to admit 'what every person on the street has known for some time': there was no *weltgeist*; the left did not know the laws of history; the class struggle was a natural process, and no vanguard would ever be able to plan and guide it; social evolution was without subject and therefore uncertain; the outcome of political action never conformed to what had been planned; instead it attained something entirely different 'which we cannot even imagine.' Referring to the history of really existing socialism Enzensberger charged that this last point was ultimately the reason for the crisis of all positive utopias.

The result of this realization on the new left was not only a widespread rejection of the Marxist utopia but also its rejection as an analytical tool. If large parts of the new left had believed that Marxist theory could explain everything, now they claimed that it could no longer explain anything. As one critic pointedly wrote, the 'misery' of Marxism resulted from the fact that it sat 'from front to back crookedly on top of the world in which it changes nothing because it fails to understand it' (Brunkhorst, 1981, p. 10–3).

With the rising public concern over the extent of environmental destruction, the new left's attack on Marxism added a new dimension. In the face of what many on the new left increasingly came to perceive as a global crisis they began to question whether Marxism had become not only an antiquated and inadequate tool for the interpretation and analysis of a system that had unleashed such an immense potential of destruction, but more importantly, whether Marxism itself might not have to accept at least partial blame for it. In short, there was a growing feeling that Marxism itself had become part of the problem. What replaced it was an anti-capitalism without Marx; a post-Marxist revolt against the whole project of modernity concentrated in an all-out attack on the industrial mode of production.

Among its leading spokespersons was Otto Ullrich, whose book *Weltniveau* (1979) soon came to be considered to be one of the classics of the ecology debate. In this book, Ullrich criticized Marxism for having bought into the bourgeois myth of progress. Marx had too uncritically adopted the bourgeois notion that increased productivity could only be achieved through a concentration of production in big industrial complexes; without much hesitation he had promoted the European model as a higher level of human development (pp. 9 and 54). By adopting the model of big industry (*Grossindustrie*) he had paved the way for the perverted form of socialism characteristic of the post-Stalinist socialist countries. In this way socialism came to be predominantly an ideology of industrialization and development rather than a guiding light for the evolution of a postcapitalist society.

A few years later, when he had become a leading theorist of the ecology movement, Ullrich extended his critique of Marxism to the project of modernity as a whole. With this he became one of the first West German advocates of a postmodern conception of the future. He called (1984, p. 56) on the highly advanced industrial societies to introduce a comprehensive program of a radical economic as well as scientific-technical disarmament of the 'overly instrumentalized, synthetic life worlds.' He saw a growing recognition that the deadly threat now facing humanity was closely connected to modernity's 'religion of progress.' After 300 years of experience with the project of modernity it was becoming clear that the translation of the 'celebrated enlightened rationality of lawfulness, unity, universality and self-control' into bureaucratic, economic, technical, and legal reality had assumed a grotesque form, not because 'of a mishap, but because of the inner logic of this cultural project.' What would have to replace the whole project of modernity was a 'postindustrial, postmodern cultural paradigm,' clearly separated from the present industrial model, that could redefine the basis of social co-existence and the norms of the relationship between humanity and nature.

Rudolf Bahro, at the end of the 1970s one of the most influential thinkers of the West German post-Marxist new left, took a similar position. In his view (1982, p. 88) the impending catastrophe was linked to 'that social dynamic which has made all written history a history of class struggle and caused the process of human development so far to hurtle forward in limitless material expansion and accelera-tion.' Like Ullrich, he attacked Marxism for having aimed too high, namely at the relations of production instead of aiming his critique at the forces of production. Marxism had accepted industrial society and the proletariat as the industrial class and attacked 'the *capitalist* form of our societies, scarcely ever the *industrial* system of capitalism.' From this he concluded that instead of focusing on the class struggle or the proletariat, the new left should launch an all-out attack on the industrial system.

What had originally begun as a critique of Marxism thus quickly turned into a full-blown attack on the project of modernity as a whole. For large parts of the new left, Marxism came to symbolize everything that was wrong with welfare capitalism: its emphasis on economic growth, the alienation experienced in large, anonymous cities like

Frankfurt or Berlin, the consumerism of the majority of West German wage earners, the malaise of the post-68 generations. This was the breeding ground for the mixture of postmodern apocalyptism and new spirituality, captured in an alternative approach to life that included a move toward subjectivity, sensibility, emotionality, and the celebration of the irrational.

. . . TO NIETZSCHE

> But Nietzsche lives! And how he lives. If certain circles today talk about a change of direction (*Kurswechsel*), then Nietzsche was its pivot. His revival . . . started the change within our minds. We will always remain the avant-garde, even if we go backwards. This marked the beginning of our farewell to the belief in progress.

With these words Wolfgang Ebert (1985, p. 65) summarized the change of intellectual climate on the new left at the end of the 1970s (see also Augstein, 1981). After the disillusionment with the working class and internationalism had shattered their *ersatz* identities, the new left began to rediscover both themselves as revolutionary subjects and their country as the privileged field of practice. In so doing, they rediscovered subjectivity and spontaneity (cf. Stamm, 1988, pp. 105–9). With this there emerged and became dominant a critical tendency on the new left which had its roots in the student literature of the early 1970s. Peter Schneider's short novel *Lenz*, first published in 1973 by the leftist Rotbuch Verlag, exemplified this tendency. *Lenz* attacked those who had subjected practice to theory, who had developed a system of categories with the goal of 'disciplin[ing] immediate impressions and the "political instinct"' (Brandt, 1980, p. 9).

Lenz tells the story of a young intellectual whose attempts to communicate his subjective experiences to others are constantly blocked by their need to integrate experiences into a system. Characteristically, it is only in Italy, the classic land of dreams and hopes of German romanticism (for example in Eichendorff), that Lenz succeeds in integrating both personal experiences and concepts and thus to gain his identity: 'Because he saw every day the needs of the students and the workers he met open before him, he did not doubt the concepts with which he expressed them' (Schneider, 1973, p. 83).

Lenz was the representative of a shift in West German leftist culture, which came to be known as *Tendenzwende* (Cf. Adelson, 1983;

Wellbery, 1985). He was the 'first literary figure embodying the *Erfahrungshunger* (hunger for experience) that inaugurated the "new sensibility" of an entire generation of young intellectuals. Theory had become suspect not only because of the innate reductionism of abstractions and slogans, but also because it had patently failed to bring about an alliance between the intellectuals and the working class, leading instead to the disorientation of the former and to a serious misjudgement about the role of the latter in contemporary society' (Burns and van der Willms, 1988, p. 54). *Tendenzwende* thus entailed both a shift 'away from the old radicalism to a new sensibility' (Schneider, 1977), including 'a willingness to embrace a *Lebensphilosophie* [philosophy of life] that placed emphasis on the uniqueness of everyday life' (Buchwalter, 1984, p. xx) and, as its critics charged, 'a cultural reversal from the political-emancipatory 1960s' to a neo-romantic inwardness for the 1970s (Berman, 1982, p. 144; also Huyssen, 1984, p. 31). But *Tendenzwende* also meant the search for personal identity and the rediscovery of emotions and suppressed spontaneity (see Schneider, 1973, p. 39; Schneider, 1977, pp. 176–7), and a tendency towards anarchism. In literature it favored 'personal concerns and aesthetic expression over collective interests and political content' (Adelson 1983, p. 5).

Few events could have better symbolized the new left's turn from theory to subjectivity than the ideological metamorphosis of the leftist Trikont publishing house. In the 1970s Trikont had specialized in problems of the Third World, publishing, amongst others, a series called *Schriften zum Klassenkampf* (*Writings for the Class Struggle*). In 1980, Trikont altered its image dramatically, dropping its reference to left-wing struggles and publishing books on mysticism, witches, and magic.[4] In a declaration that was widely-circulated in the alternative press, the publishers explained their plans in a statement which might easily have become the manifesto of the postmodern left:

> From fascism we tear away the myths which it has violated, concepts like friendship, *Heimat* (home land), nature, which it defiled; from the nobility, its lost feeling of respect, politeness, and *Minne* (romantic love); from the church, its most beautiful daughter, mysticism, which it has treated in a most unworthy fashion; from the vagabonds their freedom and neglected creativity. . . . We are hungry, in us there is a burning desire for myths. (cited in *Der Spiegel*, no.13, 1981, p. 53)

These were blasphemous words, particularly for those who considered themselves part of the West German new left. This intellectual turnabout was especially important because the new left's very tradition and self-understanding rested to a large degree on its anti-fascist credentials. It marked a growing desire on the part at least of significant segments of the new left to recuperate a lost German identity, distorted and defiled beyond recognition first by Nazism and then, after the war, by the crass materialism and consumerism of the West German *Wirtschaftswunder*.

What Anton Kaes (1989, p. 68) has written about the film-maker Hans Jürgen Syberberg, was true for the post-Marxist new left in general: they sought to find their way back to 'the spiritual home of the Germans' which they considered lost to materialism and rationalism. The result was a paradox: 'irrationalism, which the Hitler movement had appropriated and exploited, is wrested away from its National Socialistic associations' by means of a new discourse 'that celebrates irrationalism as the essence of German identity.' Examples could be found in the affirmation of Germanness by Thomas Schmid, editor of the postmodern journal *Freibeuter*, followed by his tirades against the 'imperialistic de-nazification by the god-damned Yankees' (Erler *et al.*, 1978, pp. 112–13), or Otto Ullrich's (1983, p. 445) plea for a recuperation of concepts like *Heimat*, *Lebensraum*, community, or euthanasia (*Sterbehilfe*) from fascism—concepts which in his view expressed 'more universal human desires' than to be stained forever by fascism.

Central to this reappropriation of the lost underpinnings of German identity was the argument that in the face of the immense destruction wrought upon nature and humanity as a result of the unfolding of rationality and progress, irrationalism was the only way to avert final disaster. The philosopher Herbert Schnädelbach (1984, p. 141) may have expressed it best when he challenged the view of irrationalism as intricately connected to fascism: 'The use of such labels [i.e. fascist] merely makes it more difficult to be able to pose the question of the truth of irrationalism in general.' Those who use these labels would also by necessity exclude from the philosophical field of vision re-emerging irrationalist tendencies and leave them to their own devices since they refused 'to be intimidated by these criticisms. Why then is "irrationalism" a reproach? Could it not be the truth (sic!)?'

With the growing interest in the irrational, the new left rediscovered Nietzsche. As early as 1978 Trikont published a book (*Vulkantänze.*

Linke und alternative Ausgänge [Röttgen and Rabe, 1981]) written by two spontis (see below) which represented an initial Nietzschean critique of rationalism and Marxist rationality in particular. Among the central themes of the book were (1) that rationalism ('the head') had exhausted its revolutionary potential. In the future 'the senses and our most precious vessel, the body' would take its place (p. 54); (2) that the left would have to rediscover the explosive power of mythical thinking, which had been suppressed by Athenian dialectics, Christianity, and bourgeois and Marxist rationality (p. 11); and (3) that the coming revolution would be a struggle for autonomy that would have to be based on an appreciation and re-affirmation of differences (the power 'to name oneself' [p. 21]) including that between races. Thus the authors concluded: 'Particularly through the variety of skin colors and faces, customs and rites, styles and particularities life gains its richness of colors' (p. 22).

In its rejection of the dominant enlightenment tradition and its neo-romantic celebration of irrationalism *Vulkantänze* represented an affirmation of what Allan Megill (1985, p. 34) has called 'active nihilism,' which became an important characteristic of the direction the postmodern spirit would take in West Germany in the late 1970s: 'Instead of drawing back from the void, we dance upon it. Instead of lamenting the absence of a world suited to our being, we invent one. We become the artists of our own existence, untrammeled by natural constraints and limitations.'

By the end of the 1970s, the new left increasingly adopted elements of vitalism and existentialism and turned to mysticism and new religions (Deutz *et al.*, 1979; Bacia and Scherer, 1981, p. 22; Weinberger, 1984, pp. 93–8). Hans-Dieter Hasenclever, by the end of the 1970s one of the leading West German environmentalists, wrote about his experience during those years: 'We discovered as the *meaning of life—life itself.* And we think that the essential precondition for the necessary new beginning in our society is: *Let us respect and advance life in its manifold forms!*' (Hasenclever and Hasenclever, 1982, p. 46). Translated into everyday this meant the evolution of a new subjectivity via the free expression of wants, desires, and needs, all of which Marxism had dismissed as subjectivist or even suppressed.

It was hardly surprising that left-wing critics attacked the new left's new 'cult of immediacy' (Wellmer, 1981, p. 74), its 'preference for spontaneous anarchism' and 'denigration of reason,' theoretical conceptualization, and formal social organization in favor of 'sensuous experience,' 'non-mediated being' and subjectivity (see

Berman, 1982). The new cult of immediacy was above all a rejection of representation in an effort to regain identity. As the Italian sociologist Alberto Melucci (1980, p. 220) aptly put it, the reappropriation of identity required the rejection of all mediation since mediation was seen as likely to reproduce the mechanisms of control and manipulation against which the new left was fighting in the first place. It was for this reason that the new left not only rejected political parties and the state as the classical loci of political representation, but above all the sources and mechanisms of interpretation themselves (Bopp, 1981, p. 155).

Although studies have shown that at the end of the 1970s the loss of confidence in political parties had become a widespread phenomenon, it was most profound among the new left (see Nath, 1986, p. 81). Not only did they reject the traditional mass parties, they also increasingly rejected the orthodox communist parties and their self-interpretation as the vanguard of the working class which had led them to demand absolute discipline and obedience from their members (Cf. Dräger and Hülsberg, 1986, p. 56–7). More important, however, they rejected the substitute representation and *ersatz* identity they had sought in Marxist ideology in general, and the working class, the proletariat or foreign liberation movements in particular. Instead they put forth the demand: *Wählen wir uns doch selbst!* (Let's vote for ourselves!).[5]

On an individual level the change in representation was characterized by an increasing emphasis on what Alberto Melucci has called 'the centrality of the body' (Melucci, 1980, p. 221) as an instrument of defiance and resistance and, particularly in the ecology and in some parts of the women's movement, 'as a part of nature,' as 'the seat of desires,' and as 'the nexus of interpersonal relationships.'

It was the philosopher Peter Sloterdijk who expressed and legitimized the growing importance of the body as a primary locus of resistance *vis-à-vis* the outside world. In his *Kritik der zynischen Vernunft* (Critique of Cynical Reason), he opposed cynical rationality (which he defined as the enlightened false consciousness, [1987, p. 6]) to the kynic embodied by the philosopher Diogenes. He especially emphasized the important role of bodily functions as symbols of defiance. 'The kynic farts, shits, pisses, and masturbates on the street, before the eyes of the Athenian market. He shows contempt for fame, ridicules the architecture, refuses respect, parodies the stories of gods and heroes, eats raw meat and vegetables, lies in the sun, fools around with the whores, and says to Alexander the Great that he should get out of his sunlight' (1987, p. 103).[6]

If for many who considered themselves members of the post-Marxist new left the body became the main weapon of resistance, its main target became the state. The state, however, was far from being a well-defined concept. Instead for many on the new left the state was an incarnation of everything to which they were opposed. It derived 'not so much from any analysis of the Constitutional state of the Federal Republic, parliamentarism, wage and social policies,' but from their direct experiences with the new democratic Leviathan in their dealings with the bureaucracy, judiciary and the police (Papadakis, 1984, p. 39).

Central to this understanding was Habermas's metaphor of the colonization of the life-world. In this view the state had emancipated itself from society 'spreading like a metastatic cancer, infesting and penetrating all parts of society, engulfing more and more what had formerly been separate social realms.' Its goal was the liquidation of society nationalizing as it were what remained of community and self-reliance and thus to create a 'total state society,' as a decisive step towards a new fascism (see Lohmann, 1979–80, p. 128).

For those who agreed with this view, resistance meant above all resisting the further erosion of civil society and the state's all-encompassing power. In this struggle those groups had to play a vanguard role which had still managed to preserve their autonomy. It was particularly up to the new social movements to rebel against 'abstract commodification and administratively enforced normatilization,' and to reverse the trends towards 'capitalization, disintegration, and bifurcation' (Hirsch, 1982, p. 137). Among the new social movements it was above all the spontis and the alternatives who sought to draw practical conclusions from these insights.

ALTERNATIVES TO THE MODELL DEUTSCHLAND: SPONTIS AND ALTERNATIVE MOVEMENT

The transition period between the new left's discovery of immediacy and assertion of subjectivity and their at least partial integration into the Green party in 1980 was dominated by the so-called new social movements. Because of the vast amount of literature on this subject (see Brand, Büsser and Rucht, 1983; Roth and Rucht, 1987; Offe, 1987), I will restrict myself to two movements which were of particular importance for the left origins of the Green party. These were the spontis and the alternative movement (see Stamm, 1988, ch.4).

"We are those of whom our parents have always warned us." "We have nothing to lose apart from our fear." "Even without tear gas we have enough reason to cry." "Legal, illegal, *scheissegal*." "We want everything—and we want it now!" "Marx is dead, Lenin is dead—and I am not feeling too well myself."

These popular 'sponti' slogans expressed the feelings of a generation of students who, frustrated and disillusioned with the *Modell Deutschland* on the one hand and the orthodox Marxist–Leninist cadre parties on the other, were searching for an alternative way of life (cf. Roche, 1984). 'The spontis were the decisive engine for the emancipation from the fundamentalism of '68 and its dogmas' (Sontheimer, 1988, p. 41). Although never significantly more than a radical fringe movement within a broad range of new social movements, the spontis were the most vocal and colorful representatives of leftist postmodernism in the sense in which it has been discussed above. The sponti movement originated in Frankfurt where spontanistic groups had played an important role in the new left since 1971. These groups rejected the Marxist–Leninist concepts of the vanguard; largely influenced by classical anarchists (Bakunin, Kropotkin, Landauer, Muehsam, and Buber), they 'excavated the buried and distorted anarchist traditions' (Huber, 1980, p. 26). They propagated autonomy, spontaneity of feelings, and emotions. Central to their worldview was the complete rejection of any kind of domination, especially by the state. Instead, they sought to create free space where they could develop and live out their own norms. Starting from their own needs and wishes they sought to change the totality of society (Langguth, 1984, pp. 238f.). With the rise of an alternative culture in 1974, the Frankfurt spontis increased their influence on the new left, led by Daniel Cohn-Bendit, the 'Dany le Rouge' of the May '68 student revolution in France and currently the editor of the influential *Szene* journal, *Pflasterstrand* as well as head of the 'multicultural department' of the city of Frankfurt, created after the establishment of a SPD-Green coalition government there.

After 1975 the sponti movement spread to most of the West German universities (Cf. Sontheimer, 1988, pp. 38–41). In the universities, the spontis formed so-called basis groups with often colorful names (for instance, Spontifex Marximus, Alpträumer, [one who has nightmares], *Was lange gärt wird endlich Wut* [that which has been fermenting for a long time finally turns into wrath, a spoof of the German saying 'was lange gährt wird endlich gut,'—that which takes a long time will finally turn out well], Placebo, LuSt [which stood for list of undogmatic students] or simply Anti) (Hilgenberg, 1986; Langguth, 1984, p. 235), which usually ran very successfully in elections to the student parliaments. Thus in 1979, half of the representatives of the Frankfurt student parliament were spontis. In Berlin, the rise of the spontis began at the end of 1975. In 1979 they received one third of the total votes and made up the strongest faction of the student parliament. In Heidelberg, they were the second largest faction by 1975, and in Bochum, the strongest by 1979 (Langguth, 1984, p. 235; Krause *et al.*, 1980, pp. 50ff.). In 1986, out of forty-two universities with student parliaments, fifteen were in the hands of basis groups (Hilgenberg, 1986).

The sponti movement reached its peak in 1978 (see Schlicht, 1980, pp. 140–2). In January 1978 about 6,000 spontis took part in the so-called Tunix congress (full title: National Congress of Resistance: Journey to Tunix (Do-Nothing)) in Berlin. Invited were all 'freaks, friends, and comrades . . . and all those who are fed up with "this our country".' The purpose of the congress was to discuss 'how to organize our exodus from the "Modell Deutschland",' to find out 'where Tunix is, and how to get there,' or to discuss 'how to destroy the *Modell Deutschland* and to substitute Tunix for it.'[7]

The language of the invitation expressed on the one hand the frustration of a new generation of radical students with the political situation in West Germany, on the other hand their reaction—they neither expected nor wanted anything from their country and government.

> The winter here is too sad, the spring too contaminated, and in the summer we suffocate. For a long time we have been fed up with the bad air from the offices, nuclear power plants, and factories, from the city highways. We no longer like our muzzles nor the sausage with the plastic cover. The beer is too flat and so are the narrow-minded morals. We no longer want to do the same work and make the same faces. They have ordered us around enough, controlled our thoughts, ideas, home, passports, they have beaten us up. . . . *We leave!* . . . to the beach of Tunix. There we will build our own huts, whittle our own guns and sandals. . . . We will put new strings on our violins, guitars, and celli and play 'There is no country more beautiful than our beach' with Tommy and the Stones. Those who can't sing, will collect mushrooms. . . . Let's get together, before we all leave, to this congress of resistance—let's tell each other tales, let's learn from each other, let's express this resistance movement—

and let's then leave together, together let us sail away to the beach of Tunix, which may be far away or perhaps *under the cobblestones of this country.*[8] . . . For years we have believed that we could change something with actions like 'Away with . . .' and 'Down with . . .' if we only did it skilfully enough. In the process our fantasy got mutilated, put to sleep, or buried alive. . . . We want to develop new ideas for a new struggle, which we will determine ourselves, which we won't let the technicians of the 'Modell Deutschland' force upon us. . . . We want the *Maximum for Everybody!* Everybody can formulate their own paroles and ideas, paint, sing, and we can still—or just because of it—fight together. *We Want Everything And We Want It Now!!!!!!*

The partly bitter, partly sarcastic and resigned tone of this invitation to the Tunix conference expressed the frustration and disillusionment of large parts of the new left. It can be explained, in part, as a result of the widespread feeling that 'everything was in vain, that nothing has changed, and that change is impossible anyway.'[9] In part it was a reaction to the 'proxy politics' (*Stellvertreterpolitik*) of the orthodox cadre parties and the Marxist student organizations; in part a response to the disillusioning job prospects and *Berufsverbote* that formed the experience of the new generation of students for whom the university was little more than a comfortable waiting room.[10] (This will be discussed in greater length in Chapter 3.) Finally it was a response to the determined reaction on the part of the political parties and the state to the culmination of political terrorism in the fall of 1977, which came to be known in leftist circles as the *Deutsche Herbst* (the German Fall). 'Faced with the totalitarian logic of the social state of emergency, in the fall of 1977 the radical left lost its appetite for the dialectical consciousness so profoundly that it appeared to have only been silly dreams (*Flausen*)' (Bruhn, 1987, p. 18; also Narr, 1987). Especially after the so-called Göttinger 'Mescalero,' a sponti who belonged to the group *Bewegung Undogmatischer Frühling* (undogmatic spring movement, see Langguth, 1984, p. 240), had published his famous eulogy (*Nachruf*) in which he expressed a 'scarcely concealed joy' at the news of the assassination of General Federal Prosecutor Siegfried Buback, students and the critical intelligentsia came under increasing attack from the state and the media (see Schlicht, 1980, pp. 136–40).

The immediate response to the publication of the eulogy was a wave of legal actions, house searches, and police raids against student executive committees that had published the text. In July 1977, forty-eight professors from West Berlin, Bremen, Lower Saxony, and Northrhine-Westphalia published a documentation containing the text of the eulogy. The result was a new wave of public indignation. The CDU minister of culture of Lower Saxony, Eduard Pestel, demanded that the thirteen co-authors from Lower Saxony sign an oath of loyalty to the 'free democratic order.' Among other things, the oath maintained that civil servants had a 'particular obligation of loyalty to the state.' This was a demand that they distance themselves from 'groups or tendencies which attack, struggle against and slander constitutional order.' It also demanded that civil servants in times of crisis intervene in its behalf 'in a partisan way' (cited in Mayer, 1978, p. 157). Eleven professors complied, protesting afterwards. In West Berlin, the eight co-authors who were first charged with inciting the people and defamation of the state, were later acquitted (Cf. Reichel, 1981, pp. 206f; Habermas, 1986, pp. 83f.).

The spontis' resignation reflected the growing pessimism of a whole generation. It caused Bernd Rabehl, in 1968 one of the leading figures of the extra-parliamentary opposition, to complain:

Today's generation lacks all optimism, both when it comes to politics or future careers. There is, if one is allowed to express it totally frankly, a waste of mis-planned academics—that is the one side. And the other: They neither believe in social democracy, reformism, nor in the different groups on the left. They are thrown back to subjectivism. And that expresses itself in skepticism, cynicism. That means: They are desperate, and that is the big difference to earlier days [i.e. 1968]. (cited in Körfgen, 1978, pp. 997–8).

THE ALTERNATIVE MOVEMENT

Unlike the sponti movement, which was almost exclusively confined to the large West German universities, the alternative movement included a diverse array of groups, projects, and initiatives (cf. Weinberger, 1984, ch.7). According to the SINUS survey institute (1983, p. 44), in 1982 6 per cent of fifteen to thirty year-olds considered themselves a part of the alternative movement, 42 per cent sympathized with it, 28 per cent had no opinion, 16 per cent had little sympathy with it, whereas only 7 per cent rejected it vigorously. An extensive study of the values of university students showed that almost a quarter of all students claimed to practice some form of alternative lifestyle. Between 80 and 90 per cent declared they tolerated alternative values, five per cent thought alternative life forms were the only possible way to survive, and only five per cent rejected alternative values completely (Krause *et al.*, 1980, pp. 194f.).

The alternative groups that spread throughout the Federal Republic and West Berlin after 1979 initially sought 'to create a context for the fulfilment of their own aspirations away from "established society"' (Papadakis, 1984, p. 113). The alternatives, like the spontis, rejected the state which they regarded 'not as an authority, but as a repressive apparatus . . .' (Schülein, 1983, p. 266). This sometimes led to extreme cases of isolationism in the alternative scene (Cf. Hübsch, 1980), where small groups provided new identity and community as a substitute for and opposition to society. According to two experts on the alternative scene, some members of the Berlin and Frankfurt alternative scenes 'were proud that for two and a half years they had not spoken a single word with anybody outside' (Fichter and Lönnendonker, 1979, p. 137):

The average city-indians wake up in their 'house community,' buy their rolls at the little bakery around the corner, and their granola at the bio-store, read 'Pflasterstrand' or 'INFO-BUG' [two alternative journals] while having breakfast, and then go to work in an alternative project. Every five days they work in a day care center. They have their cars patched together in a left auto-shop. In the evenings they watch 'Casablanca' with Humphrey Bogart in the 'Off' cinema and then can be found in a tea house or some other leftist bar or music club. They get their bed-time reading from the book store collective. There are medical and legal collectives, feminist self-help groups, as well as women's and men's organizations in this ghetto.

Surveys on the value system of young people considering themselves members of the alternative scene showed that for the alternatives the main goal was a reconciliation between humans and nature. This coincided with a general growing awareness among the young of the dangers to the environment. Thus, in 1982 for two thirds of those between fifteen and thirty years of age the destruction of the environment was the most important problem (SINUS, 1983, pp. 40f.). The focus on the environment led them to reject the technical infrastructure and especially large technological projects (such as nuclear power plants) they held responsible for destroying the environment. Instead they emphasized that only grassroots democratic structures would guarantee an implementation of the new values against the interests of big industry (Schülein, 1983, p. 267).

This consciousness was put into practice both in personal lifestyle (rejection of status symbols and consumer goods, environmentally conscious lifestyle and diet) and through a growing network of alternative workshops, services, and alternative presses. According to Joseph Huber, an expert on the alternative movement, by the end of the 1970s there existed about 11 500 alternative projects with an estimated 80 000 activists in the Federal Republic and West Berlin. From this number, Huber estimated the size of the movement (that is, including friends and sympathizers) at about 300 000 to 400 000 people (Huber, 1980, pp. 29–30; also Weinberger, 1984, pp. 78f., and Kreutz and Fröhlich, 1986). The vast majority of these projects were in the service sector (70 per cent). Only 12 per cent were in the productive sector (agriculture: 4 per cent, manufacturing: 8 per cent) and the rest were related to political work (citizen initiatives and citizen committees) (Huber, 1980, p. 28). In 1984 there were 124 alternative projects with 533 workplaces in Hamburg, and in Berlin in 1983 there were 260 projects with 1400 workplaces (Kück, 1985, p. 27).

The spontis and alternatives tended to oppose 'the whole' and to make a better future dependent on a radical reversal and change of the whole system. A sponti collective of 'Quinn the Eskimo, Frankie Lee, and Judas Priest' wrote after the Tunix-congress:

At the moment that the system is removed, the majority of illnesses—to give one example—will cease to exist. Therefore it makes more sense to remove this system as quickly and as thoroughly as possible, to wrestle away as much power as possible from the state which with its apparatus of coercion and violence guarantees the existence of this system, to withdraw as many areas of our lives from the disposal and administration of this state, in order to become as autonomous as possible instead of delegating more and more responsibility to this state, with the illusion that the public and universalist character of the state is in a rudimentary fashion the organ of common and mutual responsibilities. The state is in everything the opposite of what we envisage as freedom and mutual responsibility.[11]

Linked to the yearning for autonomy was the claim to a right to be different. This does not mean that the alternatives opposed universal equality and justice. What they wanted 'was *more* than mere equality and justice' (Brunkhorst, 1981, p. 105; italics in the original). Equality and justice meant that everybody had the same rights to their own individuality. Theirs was an attempt to gain power over their own lives rather than to gain political power. On the other hand, the claim to the right to be different played into the hands of groups of the new right which, at the end of the 1970s, tried to gain legitimacy by adopting the alternative label.

For the new left the alternative and sponti movements were an interlude. They symbolized and expressed the fall of orthodox Marxism reflected in the rapid decline in membership in the orthodox Maoist parties, and the revival of spontaneity, and an affirmation of immediacy and subjectivity growing out of one's own experience and life situation. Their views were largely a rejection of the reformist position seeking to preserve the legacy of modernity. Instead they believed that the discontents of the modern age *were* rooted 'in the process of modernization and rationalization itself' (Buchwalter, 1984, p. xxxii) and that disaster could only be averted if that process was radically reversed. With this they already foreshadowed those issues and themes which would dominate the postmodern politics of the Green, *bunte* (many-colored) and alternative lists that emerged at the end of the 1970s. By supporting these lists, the new left returned to politics, but this time it was a politics entirely different from the orthodox phase. Whereas in their orthodox phase, they had unsuccessfully tried to represent an elusive working class, now they tried to represent nobody but themselves.

2   From Green to Red

The *Bundestag* elections of 1983 marked the first time since 1953 that a new party successfully challenged the five per cent hurdle to penetrate what had seemed an impenetrable two-and-a-half party system. With 5.6 per cent of the electorate and more than two million votes the Green party (Die Grünen) gained twenty-seven seats in the West German *Bundestag*. Those who believed that the Green phenomenon would only be short-lived soon had to revise their predictions. After a series of successes—and some failures—in state (*Länder*) and regional elections, the Greens increased their share of the vote to 8.3 per cent in the 1987 federal elections, which translated into forty-two seats, four less than the established Free Democrats (FDP).

With the Green party the most important West German representative of postmodern politics to date entered the stage of high politics. Its parliamentary success marked the end of the new left's search for identity, immediacy, and a new political home. However, like the history of the new left's ideological transformation, the history of the Green party is complex, complicated, and often contradictory. This stems mostly from the fact that its new left origins were quite heterogeneous. The Green party project was thus as much an attempt to integrate a hodge-podge of movements and individuals, who often shared little beyond a will to escape their self-imposed ghettoization, into a viable political organization as it was meant to propose a new alternative politics to the established parties.

The history of the Green party is further complicated by the fact that in its beginnings environmental politics was dominated by the political and ideological right. This included traditional conservative, populist and nationalist and even extreme right-wing forces. The evolution and direction of Green politics was largely influenced and determined by the failure of conservative and right-wing environmentalists in the late 1970s to establish the party as a significant force in West German politics before the left could respond to the Green challenge. This is rather surprising considering the fact that in the late 1970s more than 20 per cent of the population was positively inclined towards a participation of the Greens in West German politics (see Noelle-Neumann and Piel, 1983, pp. 292–294). There are several reasons to explain this failure. The conservative and right-wing environmentalists lacked a sufficient base in the new social movements and among those individuals drawn to new politics values. Instead they sought to determine the direction of environmental politics mostly from above. Against that, the left-wing Greens were firmly grounded in a growing alternative milieu which provided them with a rather stable social base. This point will be discussed at greater length in the following chapter. The failure to appeal to those social groups most likely to support alternative politics was reflected in the political program advanced by the conservatives and right-wing environmentalists, which was 'politically at odds' with the line of direction of the new social movements (Hülsberg, 1988, p. 96). Whereas the latter represented heterogeneity and a new pluralism, the former promoted primarily a holistic program, a new grand solution. In addition, within its own ranks the Green right was far from united. This provided the left a range of opportunities to play one side against the other. Both aspects will be explored in the following discussion.

The Green party started out as a loose alliance of on the one hand various conservative and right-wing groups, on the other a variety of new left organizations. The conservative and right-wing environmentalists were united in their opposition to what they considered the worst feature of West German politics in the 1970s, namely its absolute priority of economic growth. Against that they put the regard for the needs of the individual and for nature as the most important priority. Beyond that, however, they were no less fragmented than their counterparts on the new left. Particularly in respect to the question of whether the necessary changes were possible within the framework of the existing social, political, and economic system or whether they required a radical transformation of all aspects of life there was little consensus between the predominantly conservative wing of the alliance and their predominantly populist opponents.

The new left groups, on the other hand, attributed what they considered to be a profound crisis of contemporary West German society to social conditions without, however, accepting the notion that it was enough to reform specific conditions. It was exactly the rational organization of social reality, that had contributed decisively to the overall crisis in the first place. Thus what distinguished the majority of new left Greens from their conservative counterparts (save for a populist wing of the right) was that the new left Greens envisioned a radical transformation of the basic structures of West

German society whereas most of the conservatives sought to leave them unchanged.

CONSERVATIVE ENVIRONMENTALISM

To the conservative Green spectrum belonged those Green organizations that had only regional pretensions ('Green Lists'), the most important of which was the Green List for the Protection of the Environment (GLU) founded in Lower Saxony in 1977, the Green Action Future (GAZ) founded in 1978 by the former CDU member of the *Bundestag* Herbert Gruhl, and the right-wing extremist 'World Federation for the Protection of Life' (*Weltbund zum Schutze des Lebens, WSL*) headed by Professor Werner Haverbeck. What united them was an emphasis on traditional values and a commitment to bring about fundamental change without a radical transformation of established institutions. The populist wing was represented by the Action Unity of Independent Germans (AUD), a nationalist party founded by the professional Bavarian politician August Haussleiter. Finally there was a third group which sympathized with both sides and tried to mediate between them—the anthroposophical circles of the 'Achberger Kreis' led by Wilfried Heidt and of the 'Free International University' headed by the renowned artist Joseph Beuys. These organizations (with the exception of the WSL) later formed the core of the first federal Green party, the so-called 'Other Political Union The Greens' which took part in the European elections in 1979 to gain 3.2 per cent of the vote.

The GLU was the successor to the 'Party for the Protection of the Environment' (USP), a small environmentalist party, founded in 1977 by environmental activists who had united to fight the plans for a nuclear reprocessing plant in Lower Saxony (see Hallensleben, 1984). The USP was a predominantly middle class party. Its six point program was short, mainly consisting of environmental demands. After quarrels broke out within the leadership of the party over both party ideology and strategy, the party soon split. Renaming itself 'Green List for the Protection of the Environment' the remnant decided to take part in local elections. Against all expectations they won a seat in a local parliament. Encouraged by their success the party's predominantly new middle class (particularly teachers) leadership decided to run candidates for the 1978 state elections. In these elections the GLU received almost four per cent of the vote and gained instant national attention.

The growing attraction of Green new politics was soon reflected in the expansion of the GLU's programmatic statements. Early programs had still focused primarily on the connection between industrialism and environmental destruction. In order to halt further environmental degradation the program advocated the need for a radical change of values both in the private as well as public realm rather than calling for a radical transformation of the structure of the capitalist system itself. The 1978 program saw a differentiation of demands. Although still rejecting radical structural changing, it did include topics such as women's position in society, political rights, and the call for a shortened working week. These issues were deliberately included in order to attract leftist grassroots groups and anti-nuclear activists into an otherwise conservative party.

The second conservative party, the GAZ, was a creation of Herbert Gruhl, who had left his former party, the CDU, over the latter's lack of concern for the environment. Informed by the idea that ecological politics could only be effectively pursued on the federal level, and convinced that he would be able to integrate the various environmental groups, Gruhl decided to found a national environmental party, which he called 'Green Action Future.'

The character of Gruhl's party was largely determined by the authoritarian style of its founder. It was organized from above, something many environmentalists and citizen initiatives resented. In addition, Gruhl had single-handedly written a party platform which offered no opportunity for change through discussion. This was hardly an attractive alternative to the established parties. Despite the fact that by 1979 the GAZ had managed to establish regional party organizations in all states except Bremen, it never fulfilled Gruhl's high hopes. Geared too much to the person of Herbert Gruhl the GAZ resembled a *Honoratiorenpartei* of the educated middle class with never more than a few thousand members.

Its main importance for the development of West German Green politics lay in the person of Herbert Gruhl. Gruhl believed that the economic system of the industrial countries was destroying the preconditions for human survival (Gruhl, 1978; 1980). The policy of forced economic growth would only sharpen the crisis and eventually lead to an even larger catastrophe. The 'materialist economy of waste' had failed to enhance human happiness and fulfilment. The GAZ, therefore, proclaimed that its goal was to give meaning to human life.

It claimed that the main sources of individual fulfilment were spiritual, cultural, and religious experiences as well as the social bonds of the family and the community. Mutual trust and help would have to replace economic irresponsibility. Even sacrifice could enhance 'the value of our existence' (1980, p. 28). In the work sphere, the program called for decentralization and the promotion of trades in order to secure workplaces and to further market-oriented competition. The rest of the program was devoted to environmental concerns and demands. It called for the conservation of energy and natural resources, the abolition of nuclear power plants and the creation of a nuclear-free Europe, and the production of durable consumer products. It finally demanded self-determination for all peoples, including the Germans (p. 30).

This program already revealed the basic dilemma characteristic of all of Herbert Gruhl's writings. Although he identified the economic system of the industrial countries as the cause of most ills plaguing the planet, he refused to ask whether these phenomena might not be essential to capitalism's survival. Instead he blamed the crisis on human expectations. The best state form in the world could not achieve reasonable goals as long as voters pressured their political representatives to represent their short-term material interests. In this, there existed a coalition of capital, labor, and the state, united in their pursuit of ever higher investments, wages, and taxes.

Gruhl denied that a radical transformation of the system was a viable solution to the global crisis. Instead he called for both a change in popular attitudes and values as well as a strong state. He argued that more and more people already recognized the senselessness of material rates of growth that hardly ever benefited man while destroying his natural environment (1978a, p. 118). However, in order to implement a new system of values it was necessary to have a strong state capable of compelling its citizens to make sacrifices, even if that meant a loss of freedom:

> Today we must plan for the future. And there is nowhere anyone who could do that, except for the state. But if the state does it, then it resolutely has to abolish many liberties, in order to prevent chaos. (1978a, pp. 240, 290)

Gruhl's conclusion was the logical consequence of his belief that the state was held captive by people's expectations. In order for the state to be able to act it had to reconquer its autonomy, its power to make politics. This conception, together with his authoritarian style, which both reflected a certain aristocratic attitude, were the reasons why Gruhl failed to attract a mass following in the Green movement.

The group within the conservative alliance that came closest to Gruhl's ideas was the 'Achberg Circle.' Its worldview was based on the teachings of the anthroposophist Rudolf Steiner, a leading figure within the 'life-reform movement' in the early years of the twentieth century, which sought to change the way humans lived through various reforms ranging from vegetarianism to nudism. The Achberg Circle thus tied the Green movement into the larger context of historical attempts at socio-ecological renovation (for examples see Linse, 1986; Hepp, 1987). Its main contribution to Green ideology was the notion of a 'third way,' a popular idea not only among West German Greens but also reform oriented socialists and Eurocommunists throughout Europe. Central to this idea was the notion that it was possible to reconcile conflicting ideologies and *weltanschauungen* and thus to reach a higher, more advanced synthesis between them.

One way to gain such synthesis, one leading anthroposophist believed, lay in the recovery of 'wholeness' via spirituality. In the past the development of spirituality had been hampered by the domination of 'intellectualism,' materialism and atheism over modern life. Their ideological expressions, liberalism and Marxism, however, could only answer certain aspects of the human essence (namely its individual and social aspects) while neglecting the spiritual side. The same imbalance had developed in human society. Among its three essential dimensions—economics, politics, and culture—economics (in both East and West) and politics (in the form of the monopoly of the party in Eastern Europe) had assumed primacy over the true foundation of human life, namely culture. 'Culture shapes the values of life [and] the norms and forms of conduct, without which there is neither fulfilment nor humanism [b]ut only class struggle in the socioeconomic sphere or a struggle for survival in the economic sphere. These are forms of . . . mere civilization that have squandered and destroyed its fertile soil' (Bartsch, 1980, p. 87).

Ecology was a chance, 'a new step of human evolution,' to realize the lost harmony between both the spheres of individual and social life and to unite them (Bartsch, 1980, p. 79). This harmony had to come through a process of metamorphosis, not revolution, as a result of an 'ecological ethics,' a combination of physical and spiritual forces. For 'the universe is an ecological unity that also comprises the earth and heaven. We are woven into this unity, but destroy its pattern of life

(*Lebensmuster*) that also maintains us' (p. 78). Through spirituality human beings could once again become the link between earth and heaven and thus achieve wholeness.

This emphasis on spiritual regeneration appealed not only to conservative environmentalists but also to those on the left who were searching for a new all-encompassing theory as a substitute for Marxism with which they had become disillusioned. In addition, although anthroposophists indirectly denied the necessity for class struggle, they placed great importance on grassroots democracy (Hülsberg, 1988, p. 84). They believed that individuals were capable of acting in a responsible way or at least could be educated in that direction. This view was more attractive to citizen initiatives and environmentalists whose primary motive was, after all, concern and a feeling of responsibility for the environment than the authoritarian views of a personality like Herbert Gruhl.

However, the practical side of the anthroposophists' ideas was far less important for the development of the Green ideology than their romantic anti-capitalism. With their emphasis on life, wholeness and harmony, the religious and mystic overtones of their worldview, and their preference for evolution over revolution, the anthroposophists openly expressed what were latent premises and silent conclusions of most of the other conservative ecology programs.

Politically the Achberg Circle was most influential in Baden-Württemberg. Their concepts of 'ecological humanism' and 'unity in variety' (*Einheit in Vielfalt*) became the cornerstones of the programmatic ideas of the Baden-Württemberg Greens (cf. Hasenclever and Hasenclever, 1982). But their influence could also be felt in other environmental organizations like Haussleiter's AUD. Organizationally the Achberg Circle was a small group of mostly intellectuals including the artist Joseph Beuys, the writer Robert Jungk, and the trade union activist Heinz Brandt. After the repression of the 'Prague Spring' it also provided refuge to several well-known Czech intellectuals (Ota Sik, Eugen Löbl, Jiri Kosta, and Radeslav Selucky) who promoted their own versions of a 'third way.'

If the story of the GAZ was primarily that of Herbert Gruhl, the story of the AUD was inextricably linked with the person of August Haussleiter, possibly one of the most flamboyant political figures in postwar West Germany (see Stöss, 1980). Never himself attaining the position of political power he would have wished, Haussleiter was constantly in conflict with the powerful. Haussleiter was one of the co-founders of the Bavarian CSU. He represented the CSU in the

Bavarian *Landtag* and was from February 1948 to June of 1949 its deputy chairman. In 1947, he was excluded from the *Landtag* and accused of militarism for having kept the diary of an army corps serving at the Russian front. However later he was reinstated.

Haussleiter soon clashed with the party over his populist ideas. Whereas he remained true to his conviction, the party increasingly turned conservative. This led him to leave the party in 1959 to found the 'German Community' (*Deutsche Gemeinschaft, DG*), a small party, that never led more than a marginal existence, intended as a reservoir for those without a political home. In the same year, Haussleiter was among the founders of the 'German Union' (*Deutsche Union*), one of several study circles promoting the idea of a united neutral Germany. In 1965, after several unsuccessful attempts to gain seats with the DG in state and federal elections, Haussleiter, together with other miniscule political organizations, founded the 'Action Unity of Independent Germans' (AUD) without more success at the polls. In 1968, the AUD began to seek contacts to the 'Extraparliamentary Opposition' (APO) in order to form a new party for the *Bundestag* elections in 1969. With this maneuver the party started to move to the left.

The attempt to form a new party, like so many previous attempts, was unsuccessful. But Haussleiter decided to stay on the left and soon discovered in environmentalism a new and promising political issue. In 1973, the AUD published a 'Manifesto of the Protection of Life' and sought contacts with the environmental movement. The AUD's—and Haussleiter's—ideological odyssey from rightist neo-nationalism to ecology was completed when in 1977 the AUD changed its name to 'AUD The Greens.'

In the early stages of the Green party's development, none of the leading figures provoked more controversy than August Haussleiter. His political history, especially his shifting between right and left, were the targets of often vitriolic attacks on his person. He himself once said: 'I personally was categorized by the right as on the left, and by those on the left, who did not know me closely, as on the right.'[1] This paradox was a result of two basic tenets underlying Haussleiter's thinking: in domestic politics the fear of a new fascism; and in foreign politics, his belief in the possibility of a demilitarized and neutral united Germany.

Haussleiter regarded National Socialism as a necessary stage in the evolution of German society. For him it represented a 'revolution of the masses' against the old strata of the Wilhelminian period who had preserved their status in the Weimar Republic (*Tageszeitung*, April 25, 1980, p. 9). To the extent that Nazism had removed social barriers, it had been revolutionary. Where it had failed, however, was to develop a new vision, a true synthesis between nationalism and socialism (Stöss, 1980, p. 68). Because Hitler had to depend on big business and big business had succeeded in gaining the support of small proprietors, Nazism turned into fascism. The resulting alliance destroyed any chance for socialism. Socialism, Haussleiter believed, had a chance of success only if it could show that the interests of workers were identical with the interests of the small proprietor. This belief in the crucial importance of the middle class explains Haussleiter's populist anti-capitalism, which led one critic to call the DG a 'radical–petty bourgeois party of the right' (Stöss, 1–978, p. 50).

Haussleiter's political career started with the Bavarian CSU. As one of the most influential leaders of its left wing he promoted his version of populism and neutralist nationalism. In the years immediately after the war the left wing of the CSU 'dreamed of a future united Germany, which, beyond capitalism and Stalinism, would develop the synthesis of creative human self-realization and a necessary community order, based on solidarity.'[2] These ideas were integrated into the 1946 party program which advocated among others a third way between 'doctrinaire liberalism' and 'doctrinaire socialism;' decentralization of the economy towards small and medium-size plants; the possibility for workers to share responsibility for the productive process; and the socialization of those sectors of the economy that were important for the common good, such as large banks and insurance companies. These remained among the core demands of Haussleiter's AUD and would be found again in the Green program.

His failure to attract the new left into his organization did not discourage him in his search for a cause promising enough to further his political ambitions. In the early 1970s his political instinct soon led him to realize the political potential of the citizen initiative and environmental movements. With the passing of the 'Manifesto of the Protection of Life' (*Manifest des Lebensschutzes*) in 1973, and with later party programs, Haussleiter succeeded in transforming the AUD into one of the mouthpieces of the budding ecology movement. According to Haussleiter blind faith in the progress of civilization was vanishing. 'Hunger, overpopulation, and the big conflicts resulting from them are on the increase. The limits of economic growth become visible' (*Deutsche Gemeinschaft*, October 20, 1973, p. 1). If humanity wanted to survive, Haussleiter maintained, it had to be prepared to make fundamental social and profound behavioral changes. In order to avert a catastrophe the AUD proposed a list of environmental measures. In addition, the party program also demanded an extension of democracy through plebiscites on the local and regional level, more rights for citizen initiative groups, humane working conditions, and global population control. Its goal, the AUD stated, was the transformation of the growth oriented into an equilibrium oriented society, from quantitative to qualitative growth (p. 2).

The AUD was by far the most radical of the environmentalist parties. Not only was it openly anti-capitalist, but with its mixture of Marxist, feminist, populist, and environmentalist demands—an early example of what would become characteristic of Green politics— Haussleiter succeeded in integrating his basic political beliefs (which had little to do with ecology) into an environmentalist framework which had a good chance to attract broader support, particularly from the left.

Organizationally, however, the AUD never attracted more than 2000 members. In terms of its social composition the party changed with its new focus on the environment. Whereas the proportion of members from the sector traditionally open to populist politics (farmers, artisans, and so on) dropped in the late 1970s, the number of those from a mixture between traditional and new middle class (for example, employees, public servants, scientists, journalists, doctors) increased substantially (Stöss, 1980, pp. 330f.).

Closely aligned with the AUD was a third environmentally oriented organization, the West German section of the 'World Federation for the Protection of Life' (*Weltbund zum Schutze des Lebens*, WSL). Founded in 1960, the WSL followed the writings of Günther Schwab, an obscure Austrian forester from Salzburg. Schwab had written a small book, *Der Tanz mit dem Teufel* (Dancing with the Devil, 1969), in which he described how the devil had systematically misled humanity to follow a perverted notion of progress that ultimately had to lead to human destruction. The final chaos, Schwab maintained, would result from today's greatest evil, namely uncontrolled population growth. The result would be disastrous: '[W]here there is no selection, life becomes sick' (1969, p. 452). Humanity would end as a herd of billions of incompetent, fragile, sick, and weak imbeciles, unable to exist without outside help. Misery, sickness, pain, and hunger would be the reward for 'so-called humanism' (1969, p. 544). The result would be a Darwinian struggle of all against all. Only after the destruction of most of humanity would there re-emerge harmony and justice based on poverty and reverence for nature and the earth.

With this combination of cultural pessimism, scientific facts, and mystic racism it was hardly surprising that the WSL attracted members of the extreme right interested in eugenics, biological anthropology, and human ethology as a 'scientific foundation' and justification for their racist ideas. Even after Werner Haverbeck, its new leader, and his wife strove to change its ideological direction by emphasizing environmental issues in the early 1970s, the WSL still maintained its links with the right. Refusing to disavow their admiration for National Socialism the Haverbecks claimed that the WSL was neither left nor right but tried to find a synthesis of the two. Ursula Haverbeck-Wetzel wrote in 1977: 'By now it has become evident that for a strict protection of life and the environment, biological questions and questions of political economy stand in the foreground and cannot be excluded, not even when they seem to be fixed on National Socialism or Communism . . .' (cited in Öser, 1978, p. 97; see also Haverbeck-Wetzel, 1984–85, p. 4). A positive aspect of National Socialism was 'its striving for health and the tendency to cultivate and revere traditional values such as rural culture *(Bauerntum)*, folk customs, and the beauty of nature.' Positive about Marxism was its attempt to recognize and abolish human exploitation and alienation (cited in Stöss, 1980, p. 244).

The WSL's environmental ideology was a kind of uncomitted mystical anti-capitalism that left conservative environmentalists like Gruhl enough room for interpretation to allow them, at least for a while, to accept the WSL as a partner. It maintained that the ecological crisis as well as human alienation were both caused by the dominance of economics over human life. Only the abolition of capitalism could lead to a break with the primacy of economics in social life and save the earth. For this to happen humans had to overcome materialism, renounce economic growth, and begin to value self-sacrifice.

Like Gruhl, the WSL called for a cultural, rather than social or political revolution. However, unlike Gruhl, whose authoritarian program was heavily influenced by traditional conservatism, the WSL, and particularly its chair, Werner Haverbeck, was indebted to the racist tradition of German anti-capitalism. It was this connection which led the conservatives soon to distance themselves from the WSL.

UNITING FORCES: THE SPV DIE GRÜNEN

The main impetus for the merging of the different ecological and environmentalist parties and organizations into one federal party was their plan to take part in the elections to the European Parliament in June 1979. However, initial attempts to unify the diverse Green groupings had already occurred earlier. Before the Bavarian *Landtag* elections in October 1978 there had been talks between the AUD, the GAZ, and several citizen initiatives and organizations for the protection of the environment resulting in what turned out to be a quite shaky 'election alliance.'

The Bavarian alliance already exposed the conflicts that dominated and greatly influenced the further development of the Green party after the European elections. It was basically a conflict between 'conservative bourgeois ecologists' represented by Gruhl and the GAZ and 'petty bourgeois anti-capitalist' ecologists represented by Haussleiter and the AUD (Klotzsch and Stöss, 1984, p. 1547). Whereas the former merely wanted to reform the system, leaving its basic structures (capitalism and party democracy) intact, the latter believed that the system was decayed and therefore in need of fundamental change, via grassroots democracy and an alternative to both capitalism and state socialism.

Before the Bavarian elections, the GAZ attacked the AUD as leftist or even left-socialist. The AUD, in turn, criticized the authoritarian style of the GAZ and its conservative program which, in several instances, contradicted essential elements of the AUD program (Stöss, 1980, p. 271). Similar conflicts erupted in 1978 in the GLU in Lower Saxony, culminating in the chairman's resignation from the leadership of the party and the introduction of a compromise formula stating that the GLU was neither left nor right. Despite these often acrimonious bickerings the various environmentalist groups and parties succeeded in presenting a united slate for the European elections.

The foundation of the first federal Green party occurred in March 1979 against the background of a continued conflict between the different splinter parties and organizations. After the conservatives had succeeded in excluding members of the left from the alliance, the new party, the 'Other Political Union The Greens,' included only members of the AUD, GAZ, GLU, anthroposophists, and the Green List Schleswig Holstein, a conservative ecological party led by the 'eco-farmer' and political maverick Baldur Springmann. Herbert Gruhl, August Haussleiter, and Helmut Neddermeyer, a *Gymnasium* professor from Lower Saxony (GLU) were elected chairmen of the new party.

The SPV program for the European elections was heavily influenced by the general secretary of the AUD, Max Winkler, a physicist and one-time mayoral candidate for the AUD in Munich. It was he who first developed the four basic 'dimensions of the ecological all-encompassing alternative' (*der ökologischen Gesamtalternative*) which still form the cornerstones of the Green program today: ecological, grassroots democratic, social, and non-violent (*ökologisch, basisdemokratisch, sozial, gewaltfrei*).

In a programmatic article in the AUD organ *Die Unabhängigen* (January 1, 1979) Winkler claimed that all existing political ideologies regardless of whether they were communist, socialist, liberal, con-servative, or nationalist, were fixated on economic growth. 'But since traditional economic growth cannot be created any more without immediate losses of environmental quality or quality of life and cannot be paid for without irresponsible indebtedness, inflation, and the collapse of currencies, all established parties stand helpless before the growing environmental and financial problems.' In this situation the only alternative was a 'holistic solution' of a new political theory which he called 'polit–ecology.' The new theory had to integrate all aspects of human and social life, or there would be no escape from the threatening 'chaos, barbarism, wars over resources, big technological and ecological catastrophes and finally the destruction of our bases of life.' Because the crisis was imminent, theory and practice, based on the four dimensions of the *Gesamtalternative*, had to go hand in hand. A change of individual consciousness through ecological education, and concrete measures had to be pursued simultaneously.

The *Europa Programm* of the SPV Die Grünen reflected Winkler's strategy of a *Gesamtalternative*. Its preamble stated: 'The new European politics must be a *holistic politics* (*Gesamtpolitik*), which is guided by long-term perspectives for the future and comprises four dimensions: It must be *ecological, social, grassroots democratic, and non-violent*; for today Europe is threatened by an ecological and economic crisis, by a military catastrophe, and by a constant erosion of democracy and basic rights' (Hallensleben, 1984, p. A8, emphasis in the original).

The relatively radical tone of this statement, however, was not carried over to the concrete demands of the program. Although the program stated that in order to realize a Green alternative, 'extensive changes in the human attitude towards life and the environment as well as changes in the economy and society' were necessary, it stopped short of proposing genuine structural changes. This is not to say that the SPV program was old wine in a new bottle. Not only was it quite successful in integrating some of the most pressing issues of the day into a comprehensive program, but some of the demands were highly innovative and rather radical for the time.

Among its demands, the program called for a shorter working week, the lowering of the retirement age, an extended period of education, the introduction of a baby year (a one year leave of absence for mothers after the birth of a child), and more part-time job opportunities for men and women. It asked also that the rights of minorities be guaranteed and demanded equal rights for women. It spoke of the need to educate the population in social defense as an alternative to the further militarization of society.

When it came to the question how these demands should be implemented however, the program relied predominantly on exhortations ('changes are to be made, must be made, should be made') while otherwise falling back on generalities like Gruhl's concept of a 'dynamic circulation economy (*Kreislaufwirtschaft*)' or the insistence on changing human consciousness as the key to universal change: 'The new Europe can only become reality if the *value conceptions* of the Europeans are being freed from the overestimation of the standard of living and the quantitative material one-sidedness. Human *spiritual* and *psychical self-realization* has decisive importance' (p. A9, emphasis in the original). Despite these programmatic weaknesses the SPV Die Grünen gained 893.523 votes (3.2 per cent) in the European elections. This was an impressive result, especially in view of the low level of interest that the European elections generated in West Germany. The future looked promising for the Green project. However, it soon became clear that the SPV had only been a prelude to a much larger game, a game for which particularly the conservative Green forces were ill-prepared. The conflict erupted almost immediately after the elections. Its central cause was the question of what to do with those leftist groups that wanted to join the party after its success in the European elections.

ESCAPE FROM THE GHETTO: THE ALTERNATIVE LISTS

After almost a decade of Green politics the Green party has come to be seen as the primary representative of a reconstructed left-libertarian politics (Kitschelt, 1989). In reality, the fact that the Greens would evolve from a primarily environmentalist party into a left libertarian one was neither self-evident nor was it inevitable. In fact, the new left was quite late to realize the political potential of Green politics. Initially, its members regarded both the environmental issue and its most important representatives, the citizen initiatives (Cf. Mayer-Tasch, 1976; Guggenberger, 1980), with a great deal of suspicion (see Rüdig, 1985–86, pp. 7–11). It was not until 1975, when the struggle over nuclear energy heated up quickly, that its members began to embrace environmentalism. Particularly the orthodox Maoist parties saw in the growing anti-nuclear protest 'a chance to increase their political impact' (p. 12).

In the resistance to nuclear power the new left discovered an issue which was not merely about purely technical concerns but incorporated a wide range of political questions. The central issue was the growing power of the state which refused to heed opposition and instead confronted its citizens—via its police force—with truncheons and water cannons. Nuclear power thus became for the new left—as for some conservative environmentalists—'a symbol for a repressive and environmentally destructive society' (p. 13).

The argument was spelled out most clearly in Robert Jungk's bestseller *Der Atomstaat* (the nuclear state, 1979), a concept which was made popular by the Green party (Cf. Kelly, 1983, p. 185). Jungk argued that nuclear power would inevitably lead to a police state. Nuclear power demanded such a high degree of security measures that literally every citizen would become a potential security risk and thus suspicious. 'Nuclear energy means a permanent state of emergency justified by a permanent threat and "allows for" tough laws to "protect the citizen"' (p. 143). Equipped with these arguments (which for many, faced with *Berufsverbote* and the fallout from the German Fall, reflected an already present reality) the new left made its return to politics in the form of a variety of *bunte* ('multi-colored', because they included a range of politically and ideologically diverse groups and individuals) and alternative lists.

Contrary to the majority of conservative Green parties one of the main objectives of the alternative lists was to lend parliamentary support to extra-parliamentary resistance particularly against nuclear power plants. Frustrated over the failure to stop the nuclear program of the West German government anti-nuclear activists decided to challenge the established parties not only in the streets but also at the polls. Holger Strohm, a leading anti-nuclear activist in Hamburg and one of the founders of the *Bunte Liste* Hamburg, may have put it most succinctly when he maintained:

> For the established parties nuclear energy had ceased to be a topic, especially in the election campaign. Those who were against nuclear power in the parties did not have a chance or were slowly put on ice. In this situation we asked ourselves: Who should we vote for this time? Again the lesser of two evils? Or should we not vote at all? Then we decided to vote for ourselves (Strohm, 1978, p. 126).

Politically, the members of the *bunte* and alternative lists considered themselves a left alternative to the established parties. Unlike the conservative parties, which concentrated mainly on environmental issues, the alternative lists saw their struggle against nuclear power within a broader context of a range of social issues such as the alleged assault on political freedom by the state, growing unemployment, and the rights of minorities, women, and foreign workers. This wide range of issues reflected the variegated composition of their membership which included feminists, students, anti-nuclear activists, tenants' groups, unorthodox new left groups and organizations, foreign workers, prisoners' groups, homosexuals, environmentalists, and Maoist splinter parties. However, this heterogeneity was somewhat deceiving. Although the *bunte* and alternative lists meant to be nothing more than parliamentary representatives of the various new social movements, in reality they soon were dominated by Maoist activists and 'unorthodox' Marxist groups.

In contrast to the conservative lists which predominated in the large West German states, the *bunte* and alternative lists were largely a phenomenon of the cities. Supported primarily by students they were especially successful in university cities. Among the most influential lists were the *Bunte Liste* in Hamburg, the Alternative List in Berlin, and the Green List—Voter Initiative for the Protection of the Environment and Democracy—in Frankfurt. Despite local differences they shared common concerns reflected in various programs and programmatic statements.

The lists appealed to those voters who no longer saw their interests represented by the established political parties. Claiming to represent a fundamental alternative to the existing system they offered a long list of demands designed not only to improve the state of the environment, but also to stop political discrimination and oppression and to further the right to self-determination and self-realization of a range of socal groups and subgroups—minorities, youth, students, prisoners, foreign workers, women, and homosexuals. Invariably the alternative programs also placed particular emphasis on economic and socioeconomic issues, demanding, among others, the reduction of the working week to thirty-five hours and equality for women in the work place.

Although the *bunte* and alternative lists appeared to represent the demands of a large range of social groups and movements, they were heavily influenced, if not dominated, by the organized Maoists and unorthodox leftists. In Hamburg the dominant influence came from the Communist Federation (*Kommunistischer Bund*, KB), a worker oriented, anti-fascist cadre party which, against resistance within the party, by the middle of the 1970s was slowly becoming involved in the women's, alternative, and anti-nuclear movement. The KB's involvement in the Greens ended with a split of the party over the question whether the party should continue its active participation in environmentalist politics. Whereas the majority refused further co-operation, the minority, organized in the so-called Z-Fraktion, continued to support the Greens, primarily in order to limit the influence of petty-bourgeois elements within the Greens.

In Berlin, the main organizational force behind the alternative list was the Maoist KPD (Hoplitschek, 1982, p. 83). Virulently opposed to the Soviet Union, the East German regime, and detente, the KPD called for the expulsion of the superpowers from Germany and German reunification followed by a socialist revolution.

Despite the fact that by the end of 1979 the KPD was in rapid decay and soon after folded its wing, its cadres had a considerable influence on AL politics, particularly in regard to its *Deutschlandpolitik*.

In Frankfurt, the driving force behind the Green List were the spontis. Organized in the Citizen Initiative Chaos and Quagmire and led by Daniel Cohn-Bendit the spontis sought to use parliament as a forum for 'polit-clownery,' in order to expose the absurdity and ludicrousness of West German politics via 'anti-parliamentary parliamentarianism:'

> If an anti-parliamentarian can only survive in parliament as anti-parliamentarian, then he transforms the parliament into an anti-parliament by becoming parliamentarian, or the parliament anti-parliamentarizes itself because the anti-parliamentarian parliamentarizes, or the antiment parlates the Tari-Anti, or . . . In short, IDIOCY (*Der Schwachsinn*) enters parliament, represented by US! (Fischer 1984, p. 93)

In addition, the spontis saw in the Green List an opportunity to escape from their self-imposed ghetto. 'The air in the ghetto was suffocating us, and our withdrawal into ourselves did nothing to change reality' (p. 92) This was not to say that the spontis were eager to represent the interests of the ecology movement. 'For even those spontis who had the most positive attitude did not believe in the realization of the Green dreams.' However, over time the spontis began to rethink their position. Perhaps the student militants would be able to affect politics in a positive way after all. This, however, posed a serious problem. 'The old equation is still valid: only those who have power, can make changes; but, those who have power, will also be possessed by it' (p. 94). With these words Joschka Fischer summed up the basic dilemma of left-libertarian politics.

With the emergence of the *bunte* and alternative lists the new left abandoned its largely self-imposed ghetto. If the *Tendenzwende* had primarily entailed 'a growing disinterest in politics and an increasing focus on what has traditionally been considered private' (Adelson, 1983, p. 4) on the part of many members of the new left, the new political organizations reflected their re-politization. However, as Joyce Mushaben (1985–86, p. 40) aptly put it, compared to 'the relative ideological purity that ultimately led to the self-destruction of the 1960s' movements,' this was a different new left, comprising 'a rather motley crew' of intellectuals, dropouts, marginalized social groups, and students, who were 'inclined to form ostensibly bizarre coalitions around a complex of disparate issues.'

No longer was politics reduced to one axis, one essential contradiction (that is, the contradiction between labor and capital), which relegated everything else to the periphery; on the contrary, the new politics of the *bunte* and alternative lists expressed exactly those demands which the new left not so long ago had considered marginal. This re-emphasis of politics reflected the transformation of social reality in the late 1970s, where relatively fixed social identities gave way to what Linda Hutcheon (1988, p. 58) has identified as one of the core elements of the postmodern turn, 'a flux of contextualized identities:' gender, class, race, ethnicity, sexual preference, education, or social role.

After their rather good showing in regional and local as well as the 1979 European elections, the members of the SPV Die Grünen decided to transform the SPV into a regular party to run in the 1980 federal elections. This plan immediately raised the question as to what to do about the *bunte* and alternative lists. Whereas some of the conservative forces within the alliance pleaded for excluding them, a considerable number of environmentalists particularly within the Green List sought to integrate them into one Green party for fear that they might split the vote and consequently dilute the chances of the Greens' success. This was a sensible reason if only for the fact that in previous state elections the split between Green and alternative lists had hurt both sides. However, putting this consideration into practice had disastrous results for the conservative environmentalist cause. Confronted with the organizational skills and cadre tactics of the Maoist organizations (particularly the KB) the conservative environmentalists soon found themselves outwitted and marginalized.

Although Rudolf Bahro maintained that 'red and green, green and red, go well together' (Bahro, 1982, p. 18), it soon became clear what chasm separated the two. Claiming that the Greens had already expanded their focus of concern from purely ecological issues to the general emancipation of human beings, Bahro pointed out that this was 'precisely the categorical imperative of the young Marx' (p. 18). A movement that sought to rescue West European civilization had to be capable of thinking 'on behalf of the totality' (p. 21). Concerning the future of West European civilization, he stated that West European civilization

cannot be saved and reconciled with other civilizations unless a broad concentration of political forces comes into being, mobilizing the power of the masses to change our overall direction. To me this concentration seems inconceivable without the various forces of the socialist tradition standing at the center of such a bloc. (p. 22)

He concluded that, in his view, the socialists needed the Greens, 'for survival is the precondition for them to attain their traditional goals;' and the Greens needed the socialists, 'for survival can only be ensured by disconnecting the motor of monopoly competition' (p. 22).

However, as it turned out, the socialists needed the environmentalists much less than the latter believed they needed the new left. The majority of the new left sought to transform the Greens into a left-wing party concerned with a variety of left-libertarian issues including environmentalism. By contrast, for the conservatives, the most important issue was the threat to survival of human kind caught 'between a nuclear state or nuclear war, Harrisburg or Hiroshima.'[3] For them the main cause of the crisis was the materialist disposition of the individual. Opposed to drastic changes of the economic .and political structures within society, they favored spiritual change, exhorting self-limitation and sacrifice. Thus, one of the first proposals for the preamble to the party program stated that, '[d]epending on the degree to which we free ourselves from our overestimation of the material standard of living, make our self-realization possible, and recognize our national limitations, our creative forces will be set free for the reorganization of a life on an ecological basis.'[4]

The *Bunten* and alternatives flatly rejected these ideas as reactionary, and smacking of traditional conservatism. In their view these ideas glossed over the fact that the crisis had been caused by those who wielded political and economic power. Any program that left the prevailing structures intact, was merely lending support to the power elite while forcing those too weak to defend themselves to bear the consequences of the crisis. Instead, the new left focused on the fulfilment of basic needs, demanded an expansion of social policies and grass-roots democracy and thus propagated a socialist alternative to the existing capitalist system (Klotzsch and Stöss, 1984, pp. 1540–1).[5]

This view was reflected in the new party's basic program (Die Grünen, 1980). The new left rejected quantitative growth in favor of an ecologically- and socially oriented economy, a 'dynamic circulation economy' (*dynamische Kreislaufwirtschaft*) (p. 7). They called for the decentralization of production into small enterprises to be run by the workers. They suggested the creation of 'economic and social councils' to give the population a chance to control the activities of the enterprises and to 'subject them to ecological conditions and social duties' (p. 7). They finally demanded a reduction of the working week to thirty-five hours with full compensation (p. 8). The conservatives objected above all to the latter demand. In Gruhl's view '[t]his way of thinking [was] linked with the great belief that anything can be achieved and everything put in order much, much better than hitherto, with the introduction of new laws, new organizations, and new institutions' (quoted in Papadakis, 1984, p. 162).

Under the heading 'peace and foreign policy,' the program called for the dissolution of NATO and the Warsaw Pact in order to create the basis 'for the overcoming of the division of Europe and also the division of Germany' (Die Grünen, 1980, p. 19). It spoke out against both new American medium range missiles (Pershing and Cruise) and the Soviet SS–20. It demanded the unilateral disarmament of Germany and the introduction of 'social defense,' meaning a reorganization of German society in such a way that a potential aggressor would realize beforehand that any attempt to occupy and rule the country would entail more difficulties and problems than it would increase power or gains.

Only the controversy over abortion, the most heatedly disputed point of the program besides the economic program, ended in a compromise. Although initially the new left demanded the abolition of the law forbidding abortion, they retreated from this position under pressure from the conservatives. Instead, the program stated that the abortion issue brought two Green principles into conflict, namely the support for the right of self-determination for the individual and the protection of human life. However, abortion was a question of moral conviction and personal circumstances and as such not an issue of criminal persecution. In order to make abortions unnecessary the program called for 'material and social help' as well as better methods of birth control (Die Grünen, 1980, p. 35).

However, neither this compromise nor further compromises with regard to the party's program for the upcoming elections could convince the conservative Greens that they had a future in the party. As far as they were concerned, the basic program smacked of the old socialist positions in a new guise, and these already had proven ineffective when confronted with the ecological crisis. Outwitted by the organizational talents of the cadre parties, their core beliefs relegated to a secondary position in the Green program, they soon abandoned the party.

One might speculate whether or not, confronted with the challenge from the left, the conservative cum populist environmentalists would have been able to survive as a viable party. In fact, Herbert Gruhl proceeded to found a new right-wing conservative environmental party, the ÖDP (Ecological Democratic Party), only to see it relegated to the political margins. The reason for this failure was largely that there was little support for environmentalism as a single issue. Environmental concern could only become an important political issue within a much larger political context and with a sufficiently large base of supporters. It was the new left, and to some degree the populists, which offered this context by expanding the Green political agenda from its predominantly ecological focus to a predominantly left-libertarian, postmodern program. As we will see in the following chapter, with that they succeeded also in expanding the scope of potential supporters for the party.

3 Postmodern Politics and the Greens

In the past critics of the Green project have brought contradictory charges against the Greens: on the one hand the Greens were accused of furthering rightist authoritarian tendencies, on the other of being a socialist party in ecological disguise, a 'watermelon party,' green on the outside, red on the inside (Strauss, 1984). Others have seen parallels between the revived romantic attack on progress and Nazism and warned that the Greens pose a serious threat to democracy (Bracher, 1985; Langner, 1987). Few have given them credit for what must be considered one of the most important results of the new left's return to politics in the 1980s. By organizing as a political party—even if it was initially intended only as an 'anti-party'[1]—the new left not only succeeded in reintegrating into the political process a generation of young people, who in 1978 wanted to leave the *Modell Deutschland*, by playing according to the democratic rules, the new left inadvertently gave legitimacy to a system to which they were fundamentally opposed. Thus, instead of endangering West German democracy they in fact contributed to its continued stability (see Siegert *et al.*, 1986).

However, the majority within the established parties refused to see it that way. For them, the Greens represented a challenge which went beyond the realm of the purely political. Their rejection of economic growth, instrumental rationality, industrialism, and the elite-dominated corporatist politics of the latter part of the social democratic era, threatened the very fabric and identity of postwar West German society. It pitted the champions of industrial society and the project of modernity against those who felt betrayed by the idealism and promises of the postwar era and were ready to abandon them altogether for a radical postmodern reconceptualization of politics. In the ensuing bitter struggle compromise seemed impossible.

The social democrat Richard Löwenthal (1981, p. 1087) may have expressed the majority's emotions most pointedly when he wrote for his party: 'Social democracy is a product of industrial society and a champion of democracy within the state and society. With those who declare the modern world a wrong way (*einen Irrweg*), it cannot compromise.' The Green attack on modernity, however, is only postmodern to the degree that it no longer seeks to return to a pre-modern utopia (as romantic anti-modernism would have it), but searches for a reconstitution of life beyond modernity. In this endeavor the rising new service class acquires central importance. Their experience as well as their position within the process of social and cultural reproduction make them particularly disposed towards a new lifestyle.

THE SOCIAL BASIS OF GREEN POLITICS

The rise to prominence of Green postmodern politics in the 1980s occurred during a period of significant change in the cultural and political climate of West Germany which already started in the 1970s. In the mid-1970s, as a result of mounting economic problems and rising unemployment following the first oil shock of 1973, and particularly after a doubling of the unemployment figures after the second oil shock of 1979, a growing number of West Germans began to lose faith in the blessings of science and technology. If in the mid-1960s almost two-thirds of the population considered science and technology a blessing, by 1981 only roughly one third of the population was still that confident (von Klipstein and Strümpel, 1984, p. 183). And if in 1972 60 per cent expressed a belief in progress, by 1978 that number had dwindled to roughly one third, further declining to 27 per cent in 1982. Moreover, by 1981 more than 50 per cent of respondents associated progress with fear (Noelle-Neumann and Piel, 1983, pp. 105, 514).

At the same time there was a growing awareness of the environmental crisis. Although in 1981 almost 90 per cent associated economic growth with technical progress, more than two-thirds associated it also with environmental pollution (von Klipstein and Strümpel, 1984, p. 189). By the mid-decade the vast majority of the West German population had come to regard environmental degradation as a very serious problem, second only to the protection of jobs, and as a result attributed a very high priority to measures to protect the environment (see Veen, 1985, p. 18; 1987, p. 95; Schultze, 1987, p. 7). At the same time there was a noticeable shift away from nuclear power. Opposition to the construction of nuclear plants near populated areas increased from 28 per cent in 1975 to 51 per cent in

1981. Conversely the number of West Germans still positively inclined towards nuclear power dropped from 40 per cent in 1975 to a mere 20 per cent in 1981 (Noelle-Neumann and Piel, 1983, p. 529).

Under these circumstances it is hardly surprising that the Greens succeeded quite easily in gaining the five per cent of the popular vote necessary to be represented in the *Bundestag* and entered a variety of representative bodies on the local, regional and federal level. What needs to be explained, however, is the fact that despite overwhelming public support for Green issues the party never succeeded in garnering significantly more than 10 per cent of the vote. In 1984, for example, 55 per cent of the West German electorate thought it possible to vote for an ecologist party (Inglehart and Rabier, 1986, p. 466); in the state elections held in 1984 and 1985, however, the best result for the Greens was 13 per cent of the vote (in the Berlin elections).

Two explanations have been proposed to account for the rise of the Greens to political prominence. One approach, subscribing to the influential work of Ronald Inglehart (1989), has seen the Greens as the representatives of a new generation of postmaterialists who, having grown up in a climate a material abundance and security, give priority to postmaterialist issues such as a free personal life, the democratization of political, work and community life, and a less impersonal, less destructive and more cultured life over materialist issues such as sustained economic growth and maintenance of law and order. The second approach attributes the rise of the Greens to a process of marginalization affecting particular groups in West German society (Bürklin, 1987). Both approaches heavily stress the role of the new service class. In what follows I will discuss both approaches beginning with the postmaterialism thesis.

Their rapid rise and unexpected electoral success has brought the Greens instant celebrity and rendered them one of the most well-researched phenomena in contemporary West German politics. And with good reason: on the basis of their political demands as well as their official platform and programs the Greens were considered to be the first truly postmaterialist party in Western Europe (see Müller-Rommel, 1985; Hülsberg, 1988, p. 110). Combining a scathing critique of advanced industrial society and its propensity to sacrifice the natural environment to the prerogatives of sustained economic growth with a call for greater political participation, extended democracy, and equal rights for women and minorities, the party combines what Scott Flanagan (1982, 1987) has called 'non-materialist priorities' and 'libertarian values.'

In addition, Green voters tend to be young, highly educated, predominantly urban, politically left of center, and often active in one of the new social movements (Fend and Prester, 1985, p. 376; Müller-Rommel, 1985; Hülsberg, 1988, pp. 108–118). In terms of their social composition Green supporters either come from the middle class or have already become part of the new middle class of civil servants and employees (see for example Rönsch, 1980; Fogt and Uttitz, 1984; Müller-Rommel, 1985, p. 57). In 1989, for example, 56 per cent of employed Green supporters (excluding housekeepers, students, the retired, and the unemployed) were employees and civil servants (see Noelle-Neumann, 1989, Table 1).

Additional support for the postmaterialist new middle class thesis comes from the political values and political preferences of the West German new middle class. Its members have shown a significantly higher disposition to postmaterialist values than any other occupational group (see Table 3.1). Particularly those born after 1946 showed more concern for environmental issues and were more likely to support or to be actively involved in the anti-nuclear movement than other occupational or age groups. From this perspective, the Green phenomenon in West Germany appeared to confirm Inglehart's argument about the postmaterialist tendencies of a generation that had grown up during the postwar period amidst material affluence and was therefore less likely to be concerned with fulfilling basic material needs. Instead, it was said to hold primarily postbourgeois values, ranging from the need for identity and self-actualization to the demand for an extension of civic freedoms—values traditionally associated with the left.

The Greens thus seemed to be typical representatives of a new middle class on the rise, their politics reflecting the life-style of a new postindustrial elite in search of ways to differentiate itself from established social classes in decline (Raschke, 1985, p. 28). Were those critics then right who charged both new social movements as well as the Greens with representing merely 'the luxury concerns of a wealthy elite' (Maier, 1987, p. 9)? Empirical studies show that the political reality is rather more complex. In the 1987 federal elections, for example, only roughly 10 per cent of the new middle class supported the Greens (Feist and Krieger, 1987, p. 40; Brinkmann, 1988, pp. 26–7). The majority voted for the center-right or the Social Democrats.

Even among the postwar cohort supposed to be most likely to have postmaterialist values the Greens mustered only 14 per cent of the vote (Brinkmann, 1988, p. 27).

Table 3.1   New middle class[1] value preferences (in per cent, 1987)

	Total	NMC	NMC, born after 1946
fight unemployment[2]	82	79	77
stable prices[2]	54	43	33
lower taxes[2]	44	29	27
boost economy[2]	68	72	69
protect environment[2]	67	67	73
environment priority over economic growth	58	53	66
more nuclear energy	23	26	24
anti-nuclear movement:			
support	19	22	33
participant	4	8	16

[1] The new middle class is composed of higher-level civil servants and employees as well as middle-level and lower-level civil servants and employees with at least middle-level education for those born before 1946 and secondary education or higher for those born after 1946. For detailed explanation see Brinkmann (1988, pp. 20-2).

[2] Includes only those who answered 'very important.'

Source: Brinkmann (1989, table 1).

These findings can be partly explained by the fact that within the new middle class the Greens receive support predominantly from among the new service class of social and cultural intermediaries (Nowak, 1979). These are teachers, social workers, journalists and publicists, and other social and cultural specialists with a shared set of postmaterialist and left liberal values which set them apart from both the managerial strata as well as traditional professionals (engineers, lawyers, physicians). Table 3.2, which uses Inglehart's eight-item materialist/postmaterialist battery, clearly shows the differences. Compared to all other social groups, social and cultural specialists[2] are by far the most postmaterialist in the sense Inglehart has proposed. Whereas blue-collar workers and managers put heavy emphasis on maintaining order and economic growth, social and cultural specialists assign the highest priority to expanding the right to individual autonomy, particularly an individual's freedom of speech, with aesthetic, non-materialist value priorities assuming secondary importance.

Table 3.2   Distribution of materialist and postmaterialist value types within social groupings (in per cent):

A.   Maintaining a high rate of economic growth.
B.   Making sure that this country has strong defense forces.
C.   Seeing that the people have more say in how things get decided at work and in their communities.
D.   Trying to make our cities and countryside more beautiful.
E.   Maintaining order in the nation.
F.   Giving people more say in important government decisions.
G.   Fighting rising prices.
H.   Protecting freedom of speech.

| | *Most important item* | | | |
	Managers	*Trad. Prof.*	*Soc./Cult. Spec.*	*Workers*
A.	66.7	53.8	26.4	49.9
B.	4.2	5.1	7.8	10.8
C.	8.3	35.9	55.0	32.3
D.	20.8	5.1	10.9	7.0
N	24	39	129	399
E.	40.4	28.6	27.5	47.1
F.	24.5	31.3	34.4	19.1
G.	10.6	9.5	5.6	21.6
H.	24.5	30.6	32.5	12.2
N	94	147	375	1171
	Second most important item			
A.	20.8	26.3	26.4	26.1
B.	33.3	18.4	15.5	23.8
C.	33.3	26.3	19.4	34.6
D.	12.5	28.9	38.8	15.5
N	24	38	129	399
E.	21.3	20.5	14.7	22.6
F.	18.1	24.7	28.8	23.5
G.	31.9	21.2	18.1	32.8
H.	28.7	33.6	38.4	52.9
N	94	146	375	1171

Note: Data for A–D available only for 1982. For construction of social groupings see endnote 2.

Data Source: Allbus 1980–1982–1984

These results lend support to the charge that Inglehart's issue catalog opposes primarily left-libertarian values to materialist ones (see Flanagan, 1987). These left-libertarian values stand very much in the tradition of the West European left. This might explain the relatively strong support these items receive from blue collar workers (see Table 3.2). In this sense support for left-libertarian issues represents a decidedly pro-modernist stance. It becomes postmodern only when combined with a truly non-materialist value orientation. Unfortunately, although there is much evidence for the spread of left-libertarian values, non-materialist values have received relatively little attention. One major problem is to define exactly what is meant by non-materialism. The following discussion seeks to fill this void.

Two developments have gained particular attention in the debate on the coming of the postmodern age: the rise and politization of ecology and the environmental movement, and the debate on the decline of the Protestant work ethic and the future of the working society (see Habermas, 1985). If environmentalism has become accepted as a key issue in contemporary politics, it is necessary to elaborate on the second issue.

In advanced capitalist societies there appears to be a growing consensus as to the 'declining subjective significance of the sphere of work' (Offe, 1985, p. 142) for the organization of postindustrial societies. What accounts for this decline are the reduction in working hours, both in terms of the time actually spent at the workplace as well as the proportion of an individual's life spent at work (Handy, 1985, ch. 3); the weakening of the traditional work ethic as a result of the spread of consumerism and the erosion of religious and cultural traditions (Bell, 1976); and 'the disintegration of the milieux of life which are organized in accordance with the categories of work and occupations and complemented by family tradition, organizational membership, leisure consumption and educational institutions' (Offe, 1985, p. 142). However, as real as these developments are—one need only think of the demand for a thirty-five-hour working week, early retirement, and a concomitant growth of leisure time—they obscure an equally important development which centers on growing demands for a new approach to the very nature of work itself.

If in the past work was primarily associated with either duty, necessity or both (Offe, 1985, p. 141), today there is increasing demand for work that fits into an individual's larger project of fulfilment and self-realization. This has led to a growing importance of non-materialist aspects of work such as creativity, communication, interesting work, and concomitantly to a decline in traditional goals associated with work such as rapid advancement, high income, or highly-paid overtime. In their studies on changing values in West Germany, von Klipstein and Stümpel (1985, p. 25) found, for example, that between the early 1970s and 1980s demand for interesting work rose from 71 per cent of the population in 1973 to 79 per cent in 1983, demand for more contact with other people from 47 per cent in 1973 to 57 per cent in 1981, and demand for a job in which ideas were important from 43 per cent in 1973 to 52 per cent in 1983. At the same time demand for high income declined from 67 per cent in 1973 to 50 per cent in 1983, demand for advancement declined from 62 per cent in 1973 to 54 per cent in 1981, and demand for highly-paid overtime diminished from 40 per cent in 1968 to 6 per cent in 1982.

The items in Table 3.3 seek to measure the responses of various social groups along three value dimensions relevant for politics in the postmodern age: Traditional left–right issues such as support for unions, social expenditures, and the welfare state in general; left-libertarian issues corresponding to Inglehart's postmaterialist items such as civil rights and, increasingly important, attitudes towards foreigners; and finally non-materialist values divided into environmental issues and attitudes towards work. The results strongly suggest that among the various occupational groups the members of the new service class are most consistently left-wing, left-libertarian and non-materialist. They are sympathetic to unions, without, however, being concerned about the negative effect environmental restrictions (for example on cars or nuclear power plants) and their opposition to economic growth in general would have on jobs. They place high importance on traditionally liberal issues such as the right to free speech and the protection of minorities' rights to express their identity. Their non-materialist values are reflected in their concern for the environment, the importance they attach to human contact at the workplace rather than job advancement or high income. Two other aspects deserve attention. The new service class supports higher social expenditures—a reflection of the fact that many of its members work in social services. On the other hand, however, it does not share the traditional leftist enthusiasm for the welfare state—a reflection of the aversion to the growing power of the state and its penetration of the life-world. Unlike the traditional left, the new service class is also quite ambiguous about the resort to violence in order to achieve political goals. Both issues (how to curtail the power of the state without eliminating social benefits, and the question of violence [*Gewaltfrage*]) have given rise to heated controversies within the Green party without ever being completely resolved (see, for example, Hippler and Maier, 1988).

From this analysis the West German new service class emerges as the core social base of postmodern politics. Its members satisfy the criteria set forth in the introduction for the postmodern *citoyen*. Their left-libertarian and non-materialist value orientations predispose them to place high priority on individuality, self-actualization and resistance to the process of rationalization inherent in the development of the modern welfare state.

However, it would be a gross oversimplification to see the Greens merely or primarily as representatives of the new service class. In large part support for the Greens has come from those still in training, be it at the university or the secondary level. In 1987, roughly 47 per cent from among that group supported the Greens (Brinkmann, 1988, p. 27; see also Roth, 1986, p. 66). Green support is thus quite heterogeneous with a considerable proportion coming from an age cohort which in the early 1980s was still enrolled in secondary education or had just started to enter university.

Those who see the rise of the Greens as a result of a process of marginalization of certain groups in society, focus on the latter group. In West Germany the prospects of university students and graduates deteriorated considerably in the 1980s. The influx of growing numbers of young students into West German universities and polytechnics (from roughly 220 000 students in 1960 to more than 1.34 million in 1985) led to an oversupply of qualified university graduates, and, consequently, to the realization among many university students that their prospects for the future were considerably bleaker than those of earlier student generations. According to one detailed study on political protest in the Federal Republic, as early as in the mid-1970s almost 50 per cent of all students considered their career prospects immediately after graduation to be bad or very bad, about one-fifth was very skeptical as to their long-term prospects. Interestingly enough, the perception of rapidly deteriorating career prospects was most pronounced among left-wing students. Almost two-thirds of them considered their immediate career propects to be bad or very bad, and more than a third was very skeptical about their long-term prospects. At the same time these students were most interested in a career that allowed for independence, self-expression and personal self-realization rather than merely assuring material security. For this group of students thus frustrated career expectations meant more than

Table 3.3 Value priorities and political preferences by social groupings (unstandardized regression coefficients)

	Managers	Professionals	Cultural specialists	Workers	Age	N
	Political preferences					
CDU	.490	−.195	−1.481**	−.299*	.038**	2660
SPD	−.746*	−.240	.207	.566**	−.001	2662
Greens	−.118	.614*	1.333**	−.222	−.042**	2658
	Left–right issues					
Left–Right Self-placement (high = right)	.840**	−.246	−.522**	−.170*	.188	2747
Trust in Unions (high = trust)	−.405	.025	.205	.356**	−.005	1319
Trust in Employer organizations (high = trust)	.059	.016	−.650**	−.167	.017**	1312
lower taxes vs. higher social expenditures (low = taxes)	−.137	.005	.202**	−.024	−.001	1311
lower defense expenditures (high = higher)	.471*	.022	−.578**	.009	.017**	2094
support welfare state (low = support)	.086	.268**	−.089	−.177**	.004	1324
State responsible for full employment and stable prices (low = agree)	.367*	.353**	.111	−.280**	.003	1299

Left-libertarian issues

					N
citizens lose right to strike and demonstrate if they threaten public order (low = disagree)	.017	−.518*	−.395**	.159	.023**	1425
in every democracy there are conflicts that can only be solved by violent means (low = disagree)	−.517	.165	.143	−.190	−.008**	1426
when jobs get scarce foreign workers should be sent back (high = agree)	−.475	−1.114	−1.275**	.374**	.016**	2720
foreign workers should adapt to the West German life style (high = agree)	−.661**	−.895**	−.770**	.350**	.022**	2720

Non-materialist values

					N
Importance in respect to job (low = unimportant)						
high income	.157	−.340*	−.498**	.290**	−.003	2103
advancement	.749**	.144	−.578**	.185**	−.017**	2094
contact with people	.438	−.389*	.352**	−.203**	.003	2100
Sources of Pollution (low = very much)						
cars	−.106	−.206*	−.261**	.133**	.007**	1325
industry	.008	−.280**	−.245**	.129**	.012**	1316
nuclear power	.186	.150	−.424**	.104	.012**	1277
nuclear power should be increased to cover energy needs (high = agree)	−.301	−.416	−.904**	.082	.022**	1393

Note: For construction of social groupings see endnote 2.

Data Source: Kumulierter Allbus 1980–1982–1984; * < .05, ** < .01

material insecurity; they represented an attack on the very basis of their value system (Infratest, 1980, pp. 69–70). Evidence presented below indicates that a considerable number of these students would eventually find their way into the alternative movement and from there to the Greens.

The rise in graduate unemployment proved that the students' perceptions had hardly been exaggerated. Between 1975 and 1988, the number of unemployed university and polytechnic graduates rose from roughly 30 000 persons to almost 140 000 (Teichler, 1989). Two-thirds of them were under thirty-five years of age, 26 per cent were teachers. As a result, traditional patterns of acquiring elite status via education began to break down. As long as there had been a shortage of qualified applicants for higher careers, 'successful graduates could be assured of the traditional highly privileged positions both in life and at work' (Liebau, 1984, p. 274). What new graduates had to learn was the lesson of positional goods: the greater the proportion of people attaining high levels of education, the more education loses its status as a valued commodity on the job market (Paterson and Thomas, 1986, p. 9).

With the overabundance of graduates the gap between qualification, career prospects, and life chances widened (Bürklin, 1987, p. 114). The result was a fragmentation of the young educated class ranging from 'genuine poverty caused by unemployment, via a grey area of more or less short-term jobs which at least provide a livelihood based on employment—if a very insecure one—via qualified administrative positions which have been created in large numbers as a result of "downward qualification" in companies and administration to the traditional graduate occupations in the public and private sector' (Liebau, 1984, p. 274; also Krais, 1980, pp. 76–9).

In the early 1980s a growing number of university graduates joined the ranks of a new highly-qualified, but superfluous social stratum which depended largely on outside resources for survival. In 1984, for example, more than 40 per cent of the young educated class were supporting themselves from sources other than gainful employment—parental support, social security, or unemployment benefits (Bürklin, 1987, p. 116). Particularly hard hit were those disciplines dominated by 'educational climbers' (Liebau, 1984, p. 273) from the lower classes who thought to gain upward mobility via graduate education: teachers and graduates in the social sciences, psychology, and social work (Liebau, 1984, p. 274); also affected were the humanities as well as some fields in engineering and the natural sciences (cf. *Der Spiegel*, no. 20, 1985; Tessaring, 1989, p. 20). In 1985, for example, the ratio between applicants and open positions in engineering was roughly 2:1, in medicine and pharmacy 7:1, whereas it was 66:1 in the social sciences, and 67:1 in education, the humanities, and journalism (Bodenhöfer *et al.*, 1986, p. 7). Among biology graduates, in 1980 only one third had found a stable position five years after they had graduated from university. The rest were either unemployed, or continuing their studies for lack of other options, or they occupied insecure, temporary positions (Kaiser, 1981, p. 3).

The new stratum of the 'postindustrial non-established' (Bürklin, 1985) confronted this situation with growing resentment at the persistence of social inequality and the continued unfairness in regard to social mobility (see Sandberg, 1983, esp. pp. 194–6) which found expression in political cynicism and a tendency to escape into an alternative lifestyle. This was particularly prevalent among students in the humanities and the social sciences with lower-class social background (Krause *et al.*, 1980, p. 204–5), where the job prospects were bleakest. According to one study on alternative projects (Kreutz and Fröhlich, 1986), in 1982, two-thirds of those actively involved in alternative projects were university students or graduates, two-thirds of whom came from the social sciences or humanities, teaching, or social work. In addition, the likelihood of alternative tendencies increased with the number of semesters spent at the university, with those who had spent more than ten semesters there most inclined to be actively involved in the alternative scene. The rationale was that those who were unable to find open positions would remain at the university lest they lose basic social benefits like health care (Minks and Reissert, 1985).

If in the early 1980s the alternative scene had become the main locus of protest of the young highly educated stratum, with the rise of the Greens it found a new political home. Various studies have pointed out that high levels of education, age, and material insecurity and/or 'blocked chances of social mobility' (Alber, 1985, p. 220) correlate with electoral support for the Greens. Thus a combination of higher education and unemployment doubled the likelihood that a young man or woman would vote for the Greens (Feist *et al.*, 1984, p. 13). In 1984, for example, 47 per cent of unemployed university graduates and secondary school graduates preferred the Greens (Alber, 1985, fn.5; see also Roth, 1986, p. 66). The insecure economic situation of many Green supporters might also explain the fact that in 1983, a larger percentage of Green supporters (almost 90 per cent) considered unemployment a very important political issue than was the case for environmental protection (80 per cent, see Schultze, 1987, p. 7). In addition, with regard to the young and highly educated stratum there was also a strong correlation between perception of one's own economic situation and Green preference. The worse an individual's perceived economic situation, the more likely he or she was to support the Greens (see Table 3.4). These findings did not go unnoticed by the Greens themselves. In 1987 two advisors of the Greens pointed out that the majority of Green voters come from students and others outside the labor market. In 1983–84, almost two-thirds of Green

Table 3.4   Percentage Green preference by education, age and economic circumstances

Education: No degree or not more than primary school degree (*Hauptschulabschluss*)

Age	Material circumstances			
	good	partly	bad	
18–30	16.9	25.2	32.7	(N = 59)
31–38	17.9	23.3	13.5	(N = 47)
39 plus	10.3	10.5	11.5	(N = 130)

Education: Middle level degree (*Mittlere Reife, Fachschulabschluss*)

Age	Material circumstances			
	good	partly	bad	
18–30	31.7	32.4	42.3	(N = 72)
31–38	14.7	36.4	40.0	(N = 26)
39 plus	14.2	15.6	15.4	(N = 46)

Education: Secondary school degree (*Hochschul-, Fachhochschulreife*)

Age	Material circumstances			
	good	partly	bad	
18–30	26.3	44.0	60.7	(N = 70)
31–38	44.8	38.5	33.3	(N = 49)
39 plus	19.9	31.6	33.3	(N = 54)

Data source: Kumulierter Allbus 1980–1982–1984 (ZA No. 1335).

supporters were without gainful employment. And in 1985, more than 20 per cent of all unemployed and almost 50 per cent of unemployed secondary school and university graduates preferred the Greens (Jurtschitsch and Rieckmann, 1987, p. 63).

UNEASY PARTNERS: THE POLITICS OF DISCONTENT

The evidence presented so far suggests that neither the new middle class thesis nor the marginalization argument fully account for the rise of the Greens and their electoral support. The Greens represent instead an often uneasy coalition of at least two distinct social groupings, separated not only by age, but also by their respective life situation: a new service class faction that comes primarily from the 68-generation, and a significant portion of the generation of 1978, consisting of the 'new plebeians' (Vester, 1983) already caught in 'the ghetto of the unemployed' (Glaser, 1987), in addition to those who were still 'studying towards unemployment,' as one Green-alternative journal ironically put it (Esser, 1987, p. 24), and finally those from among the 'superfluous generation' (Richter, 1979) who were entering the universities well aware of their bleak job prospects, but who saw few alternatives.

This has proven to be an uneasy alliance, held together primarily by the shared disaffection with social democracy and the welfare state. What led many young leftists in the late 1960s and early 1970s to become teachers, social workers, or to study socially critical subjects like sociology or political science was the expectation to be able to affect profound social change. Thus for example the 1972 OECD report on West German education (OECD, 1972, p. 70) warned 'of the danger that the new young teachers may bring to their tasks a new dogmatism, presently instilled by more militant left wing factions within pedagogical seminars and institutes.' Some of the most outspoken critics of West German society entered university careers. Thus among seventy-five of APO's leading figures one third remained at a university (fourteen in Berlin alone) to teach primarily sociology and political science. Above all the older generation of APO leaders (those born between 1938 and 1942) succeeded in establishing themselves in academic careers. A second, considerable segment of the APO activists became professionals in the culture industry (publishing, film, theater) and the media (Fogt, 1988).

The new left's hope for substantial reform was sustained by the Social Democratic reform program and particularly its core concern—educational reform. The objective of the SPD reform program was to promote greater equality allowing a greater proportion of the population to participate in the material as well as cultural wealth of society. A classical statement of this objective was the 1970 report on education (quoted in Katzenstein, 1987, p. 332) which stated:

> Education should help people to shape their own lives. The younger generation must experience the possibilities of greater flexibility and freedom, so that they can learn to choose usefully for themselves. Education should create a permanent basis for liberal co-existence through learning and experiencing democratic values and through an understanding of social development and its changes. Education should awaken joy in independent, creative work.

The realization of the social democratic objectives in education, social welfare, and the administration of the economy led not only to the creation and expansion of large state bureaucracies and a potential social democratic clientele, it also raised expectations that the state would continue to employ the growing number of those who were taking advantage of the opportunities for upward mobility via education. However, the economic downturn following the second oil shock thwarted many of these expectations. After Helmut Schmidt's politics of 'crisis management' had already cut back on many aspects of Brandt's reform program, now even the prospects for employment quickly faded away. In the early 1970s the finance ministers of the different *Länder* announced that they had filled all available positions. For financial reasons an extension of the public sector was out of the question. In the future the public sector would hire 15 per cent of university graduates at the most. At the same time the private sector anounced that it too was cutting down on new positions for graduates. In the future it would only by able to provide employment for one fifth of the university graduates (Schlicht, 1980, p. 124). As a result, if in the early 1970s more than 60 per cent of graduates found jobs in the public sector, by the end of the decade that proportion had declined to roughly one quarter (Teichler, 1982, p. 164; also Frackmann *et al.*, 1981, p. 60).

The result of this process was growing disillusionment on the part of the 68-generation with the unkept ideological promises of the Social Democratic reform period, and disenchantment of the 78-generation with its unkept pragmatic promises. The ensuing anti-SPD alliance which found its expression in the Greens is reflected in the political origins of Green supporters. In 1980, 36 per cent were former SPD voters, 50 per cent were first-time voters and former non-voters (Veen, 1987, p. 73). Andreas Huyssen (1987, p. xi) has aptly characterized these two generations:

> Cynicism and resignation . . . are indeed dangers for a generation that had its formative political experiences in the 1960s and that has since then seen its hopes not so much dashed as crumble and fade away. The situation is even worse for the subsequent generation, the no-future kids and dropouts (*Aussteiger*) of the 1970s who were too young then to feel anything but contempt for the 1960s nostalgia of their elders who have the jobs, while they face diminished opportunities and an increasingly bleak labor market.

Huyssen's observation not only captures the two generations' motivations, but also the uneasiness of their coalition. For in many regards, the 78-generation has defined itself in opposition to the previous generation. It is they who are fighting 'the last battle against the hegemony of the 68-generation in culture and in the media.' It is they who are suffering because 'where-ever they look—the 68-generation is already there' (Sontheimer, 1988, p. 44). And it is they who are primarily rebelling against the rationalization of the life world by the state and those who serve it, the domination of life by critical discourse and those who promote and perpetuate it—which includes a significant part of the 68-generation. As Bernd Ulrich (1988, p. 34), a leading spokesman for the 78-generation within the Greens, has noted, 'what is rational or intellectual is determined not least by those of the 68-generation who became professors and teachers.'

Despite these misgivings, the 78-generation has continued to support the Greens whose most important positions have been dominated by the previous generation. As Helmut Fogt (1983, 1986) has shown, in the early 1980s the majority of the party's elite belonged to the generation whose experience had been formed by the student movement. Most of them held jobs, primarily as public servants or public sector employees, and here predominantly as teachers or social scientists. From among 235 Green members in top party or parliamentary positions, between 1979 and 1985 only 15 per cent were without occupation (Fogt, 1986, p. 22). The result was an inverse relationship between Green representatives and those they represented: whereas the majority of Green voters came from a generation which was mostly concerned about its own future, the majority of Green representatives came from a generation which could afford to worry about global issues. In 1982, for example, those aged between between 18 and 29 accounted for more than 50 per cent of the vote; however the proportion of Green *Bundestag* candidates in 1983 from that age group was only 20 per cent. Against that, two-thirds of the candidates were between the ages of 30 and 48, a cohort which accounted for only 20 per cent of the vote (figures calculated from Fogt, 1983, p. 505; and Rönsch, 1983, p. 101).[3]

From the previous two sections the Greens emerge as a rather heterogeneous assemblage of members of the new service class and what Claus Offe (1987, p. 78) has called 'peripheral or decommodified groups,' whose situation is not directly defined by the labor market. What they shared was a desire to advance personal autonomy and individual identity against the centralized, bureaucratized, technology and growth oriented old politics of the established parties. This appealed not only to the members of the new service sector but also, as Bernd Ulrich (1988, p. 35) has aptly pointed out, to the marginalized segments of the 78-generation:

> The threat of unemployment confronts us to a much larger extent than the 68-generation . . . And yet—and this is a significant achievement—there is a greater number of discriminating unemployed than ever before; despite the threat of unemployment, not many of us want to be locked into a meaningless forty-hour jail.

Both the heterogeneity of the social base of the Greens as well as their left-libertarian, non-materialist aspirations are reflected in the programmatic vision of Green politics. This will be discussed in the following section.

POSTMODERN FREEDOM AND EMANCIPATION

It is hard to dismiss the charge that the postmodern drive of Green new politics found its most pronounced expression in the Greens' opposition to the project of modernity in its various aspects. As we have already seen in the previous chapter, their opposition ranged from a vehement critique of industrialism in both West and East, to a condemnation of its fetishism of economic growth and its consumerism. Increasingly this critique included also a rejection of the special role Marxism had attributed to the working class and the privileged position of instrumental rationality central to the social democratic project without, however, renouncing the Marxist attack on the capitalist system. Rudolf Bahro (1982, p. 25), among the most vocal Green critics of modernity, put it perhaps best when he said that the 'entire Green critique of the existing economic order is directed, whether deliberately or not, avowedly or not—at the mechanism that has effected the tremendous technical and scientific progress in Europe since the first industrial revolution'—capitalism.

However, it would be an inordinate simplification to put the Green postmodern position into the anti-modernist corner. The Green attitude towards modernity is better characterized as a profound ambivalence. Although there is broad agreement among the different Green factions that the project of modernity is seriously flawed as far as it has led the world to the brink of global ecological and nuclear disaster, and that the system as a whole is bankrupt and needs total transformation (Kelly, 1983), the project of modernity is not dismissed in its entirety.

As Stephen Brockman (1989) has rightly suggested, what Green postmodern politics attacks is advanced capitalism, the *société de consommation*, and its hold over modernity. Informed by the realization that modernity's quest for control over the world has led to a world out of control and that a reversal can only be successful if the left transcends its traditional focus on class struggle and embraces as its goal the abolition of both human exploitation as well as the exploitation of nature (cf. Bahro 1982a), the Green critique starts with an almost Baudrillardian attack on the engine within the modern machine: Green postmodernism expresses 'a critique of both production and consumption of everything from hamburgers, automobiles and hairdriers to books, movies and scholarly articles. (. . .) Rather than emphasizing rapid and meaningless style changes and the compulsory elimination of the old . . ., it emphasizes economic, political, and cultural recycling' (Brockman, 1989, p. 11). This, however, reflects a decisive break not only with the logic of the postmodern *société de consommation*, but also with the logic of modernity—their shared fetishism of the perpetual new (Wolin, 1984–85, p. 16). As such, Green postmodern politics is directed both against the production oriented Marxist–Leninist left as well as the growth oriented post-Marxist social democratic left.

From this rejection of the tenets of traditional left-wing politics it follows that the Greens had to find a new social actor. If the established parties increasingly sought to appeal to a broad majority of the West German population who supported progress, industrialism, and economic growth, the Greens sought to appeal to those social groups which had become marginalized. Seen from this perspective Hans-Joachim Veen (1985, p. 9) is quite correct to assert that the Greens reflect crisis tendencies inherent in modern, increasingly pluralist industrial society. The Green emphasis on the marginalized stands in opposition not only to those groups which were still defining themselves in terms of their position in the work process—'workers, employees, the self-employed, and the majority of the public sector' (Löwenthal, 1981, p. 1087), but to the privileged position Marxism attributed to the working class in general. Instead they seek to appeal particularly to those groups that have 'traditionally [been] excluded from the dominant Marxist concept of the historical subject' (Jay, 1984, p. 531): women, minorities, homosexuals and other marginalized groups such as the unemployed.

What emerged from this emphasis was a new type of politics. No longer was politics reduced to primarily one privileged axis (material distribution), or one essential contradiction (the contradiction between labor and capital), which relegated everything else to the periphery; on the contrary, the postmodern politics of the Greens expressed exactly those demands which the new left had tended to dismiss as marginal compared to the central contradiction between capital and labor: the abolition of discrimination based on gender and sexual preference, the reorganization of society apart from and against the state, or guaranteed rights for minorities. These new politics demands reflected as much the views of the social basis of the Greens as it reflected broader changes of social reality in the late 1970s. It was in this period that relatively fixed social identities were beginning to give way, at least on the margins, to what Linda Hutcheon (1988, p. 58) has identified as one of the core elements of the postmodern turn, 'a flux of contextualized identities: contextualized by gender, class, race, ethnicity, sexual preference, education, social role, and so on.'

It was particularly this heterogeneity of the Green party which accounted for its ideological ambiguity expressed in the celebrated claim that they were neither left nor right, but ahead (*vorne*). Its heterogeneity found further expression in party programs. A hodge-podge of variegated demands stemming from a variety of political traditions and ideological directions (Cf. Hippler and Maier, 1988,

p. 12) while resisting categorization according to the old totalizing political narratives (liberalism, socialism, or communism) they reflected both strength and weakness; strength, because heterogeneity encouraged creativity and allowed for dissent; weakness, because it was prone to lead to intra-party stalemates, endless discussions, and more often than not exhausting and at times bitter internal fights between a growing number of opposing factions (Murphy, 1986).

It is certainly true that many of the Green political demands that stressed extended democracy in terms of individual and minority rights represented a radicalized claim to the modern tradition of Western liberalism and social democracy (which is not to say that these claims would not threaten the Social Democratic *Modell Deutschland*) rather than a 'comprehensive rejection of them' (Offe, 1987, p. 90). However, what differentiated the Greens from these traditional approaches was the fact that they no longer subcribed to comprehensive visions, grand designs, or claims to absolute truth which these approaches represent. As Tine Stein (1988) put it, the Greens question

> closed concepts, unequivocal answers and universal formulas.— Wherever something claims to be the sole representative of truth, wherever one perspective is elevated to represent totality, Green skepticism is necessary. *The* truth no longer exists—we rather accept a pluralism of truths, which, depending on the case and without being generalizable, can claim validity.

From this perspective Green postmodern politics seeks to recover the promises of individual and social emancipation and democratic rights inherent in the project of modernity. The preamble to the federal programme expresses this vision succinctly stating that the Greens 'support self-determination, the free development of every human being and want that people be able to lead their lives creatively and in harmony with their natural environment, their own desires and needs, and free from external threat' (Die Grünen, 1980, p. 5). However, this emphasis leaves Green postmodern theory and practice with a paradox: they are ultimately grounded in a rather universalist claim to the right of the individual to self-realization and individuality. This claim finds expression in the Greens' identification with the causes of women, gays, foreign workers, and political refugees, handicapped people, and other clients of the welfare state. However, this paradox is dissolved by the ultimate Green political objective—namely to effect the restitution of subjectivity in the face of a web of totalizing structures surrounding the individual as the precondition for the 'constitution of the democratic subject' (Marmora, 1985, p. 109).

With this conceptualization of an alternative politics the Greens put into practice what Jean-François Lyotard has regarded as the core of the postmodern condition, namely the replacement of the grand narratives of history with a myriad of competing language games. To be sure, some influential Green theorists like Rudolf Bahro (1982, 1982a) or feminists like Manon Maren-Grisebach (1982) tried to introduce holistic thinking into the Green discourse and thus to ground it within a larger ideological framework. However, neither Bahro's attempt to develop a communitarian alternative to what he considered the 'exterminist' logic of Western civilization and capitalist industrialism, nor Maren-Grisebach's effort (under the guise of a 'Philosophy of the Greens') to develop a new philosophy persuasive enough to support a universal ecological ethics succeeded in capturing the Green imagination long enough to translate these approaches into a coherent Green grand narrative. Instead the often wild ideological gyrations of Green politics were largely the outcome of the mood of the moment, reacting to momentous events like Chernobyl or the INF conflict, or the seduction of political power.

The claim to emancipation, self-realization, creativity, and subjectivity informs particularly those aspects of the Green vision which deal with social issues. In what follows I will restrict myself to a short discussion of Green women's policy, which has become one of the most important areas of Green politics (see Kolinksy, 1989).

The goal of Green women's policy is above all to recover individual autonomy in the face of centuries of oppression and exploitation, injustice and discrimination, legitimized by an ideology that has claimed that women are subordinate to men—either as housewives or sexual objects (Die Grünen, 1980, p. 32; 1989, p. 15):

> We want meaningful jobs which are more than just making money. We want to be active culturally and politically, we want to be free to decide for ourselves whether we should chose a life with or without children . . . . We want to decide freely and without discrimination how we want to live—whether alone or with others—and whom we love—men or women. (Die Grünen, 1987, p. 6)

However, these demands can only find realization if those who make them are able to deconstruct the dominant ideology and expose the allegedly natural division of gender roles as socially and historically constructed. Since in today's societies women are still predominantly defined through their husbands and children, self-determination can only come as a result of a process of emancipation from assigned roles. It is for that reason that Green women's policy centers on the following three core demands: the abolition of the gender-based division of labor which 'prescribes social roles for women and men and leaves little room for personal fulfilment'; equal access to work in order to provide women with a material base which alone offers the opportunity to achieve independence; and finally the abolition of laws discriminating against women by allowing others to make decisions for them, particularly the law restricting the right to an abortion (paragraph 218). Behind all three demands, as well as other proposals connected to them, is the objective to create a society in which women no longer have to fear repression, in which they no longer have to submit to authority, and in which prescribed roles have been abandoned and women are able to define themselves as individuals. The latter has found expression in a Green proposal which provides that every person keep her or his name after marriage and that children should adopt the name of the mother rather than their father.[4] Although women's policy has assumed a prominent place in Green politics (the Greens were the first party to introduce a women's quota; since 1986 at least 50 per cent of all posts in the Green party organization and in the parliamentary faction must be held by women) it is tightly integrated into the heterogeneous universe of Green issues. Thus Green women have been particularly concerned with the situation of foreign women who have a right to stay in the country only as long as their husbands are permitted to work. Their situation represents thus the most extreme case of women's role as 'appendages' to their husbands without their own identity. It is for that reason that the Greens demand that foreign women have a right to stay and work in West Germany independent of whether they are married or not (Die Grünen, 1987, p. 9). In addition the Greens demand that the West German courts recognize gender-related persecution as a reason to grant asylum.

This concern for minorities is not without internal contradictions. Thus in the mid-1980s the Greens prepared an Anti-Discrimination Legislation which would have proposed a minimum sentence for rape. However, this provision conflicted with traditional Green support for prisoners who according to the federal programme 'had to be seen as victims of an inhumane system of law enforcement and as deprived of their rights' (Kolinsky, 1989, p. 202). As a result of internal protests and dissent, the rape clause was initially deleted from the draft proposal in 1987 and only reintroduced after long debates in 1989.

Green women's policy reflects the strong left-libertarian pro-modernist tendencies of Green politics. Its postmodern tendencies are reflected in the Green approach to the question of the future value and nature of human labor, which according to one observer is the central issue for an alternative model of the future (Jansen, 1987, p. 68). As the programme for the 1987 federal election put it:

> Our goal is a society where all socially necessary labor—housework, child rearing and wage labor – is redistributed among all and thus the gender-specific division of labor is abolished. That does not mean a mere integration of women into the existing labor market. Rather do we strive for a fundamental qualitiative transformation of gainful activity: towards self-determined, meaningful activity for all. (Die Grünen, 1987, p. 7)

The reconceptualization of the nature of work has become a central concern of Green postmodernism and puts the party and its supporters in a fundamental conflict with the politics of the established parties (see, for example, Rönsch, 1983, p. 105). Whereas traditional left and right politics is grounded in a conflict between employers and wage dependents over the just distribution of the fruits of labor, the Green reconceptualization of the nature of work questions the alienating character of wage labor in general. Instead it envisions 'a utopia of non-alienated activity, whereby work encompasses both the production of life and self-determined, free activity' (Bishoff *et al.*, 1983, p. 74).

In order to achieve this goal, the Greens have proposed measures that would separate income from work and thus liberate the individual from 'wrong labor' (Schmid, 1986) and allow him or her to engage in 'free and self-determined activity' in order to find self-realization (Die Grünen, 1983, p. 7). Concrete proposals are the adoption of a 'basic security' for everyone in need (*bedarfsorientierte Grundsicherung*), or a 'guaranteed minimum income' (see the essays in Opielka and Zander, 1988). Not only would a guaranteed minimum income free the individual from having to accept objectionable, low-paying work, it would also advance the Green vision of a 'right to less work' by providing for 'security and an income guarantee for those who consider the option "free time" more valuable than the option "full income"' (Wiesenthal in Opielka and Zander, 1988, p. 52). This proposition clearly reflects the non-materialist aspirations of the Green clientele. It is thus hardly a coincidence that among the concrete policy suggestions is the proposal that all students eighteen years of age or older be given DM 650 per month (for those living at home), or DM 1000 (for those living on their own) (Die Grünen, 1986, pp. 95–7).

The Green vision of self-determined, unalienated work, although only one among several Green essential ideas, is the clearest example of postmodern new politics. In terms of its conceptualization it seeks to bridge the interests of the Green clientele and a larger vision of a postmodern future. Not only does it promise an end to material insecurity, the accelerated individualization of social problems and the need to sell oneself on the market, it also opens up opportunities for choice, individuality and existence design beyond wage labor, and greater equality (see, for example, Schmid, 1986, pp. 12–13). It thus potentially appeals to all forces relevant within the Greens: socialists, feminists, and the critics of economic growth. On the other hand, particularly the notion of a guaranteed minimum income in form of what is also often referred to as a 'citizen wage' offers a potential solution to the dilemma the Greens have had to face when pushing for a preservation or an expansion of existing welfare benefits, namely that every increase in welfare benefits leads to an expansion of the power of the welfare state bureaucracy over its clients. A guaranteed minimum wage would among others also abolish this client role and restore individual autonomy to those dependent on transfer payments (see Schmid, 1986, p. 12).

From this perspective the Greens emerge as the core advocates of a comprehensive postmodern politics. Representing the left-libertarian values of a new service class whose origins lie in the student revolution of 1968 and the non-materialist values of a generation of highly-educated yet materially insecure young people they reflect the demands of both groups for greater self-expression and participation, and an improvement in the general quality of life in advanced capitalist society. Central to the Green project is a struggle against those who defend formal rationality and the project of modernity in favor of a totally different life beyond modernity based on need satisfaction and self-realization. It is in this sense that Green postmodern politics represents adversary politics.

It is rather unlikely that adversary postmodern politics will disappear in the future. Even if the electoral appeal of the Greens should diminish, the impact of left-libertarian non-materialist politics can be expected to prevail within all major fields of political discourse. Not only ecological concerns, but also anti-nuclear, pacifist and feminist impulses have moved 'into the zone of respectability' (Joffe, 1989, p. 52). The postmodern agenda has penetrated mainstream politics and determines its outcomes to a significant degree. However, the assault from the postmodern left has not gone unchallenged. During the rise of Green politics this challenge came largely from the established parties of the center right. In the late 1980s it has increasingly come from an emerging new right. The rise of new right ideology and politics will be the topic of the following two chapters.

4 Postmodern Anti-Modernism

In the early spring of 1989 the results of the state and local elections in Berlin and in the state of Hesse sent shock-waves through the West German political establishment. In Berlin, the right-wing radical, populist *Republikaner* came—so it seemed—literally out of nowhere to gain more than 90 000 votes (7.5 per cent of the vote) which translated into eleven seats in the city parliament. A few weeks later, in Frankfurt, the right-wing extremist National Democratic Party of Germany (NPD) gained 6.6 per cent of the vote and seven seats in the city parliament. In addition, in the two districts where they were able to offer candidates, the *Republikaner* won 10.5 and 7.0 per cent of the vote. Polls taken immediately before the elections indicated that had they run candidates in Frankfurt, the *Republikaner* most likely would have surpassed not only the NPD, but would also have improved their previous result in Berlin.[1]

Those who thought that the right-wing radicals and extremists had profited from local circumstances confined to Berlin or Frankfurt and would therefore hardly be able to duplicate their success on the federal level, soon had to revise their predictions. Despite attempts by political observers to downplay the extent of support for right-wing radicalism, the European elections in June brought the breakthrough for right-wing radicalism: capturing 7.1 per cent of the vote the Republikaner were responsible for the painful losses of the ruling Christian Democrats and their sister party, the Bavarian CSU. In addition, the DVU (German People's Union), an extremist neo-Nazi party alligned with the NPD, gained 1.6 per cent of the vote, increasing the total right-wing vote to almost 9 per cent.

Particularly in Bavaria, for decades a stronghold of the center-right, the ruling Christian Social Union (CSU) suffered a stunning defeat which surpassed even the worst fears of CSU activists prior to the election. Not only did the CSU lose almost 12 per cent of the vote, with 45.5 per cent it also lost its absolute majority statewide. The *Republikaner* gained 14.6 per cent of the vote and became the third largest party in Bavaria. Despite a series of surveys predicting that the *Republikaner* were on their way out, they gained significant support in local elections later in the fall in Northrhine-Westphalia and Baden-Württemberg. Thus by the end of the year it was no longer possible to ignore the potential political significance of right-wing radicalism in West German politics.

What can explain this sudden rise of right-wing radicalism in the Federal Republic? It was only in 1988 that Richard Stöss (1988, p. 35), one of the leading experts on the development of West German parties, discounted the prospects of a revival of right-wing radicalism in West Germany. 'In the face of the enormous integrative power of the two bourgeois parties, the CDU/CSU and the FDP, and their virtually hegemonic position within the bourgeois camp, the prospects for right-wing extremism in West Germany were and are very poor.' At the latest since the European elections this conclusion seems to need revising. With the success of the *Republikaner* and to a lesser degree the NPD, right-wing radicalism has re-emerged as a significant factor in West German politics for the first time since the late 1960s, when the NPD won seats in several Länder parliaments.

On one hand the rise of right-wing radicalism in West Germany is hardly surprising. One might even suggest that West Germany represents merely the rearguard of a development which has affected most parts of Western Europe. The French National Front, the Austrian FPÖ, the Swiss *Vigilants*, *Action National*, and the *Autopartei*, the *Vlaams Blok* in Belgium, and the 'progressive' parties in Norway and Denmark are among the most prominent examples of a rising tide of right-wing populist and radical parties in Western Europe (see Kirfel and Oswalt, 1989). Describing themselves as 'national-conservative' or 'right-wing conservative,' they pursue similar objectives: the protection of national identity against 'foreignization' by Third World immigrants, foreign workers, and particularly refugees; the re-establishment of strict law and order to combat rising crime rates associated with drugs; and the enforcement of traditional moral values in the face of a rising number of abortions and a threatening AIDS epidemic.

On the other hand, if right-wing radical and populist parties have become a rather common phenomenon in most advanced West European countries, the emergence of right-wing radicalism in West Germany evokes particular interest and concern both in West Germany as well as abroad, especially, but not only, for historical reasons. Particularly at this very moment, confronted by a newly uniting Germany, its neighbors are understandably concerned about any stirrings of right-wing radicalism. West German critics in particular have argued that the new right-wing parties represent a grave threat to German democracy (Backes and Jesse, 1989, von Hellfeld, 1989). Not only do they evoke the specter of Weimar whose multiparty system, large number of anti-system parties, and electoral volatility have been largely held responsible for the permanent political crisis of Germany's first democratic republic and its ultimate collapse in the wake of the rise of Nazism, they also give rise to doubts about the stability of the postwar West German political consensus.

For an assessment of the validity of these charges, it is important to understand the roots and evolution of contemporary German right-wing radicalism as well as the conditions which facilitated its rise. On the surface, contemporary right-wing radicalism might be seen as strictly German nationalist focusing only exclusively on the German question. However, upon closer scrutiny right-wing radicalism becomes part of a larger context of a renewed concern with cultural and national identity that has emerged throughout industrial and postindustrial Europe. As Peter Koslowski (1989, p. 24) has argued, right-wing radicalism represents primarily a response to the 'cultural deficits of modern industrial societies,' setting, not unlike the new social movements and the Greens, a set of cultural principles against the 'discourses and societal decision-making systems of the market and of democracy.' In contrast to Green postmoderism, however, which seeks to transcend rather than eliminate modernity altogether, right-wing radical ideology is grounded in a theoretical and philosophical tradition which is deeply hostile to modernity and its claims to universal emancipation.

The core of right-wing anti-modernism is its claim to particularity and diversity against the 'levelling' tendencies of the Christian, Marxist and liberal grand narratives. Postmodern society has a choice: it can either recover and preserve its national and cultural identity or it will join modernity in decay. Particularly at a time when there is growing public concern over the influx of Third World refugees into the affluent societies of Western Europe, this message gains urgency. As one voice put it succinctly (Uhlitz, 1987, p. 51), West Germany has to make a choice between 'the German people or a "multicultural society".' In contrast to left-libertarian postmodernism which grounds diversity in the emancipation and self-realization of the individual, right-wing anti-modernism argues that human beings are different by nature and can only preserve their particularity if they accept themselves as a part of a natural, hierarchical order. The highest unit of order is not humanity but the people constituted as a nation. The most important goal of politics is the preservation of national identity and particularity, and, as a result of this process, the reconstitution of the nation as a historical subject.

NEW RIGHT POSTMODERNISM

The core of the new right's *weltanschauung* is a radical and complete rejection of any kind of universalism in the name and in favor of an allegedly postmodern pluralism. Armin Mohler, at one time Ernst Jünger's private secretary and today a leading figure of the West German new right (Leggewie, 1987a), whose thinking was heavily influenced by the ideas of the so-called 'Conservative Revolution' of the Weimar period, was the first to claim postmodernism for the right. Conservatives were especially called upon to study the postmodern turn because 'this intellectual tendency represents an elaboration of conservative ideas which has taken place outside the so-called "conservative camp"' (Mohler, 1987, p. 38; also 1988, p. 81). In his view, what united postmodernists like Lyotard and the West German new right was a common enemy—the 'second enlightenment' (1986, p. 158). With this concept he referred to what he called the 'one-dimensional' egalitarianism in its universalist form which had spread throughout the world and led to a 'uni-linear thinking which claims to be able to explain the world in a logical fashion and solve all riddles' (ibid.). Like many other rightists, Mohler too saw Marxism (which he considered 'dead' [Leggewie, 1987a, p. 220]), Christianity ('the most imperious universalist teaching' of modern history [Mohler, 1981, p. 68]), and liberalism ('which makes us sick' [Mohler, 1981, p. 70]) as the most important, and dangerous types of universalism.

Reviewing a book on postmodernism by the West German philosopher Wolfgang Welsch, Mohler (1988) agreed with the author that postmodernism's great merits were to have rediscovered pluralism as a 'basic revision' of modernity and to make every effort to save this rediscovered pluralism from renewed 'totalization.' But he was also quick to point out that the revival of pluralism was hardly as new as the growing interest in postmodernism might indicate. As 'nominalism' it had been advocated by the new right, and particularly by Mohler himself, for some time (1988, p. 83).

According to Mohler (1981, pp. 58f.; 1981a, pp. 34f.), at the bottom of the nominalist creed was the question of the universal (*Das Allgemeine*) versus the particular (*Das Besondere*). The universalist believes that reality is based on a spiritual order. He believes in the existence of universals (such as humanity) from which the particular (such as the individual, a people, or a nation) can be derived. Against that the nominalist holds that there is only the particular. Universals are mere names given by man to the particular without, however, corresponding to anything in reality. The nominalist refuses to accept the notion that the human intellect is capable of gaining true knowledge of reality. Above all he rejects the universalist's pretension to speak and act in the name of 'the whole,' of a 'universal order' (1981, p. 62). In the face of an 'infinite chaos' (1981, p. 71), an 'immense jungle of reality' (1981, p. 62; similarly 1981a, p. 32) frustrated universal pretensions tend to lead to totalization and totalitarianism complete with mental institutions and concentration camps (1981, p. 63). The nominalist, on the other hand, deals with the overwhelming complexity of reality by focusing on the particular; his answer to the infinite chaos of reality is the 'lucid' (*übersichtliche*) form. This was essentially what separated the conservative from all other political tendencies (1981, p. 71; 1981a, p. 35).

However, the new right's focus on the particular must not be equated with a preference for the individual. In fact, Mohler as well as other new rightist writers argued that individualism was merely one aspect of the egalitarian, universalist ideology which they despised. For, as one new right author commenting on the rise of postmodernism charged, individualism and the idea of emancipation had led to the complete dissolution of all human bonds (*Bindungen*). 'All of "society" is atomized—one only thinks in terms of particular human beings and above them, one single humanity' (Fiedler, 1987, p. 6). In a similar vein Pierre Krebs (1982, p. 26), the head of the right-wing 'Thule-Seminar' (see Feit, 1987, pp. 77–82), accused those, who believed in the equality of all human beings, of the 'greatest possible intolerance' since they condoned the destruction of diversity, originality, and particularity. These terms evoking the charge of totalitarianism (Krebs, 1982, p. 29) were used to support the claim that human beings could only develop their particularity in the framework of a (hierarchically structured) whole, be that 'a group, or a people which is different from the people next door' (Mohler, 1981, p. 68). (Whereby Mohler emphasized that 'different' had nothing to do with 'better.')

By defining pluralism/postmodernism in this way the new right sought to justify their call for an end to the influx of foreigners, particularly refugees, into Europe as one precondition for the revival of Europe's cultural heritage. Thus Mohler (1981a, p. 37) criticized the decision to allow Southeast Asian refugees to settle in West Germany questioning whether this 'transplantation into an alien environment, in which these human beings cannot live according to their particularity,' might not 'make up for the murder, from which these refugees just escaped.' However, a quick glance at Pierre Krebs' programmatic essay on the 'revival of Europe' makes it clear that the main purpose of the new right's concern for the cultural survival of foreigners was to legitimize their efforts to preserve European culture in the face of what they considered a growing 'subversion' from abroad. Laying claim to the heritage of European culture, Krebs asserted that all the new right wanted to achieve was to strengthen 'the Europeans in their particularity and difference' and, at the same time, to encourage all 'other races to preserve their particularity.' New right humanism wanted 'to take up responsibility for all of Europe's cultural heritage' and sought 'to regain all of the mysterious wealth which is contained in the history of our peoples, but also all those human values which were forgotten, exploited, or mutilated during 2000 years of Christianity' (Krebs 1982, p. 27).

As far as the West German case was concerned, the new right's postmodern agenda focused on two particular issues: the growing number of refugees from Third World countries seeking asylum in the Federal Republic; and the growing interest in identity, the national question, and West Germany's position in Europe and in the world. Together they formed the foundation of the new right's concrete political agenda, an agenda which at a later date would find expression with the rise of the Republikaner.

ECOLOGICAL RACISM

In July 1983, the well-known ethologist Irenäus Eibl-Eibesfeldt, head of the research department of human ethology at the Max Planck Institute of Behavioralism in Seewiesen, wrote in the liberal *Süddeutsche Zeitung* (July 3–4, 1983, p. 111):

> The present confronts us with many problems which frighten us. We experience fears based on economic worries, fears resulting from uncontrolled population growth and the damage to the environment resulting from it; and, finally, social fears, the result of the crowdedness and anonymity of mass society and a policy of

immigration the consequences of which the politicians have failed to recognize in time.

The connection between pollution, overpopulation, and an allegedly misguided 'policy of immigration' (that is, the recruitment of foreign 'guest workers' during the period of economic boom) was characteristic of the direction of the struggle against the 'foreignization' of West Germany in the early 1980s. Referring to the popular writings of respected scientists like Eibl-Eibesfeldt and particularly Konrad Lorenz (see Feit, 1987, pp. 94–8) the new right was quick to combine demands for the protection of the natural environment with calls for the protection of the 'ethnic' environment from cultural 'pollution' (Mohler, 1981a; Krebs, 1982; Künast, 1983).

Central to the new right's justification of xenophobia and racism was the claim that a people's economic and cultural wealth depended on its ability to preserve its specific national environment. Every interference from outside disturbed the ecology of the people with potentially disastrous consequences. Therefore only if individual peoples maintained their uniqueness would humanity be able to preserve the ethnic variety to which it owed its adaptability.

These arguments were nothing new. What was new was that as a result of the renewed increase in the number of unemployed in the late 1970s they gained a growing sympathetic audience in the early 1980s. As early as in 1979 one 'national revolutionary,' writing for the national revolutionary journal *wir selbst*, had argued for an ecological justification for supporting ethnic diversity. To assume, the writer argued, that humans were equal and had equal needs was profoundly unecological and represented an incorrect view of human nature in general. The diversity of human beings, peoples, and their cultures justified the struggle of all ecologists against the 'degeneration' of humans into masses and against the levelling of the human spirit (Laubenheimer, 1979).

A few conservative ecologists agreed. In a 1981 memorandum the ultra-conservative WSL advanced the 'question of foreign workers as an ecological problem.'[2] Its authors argued that the foreign workers had been called into Germany to 'swell (*aufblähen*) the economic power of an industrial country' without regard for ecological consequences. They had thus contributed to the destruction of the West German environment. Equally important, the implantation of human beings from a different culture into West Germany had inevitably led to alienation, the loss of cultural identity, and human dignity. It was wrong, the author asserted, 'both from a human as well as an ecological point of view, to take these human beings out of their homeland, out of their culture, only for the purpose of being the workforce which was allegedly needed for the continuous and unhealthy expansion of the economic capacities in the industrial countries' (p. 69).

With this twist of the argument the new right found a way to present both West German society as well as foreign workers as victims. Thus both the supporters of a 'Citizen Initiative Ausländerstopp' (founded in 1980) and the right-wing extremist National Democratic Party were quick to point out that their demand for a reversal of West Germany's policy towards foreigners had nothing to do with xenophobia or open hostility towards foreigners (*Ausländerfeindlichkeit*). In fact they claimed that they regarded foreign workers as allies. Since the attempt to 'melt' foreign workers into German society destroyed not only German culture but theirs as well, a policy of returning the foreign workers to their homelands was both in the interest of Germans and foreigners.[3]

Probably the most influential attack on the foreign presence in West Germany was the so-called 'Heidelberger Manifesto' (1982), signed by fifteen professors from leading West German universities (*Die Zeit*, February 2, 1982). 'With great worry,' the authors began, 'we observe the subversion of the German people by the influx of many millions of foreigners and their families, the foreignization of our language, our culture, and our national characteristics.' Peoples were '(biologically and cybernetically) living systems' with different system characteristics. Every people had a right to be able to preserve these characteristics, its identity. 'Therefore the integration of large masses of non-German foreigners with the simultaneous preservation of our people is impossible and leads to the well-known ethnic catastrophes of multicultural societies.' The authors were particularly concerned about the survival of Europe, and, within it, the future of the German question. For, they argued, how could a reunification of Germany be possible in the future, 'if the parts became ethnically alien?'

One of the co-signatories of the manifesto, Professor Siebert of Mainz, re-emphasized that this thinking had nothing to do with racism or xenophobia. It was merely the result of the recognition of the differences between peoples and a 'need to protect' not only Germans but also the foreign peoples, 'which also have a right to the recognition and the cultivation of their special existence and particularity.'[4]

With this interpretation of the postmodern call for subjectivity, diversity, and particularity the new right sought to influence the beginnings of a debate on the question of whether West Germany was on the way toward a multicultural society. This the new right rejected arguing that the Germans had a right to preserve their identity. However, German identity was not only threatened from within by the growing number of non-Germans living in the Federal Republic; it was also threatened from without, particularly by the military strategy of the United States. These feelings reached a new urgency with the NATO plans in the late 1970s to introduce new theater nuclear weapons in Europe.

THE RETURN OF THE NATION

Because of its exposed position in the East–West confrontation the question of national identity assumed particular importance in the West German part of the divided country (Betz, 1988, pp. 127–9). In the early 1980s a number of writers, political observers, and pundits suggested that West Germany was going through a severe crisis of identity (*Identitätskrise*). Between a new wave of affluence and renewed fear of nuclear disaster and a new Cold War in the wake of the 1979 INF decision, the majority of West Germans began to confront a reality they had chosen to ignore for a long time: that West Germany was neither a nation, nor 'a culture, hardly a society but an entity, a country which has been economically successful, and one in which economic success has been closely linked to the success of political institutions' (Dahrendorf, 1987, p. 141).

The crisis of identity of the 1980s has given various groups and individuals on the far right an opportunity to regain long-lost legitimacy for their views and ideologies. In the process, a new ideology emerged on the right, partly modified compared to traditional right-wing demands, partly incorporating new issues into an ideology for the postmodern 1980s, so that one can legitimately speak of a West German 'new right' (see Feit, 1987). What united the new right was the absolute priority its members accorded to nationalism and the nation. To quote one of the leading West German neo-nationalists (Willms, 1986, p. 214):

Those who love 'peace' more than the nation and its freedom resemble bleating sheep. Those who love 'man' more are true simpletons; and those who love 'democracy' or 'socialism' or 'the constitution' more than the idea of the nation, sentence themselves to be cannon-fodder in the hands of the concentrated nationalism of the superpowers.

The ideology of contemporary new right neo-nationalism was heavily influenced by the thinking of the so-called new nationalists (see Stöss, 1978). The new nationalists broke off from the extreme right (particularly the NPD) at the time of the student revolution in the late 1960s. They rejected the dream of the old nationalist organizations like the NPD of a reunited German Reich in the borders of 1937 as outdated and reactionary, and called instead for a 'national revolution' from below, modeled after the struggle for independence in the Third World. They attacked the superpowers and the multinational corporations for their imperialism and advocated a 'third way' between capitalism and communism, and East and West in the form of a united, but neutral and largely demilitarized Germany (Stöss, 1978, p. 50).

The main representatives of new nationalism were the AUD and the 'national revolutionaries.' As we have seen earlier, the AUD succeeded the nationalist *Deutsche Gemeinschaft*, one of August Haussleiter's creatures. The program of the DG for the *Bundestag* elections in 1961 was an example of the continuity between new nationalism and new right neo-nationalism.[5] Appealing to the spirit of von Stein and Fichte, the DG demanded an end to the division of Germany, an end to 'the open and concealed foreign rule,' and advocated a 'free and peaceful,' a 'social and independent, united Germany.' According to the DG, Germany represented a colony of foreign imperialist powers. Its status could only be changed if Germany rejected 'Western as well as Bolshevist colonialism' and turned to the newly independent countries in Asia and Africa. Permanent peace in Europe could only be attained if all foreign powers left Germany, and Germany promised to be 'a stronghold of freedom' *vis-à-vis* the West, and a 'stronghold of peace' *vis-à-vis* the East. 'The German people knows that the German states which are integrated into foreign pact systems must assume the role of firebrands. True, enduring security can only be found in the independence of all of Germany.' These changes could only occur, however, under the condition that the German people claimed its identity by acknowledging German history and German culture, that there occurred a 'moral and spiritual rejuvenation of [the German] people in the spirit of its great poets and thinkers,' and that there was an end to the 'mendacious and one-sided Morgenthau-re-education of our children.'

The West German national revolutionaries emerged in response to the student movement of the late 1960s. Young rightists who were dissatisfied with the old right's antiquated and reactionary views and opposed to the new left's faith in what they considered an outdated Marxist ideology and its disregard for the national question, joined together with the objective of developing a comprehensive alternative worldview (Singer, 1971). Central to their thinking was the question of how to 'combine a redefined nation with the democratic and socialist idea in such a way as to give Germany the opportunity to play its role in Europe as a bridge between East and West, socialism and liberalism, and as the country of the center once again. At stake were the perspectives of an internal, spiritual liberation of Germany as a precondition for her reunification in a Europe liberated from foreign domination.'[6]

Like the DG before them, the national revolutionaries attacked both superpowers for dominating and exploiting other peoples (*Völker*) and thus preventing their autonomous development. They believed that nationalism was the only effective weapon against superpower imperialism. Nationalism, 'as an element of identity against multinational alienation,' would integrate the individual into the community of his or her people, would lead to equality and solidarity, and thus 'make possible the struggle against the common enemy of the peoples, against every form of imperialism and totalitarianism.'[7]

In the worldwide struggle for national liberation, Germany's place was with the countries of the Third World. Like them, Germany was a colony, divided and dominated by the superpowers.[8] Germany could only be reunited if the German people liberated the whole of their country from superpower domination. A united Germany, transformed by a national, social, cultural, and democratic revolution, would bring peace to Europe. To quote from one leading national revolutionary: 'The precondition of unity is freedom, and freedom is the precondition of a lasting peace' (Meinrad, 1973, p. 7).

One of the central notions advanced by the national revolutionaries was the question of national identity. Particularly Henning Eichberg, a cultural anthropologist and editor of the leading national revolutionary journal *wir selbst*, was instrumental in popularizing this idea on the right. His book, *Nationale Identität* (1978), was one of the first to address the question of national identity in West Germany. In this book, Eichberg defined identity as 'collective identity' (Eichberg, 1978, p. 7), based on differentiation, and the recognition of one's own ethnic and national particularities and the particularities of others. Proceeding from this definition Eichberg propagated what he called 'ethnopluralism,' the decentralization of large national units ('balkanization for everybody'), and regionalism. Germany was in his view an 'occupied country,' both militarily and culturally. To overcome occupation and division, Germany had to secede from the sphere of superpower competition, in an act of decolonization.

> Creating the German nation means *decentralization*, breaking away from the headquarters of Wodka-Cola, secession from the metropolises. German nationalism means: recognizing that we are a minority that has to fight against internal colonialism, and the alienation in our brains like the Bascs [Basques] and the native Americans. Therefore: *decolonization, decoupling*. Ceasing to be the 'FRG-citizen' with Americanized language and ITT-consciousness—but [gaining] German identity, this is one step towards '*balkanization for everyone*' (Eichberg, 1981, p. 68).

Whereas Haussleiter's AUD was absorbed into the Green party, the major national revolutionary organizations disintegrated in the 1980s, however not before they had played an important role in the development of West German neo-nationalism of every *couleur* (see Klönne, 1984; Honolka, 1987). They bridged to some degree the gulf separating the left and the right with an ideology that seemed to oscillate between the two camps. Before long, in the wake of the controversy over the INF decision, neo-nationalists of the right would follow their lead and adopt central arguments of the peace movement in order to legitimize their demands for German reunification.

In his attack on the West German peace movement, the French philosopher André Glucksman (1984, p. 183) observed that West Germany's 'geopolitical inferiority, whose end cannot be foreseen, is slowly being experienced as a second Versailles. The reparation demanded from the Germans, this time both in political as well as moral terms, threatens to turn into a philosophical curse, which is justifiably felt as intolerable.' These words were written at the height of the controversy over the deployment of new intermediate-range nuclear missiles that shook West Germany in the early 1980s. In the course of this controversy, largely carried out in the streets, the central issue for both the left as well as the right became increasingly the status of Germany as a defeated, divided, occupied country, forty years after the end of World War Two.

In the prevailing political climate of uncertainty, *Angst*, and a growing opposition to United States policy on the part of a sizeable segment of the West German public, right-wing neo-nationalists saw a new opportunity for the promotion of their ideas. They argued that durable peace in Europe depended on the solution of the German question. One example of this approach was an appeal to both German governments and the peace movement entitled, 'Save Peace—Unite Germany!' which appeared in February 1984 in the left-liberal newspaper, *Frankfurter Rundschau*. Initiated by a group of national revolutionaries, the appeal carried the signatures of prominent neo-nationalists of various ideological persuasions.[9] The co-authors expressed 'the silent hope' that the growing danger of nuclear war would provide Moscow and Washington with new insights. Perhaps it no longer was absurd to make the salvation of humanity from nuclear extinction dependent on the reconstruction of Europe as a mediator between the superpowers. Without an end to the division of Europe and freedom for all its peoples, 'we might all end one day in a nuclear inferno.' The co-signatories appealed to both German governments to solve the problem of the growing military buildup in Germany by concluding a peace treaty with Germany and uniting the two German states within a confederation.

The claim that the dissolution of the hostile blocs in Europe and the reunification of Germany were the sole way to avert a nuclear holocaust, and the idea of a German confederation became central elements of West German neo-nationalism, both on the right as well as on the left (see, for example Ammon and Schweisfurth, 1985). Among the most influential proposals was Wolfgang Venohr's conceptualization of a confederation that would allow both German states to remain in their respective economic and military alliances. This arrangement would alleviate the fears of Germany's neighbors while simultaneously extending its sovereignty and allowing its citizens to move freely between the constituent parts of the confederation (Venohr, 1985, pp. 216–17).

With the advantage of hindsight, one cannot help noticing the prophetic quality of these propositions. Of course, at the time, they were quickly dismissed by the political establishment and its advocates relegated to the slightly lunatic margins of West German politics. This foresight might caution us to dismiss as irrelevant the central line of argument which increasingly came to dominate the neo-nationalist debate. During that debate it became increasingly clear that for a majority within the right these and similar ideas of a German confederation aligned with the superpowers were far too moderate. What they envisioned was a militant German nationalism, grounded in anti-Americanism, historical revisionism, and a reconceptualization of German foreign policy.

By far the most important charge levelled primarily at the United States by the new right was the notion that Germany was still an occupied country. 'Germany under Foreign Occupation' was the title of an article by Harald Rüddenklau which appeared in Wolfgang Venohr's influential collection of essays on the German question, *Die deutsche Einheit kommt bestimmt* (1982). Three years later Peter Dehoust (1985, p. 3), the editor of the right-wing extremist *Nation Europa* asked, 'When will the foreign rule end?' Like Henning Eichberg, the right saw foreign occupation as transcending military occupation. In their view, the nature of Germany's occupation was above all psychological. The primary instrument of psychological occupation had been the American policy of re-education immediately after World War II. Re-education taught the Germans to accept responsibility for the lost war and to feel guilty. It imposed on the German people 'the special status of the criminal people alone responsible for the last war' (Jäckel, 1984, p. 24). By imposing their narrative and their alien way of life on the Germans, the United States was depriving the Germans of individuality and identity, two essential bases for resistance. Denied the right to speak for themselves, the Germans were without patriotism, without love for the fatherland. 'Patriotism is nothing but self-determination, the emancipation of the nation! And only patriotism can provide a people with a spiritual nature' (Venohr, 1982, p. 726).

For the new right, national independence and autonomy thus entailed not only political but above all psychological and ideological emancipation from the superpowers (Maschke, 1987, p. 141). This entailed emancipation not only from the Soviet Union, but also from the United States. The result was a growing anti-Americanism which harped on old cliches and stereotypes about America's lack of culture while integrating new right anti-universalist ideas (see Krebs, 1981). Its goal was a reversal of an American-inspired foreign policy that sought to disseminate universal ideals in favor of one that pursued national self-preservation (Mohler, 1982). One example might suffice to show the degree of the new right's hatred and contempt for the United States. Pierre Krebs (1987), dreaming of a resurrected European empire, wrote: 'With it we will be able . . . to throw Michael Jackson and the melting pot cosmopolitans into the trash can, and send the Dallas thugs and Ronald Reagan back to their cow pastures.'

The attacks on re-education, confrontation with the past, and the United States were evidence of the way the new right sought to reconstruct German national identity. Germany could only regain its former position of power and strength if it rediscovered its national characteristics, the uniqueness of its history and if it escaped forty years of foreign indoctrination. As a result of national liberation, Germany would be able to be a 'normal nation' again, regain national sovereignty, and the capacity to conduct an independent foreign policy.

With the growing controversy over the dual track decision of 1979 the new right saw an opportunity to promote these ideas. Hellmut Diwald, author of the controversial book, *Die Geschichte der Deutschen* (1978), argued that foreign powers had transformed Germany into what he called 'the decisive battlefield.' There were more missiles, nuclear war heads, and missile launchers on German territory than anywhere else in the world. The superpowers claimed to guarantee Germany's security; but in reality security only meant 'to be doomed to be destroyed as the nuclear battle field in the center of Europe.' Therefore the restitution of German unity was an existential question, not only for Germany, but also for Europe. For Europe's sovereignty depended on German unity. 'Even if the Germans had no interest in changing their situation: the European states would have to demand the restitution of Germany for the sake of Europe's independence' (Diwald, 1985, pp. 64–8).

The 'Declaration of the German Council,' an attempt by several influential right-wingers to work out a common platform on the national question, which appeared in the spring of 1984 in *Nation Europa*, stated that recent events had shown that Germany, in the case of a war between East and West, would be abandoned to nuclear destruction. 'This is the situation: Germany's past is characterized by defeat and guilt, her present by division and foreign domination, her future appears hopeless.'[10] In this situation the Germans should remember the principle of national politics that only those who determined their own destiny were free. This meant in the German case 'the decriminalization of our history as the precondition for a normal national consciousness.'

Among the co-signatories of this declaration were a political scientist, Bernard Willms, and a professor of comparative law,

Wolfgang Seiffert. Bernard Willms, one of the leading theorists of West German neo-nationalism (Klönne, 1987), has been one of the most ardent and outspoken neo-nationalists on the right. Willms recognized quite early in the debate on the national question that the political climate was changing and that this might open new opportunities for the right. In an article for *Nation Europa* he observed that it had become possible again in Germany to talk about the nation in a way which had been politically unacceptable only a few years before. What had happened was a dramatic movement in the 'political-intellectual spectrum.' What once had been dismissed as extreme rightist, had come to be seen merely as right-wing (Willms, 1984, p. 8).

This may explain why *Politische Vierteljahresschrift*, a leading political science journal, gave him the opportunity to present his views to the academic establishment. There he settled accounts with the victors of World War II who had fought the war as a crusade of the 'better part of humanity' against *the* enemy of humanity, and who had indoctrinated the Germans with their interpretation of the nature of this war. 'The last power of resistance had to collapse when the victorious powers were able to use, and did use, the revelations about the national socialist practice (*Praxis*) of the concentration and extermination camps to attribute to the shocked Germans collectively the guilt for national socialism, the crimes it had committed, and, above all, the war itself and all its consequences' (Willms, 1984a, p. 54). In this way the victors not only destroyed German self-confidence but also made it clear to the Germans that they could no longer count on being recognized as a normal nation (Willms, 1986, p. 36).

If Germany wanted to regain its national consciousness the West Germans had to remember Carl Schmitt's famous words that politics meant above all to distinguish between friends and enemies. In terms of foreign politics, that meant that enemies were everyone who denied 'a people, a state, a nation its own, independent existence' (Willms, 1984, p. 12). In Germany's case, this included both superpowers and their allies in East and West. The objective of West German foreign policy should be to create opportunities to escape its position, even if that meant a reversal of West Germany's traditional foreign policy direction. 'If the USA and the European West absolutely refuse to want to have a reunified Germany, then the Germans have to develop a policy which at least enquires of the other superpowers about a price [for reunification].'

If Willms refused to go into detail as to the nature of a possible reversal of Germany's relationship with the Soviet Union, other neo-nationalists were less cautious. As early as in 1979, Wolfgang Venohr said in an interview with a national revolutionary journal that national interest had to be separated from ideologies. 'To entice the Muscovites with the Chinese card can be a good short-term tactic, if the long-term strategy remains clear: in the long run, only a close, absolutely equal partnership of the two great nations of the Russians and the Germans can guarantee peace in Europe.'[11]

The leading advocate of such a rapprochement became Wolfgang Seiffert. Once a personal acquaintance of Erich Honnecker and one of East Germany's leading experts on international law, Seiffert left the GDR in 1978 disenchanted with Honnecker's policy of demarcation (*Abgrenzungspolitik*) *vis-à-vis* the Federal Republic. Once in West Germany, Seiffert, like other East German expatriates (see von Berg, 1986, 1987; Obst, 1987), became an ardent advocate of German reunification (Seiffert, 1986, pp. 123–5).

Seiffert contended that the division of Germany could not be separated from the larger context, namely the division of Europe. 'But even from this perspective, there is only *one* country, only *one* people, only *one* nation in Europe divided by two incompatible political systems, and that is Germany, the *German* people, the *German* nation' (Seiffert, 1986, p. 165). Therefore, the solution of the German question depended on the Germans themselves. Because the GDR—as a result of her economic and technological back-wardness and the legitimation problem of her leadership—had been incapable of taking the initiative, it depended on the Federal Republic to devise a policy capable of 'improving the conditions for attaining the national goal and using opportunities offensively' (p. 195).

In Seiffert's view, history was offering such an opportunity to the Germans today. Because the Soviet Union was 'much weaker than the West believes . . . politically, militarily, and economically,' its leaders might be forced to re-evaluate their policy towards Europe. In the process they might be tempted to 'make the German question a topic of operative politics' (Seiffert, 1984, pp. 25–6). Such an opening would be beneficial both to the Soviet Union and West Germany, at a point in time when the new technologies of computers and microprocessors force the Federal Republic to open up new markets. If the Federal Republic wanted to retain its position as a leading industrial nation, and if it wanted to counterbalance Japanese and American dominance in Asia and the Pacific region, it had to turn to Eastern Europe, CEMA, and the GDR (p. 28). Under these circumstances the Soviet Union might be willing to permit the reunification of Germany in exchange for a long-term and comprehensive economic co-operation 'which at the same time could lead to a long-term political alliance with the Soviet Union' (Seiffert, 1986, pp. 128, 158).

Seiffert's propositions were the most detailed example of a growing tendency among right-wingers to develop scenarios for an accomoda-tion with the Soviet Union in order to restore Germany's position as a great power in Europe (cf. Feiler, 1984, Aigner, 1987, Feldmeyer, 1988). Günter Maschke (1987a, p. 369) put it most frankly when he explained why nationally-minded conservatives could not return to the anti-Soviet foreign policy of the Adenauer era: 'With this form of nationalism nothing can be gained, because the key to reunification lies in the Kremlin, not in the Californian orange groves. It is up to us to summon up the will and the energy to get it. That includes a readiness to come to an arrangement with the predominant power in the East.'

These sentiments marked a significant departure of the West German conservatives from their traditional anti-communism and hostility towards the Soviet Union. Their perception of the swift deterioration of the Soviet economy and particularly their assessment of the consequences and opportunities this would entail for Eastern Europe and particularly the two German states proved to be remarkably far-sighted. With the double theme of xenophobia and neo-nationalism the conservative right had found an ideological platform which they could exploit for political gain. What they lacked was a political party to translate cultural gains into political success. However, as far as a political strategy was concerned, the situation appeared bleak in the early 1980s. The traditional representa-tive of right-wing nationalism, the NPD, had become politically irrelevant. As a result, right-wing supporters had either turned to neo-Nazi groups or opted out of politics altogether.

CONSERVATIVE META-POLITICS

The only promising attempt to revive a politically relevant German conservatism came from a number of conservative and right-wing intellectuals who sought to develop a genuine conservative agenda.

Politically the revival of German conservatism was a direct response to the unfulfilled promises of the new CDU/CSU-led government of Helmut Kohl to execute a complete turnaround (*Wende*) in West German politics after coming to power in 1983. The response was initiated by prominent conservative and right-wing academics and publicists with the goal of creating a genuine conservative alternative to the center right parties in power.

The conservative critics of the Kohl goverment attributed its failure to embark on a radically new course in West German politics to the strategy of leading moderates and modernizers within the CDU to attract new middle class voters by adopting new issues (such as women's rights) and responding to the spread of new values (Rohrmoser, 1987). The conservative critics were particularly disappointed by the government's refusal actively to pursue the question of German reunification as the central objective of German foreign policy. They feared that without a new party willing to promote German interests, the interests of the nation would 'cease to play a role even on the margins of West German society,' and those citizens who were still nationally-minded would turn into an irrelevant group on the fringes of West German politics (Hartmann and Fürst, 1986, p. 73). In their view it was thus of crucial importance that the right solve the question of German identity which they considered endangered and threatened by three issues: the continued division of the country; the influx of a growing number of foreigners into the country; and finally the heritage of the past.

In order to solve these issues the conservatives had to offer a strong core message. Under the circumstances this message had to assert vigorously the will to German identity expressed in the motto, 'we want to remain German' (Hartman and Fürst, 1986, pp. 173–4). All other demands would logically follow, whether they concerned the national question, the 'chances of the biological survival of our people,' or the problem of foreign immigration. Above all, in order to neutralize past indoctrination of the German people by the victorious powers, which had led to the 'criminalization' of German history, the conservatives would have to concentrate on a reinterpretation of history in order to recreate a sense of identity. In addition, they would have to offer a variety of 'alternative' values capable of appealing to the German cultural traditions, such as an emphasis on style, morals, character and inner attitude. Only by achieving a 'value change' in the West German public could the conservative right hope to break the left's intellectual and spiritual hegemony dominating West

German society since the 1968 cultural revolution (Weissmann, 1988, p. 51).

The revival of German conservatism, or what some observers have called the German new right (Feit, 1987), was an important cultural and political event marking the beginning of the post-postwar era of contemporary German history. As will become clear in the following chapter, the conservative critique of the dominant consensus within West German society was a sensitive response to a shift in West Germany's political climate. However, in its effort to revive a genuine German intellectual conservatism, modelled to some extent after the ideas of the 'conservative revolution' of the interwar period (for example, Moeller van den Bruck, Ernst Jünger, Edgar Jung) it ultimately failed to become a significant political force. The core of its political philosophy was a vigorous attack on the German turn to modernity, exemplified by West Germany's embrace of Western, and particularly American values in the immediate postwar period and coming to its fullest fruition with the cultural revolution of 1968.

The conservatives' rejection of modernity led to often vicious attacks on the United States which they considered had subjected the Germans to re-education and thus infected West Germany with the bacillus of modernity (cf. Mohler, 1982), on the dominant political theory underlying the postwar consensus whose main representative they saw in the Frankfurt School and particularly in Jürgen Habermas (Künast, 1983, Kraus, 1986), and on the new left heirs to 1968 who had instigated the cultural revolution of the 1960s. It was hardly a coincidence that a leading conservative figure celebrated the rise of postmodernism with the argument that postmodernism had succeeded in bringing down the cultural revolution (Mohler, 1988, p. 81).

However, despite their rejection of the politics of the center-right parties and despite a number of programmatic statements on the political situation in West Germany the conservatives hesitated to organize their own party. Following the strategy of the French 'nouvelle droite' they concentrated instead on creating and cultivating a network of intellectual circles and a number of journals of varying quality with the ultimate goal to wrest 'cultural hegemony' from the left, to eliminate the left-libertarian heritage of 1968, and thus to prepare the ground for a truly conservative revival in Germany.

The sudden emergence and electoral success of right-wing radical parties in 1989 confirmed the conservative perception of a transformation of the political climate in West Germany which would open up opportunities for a party on the right of the Christian Democrats.

However, despite the fact that the successful right-wing radicals adopted the core of the conservative agenda, their populist appeal was a far cry from the genuine intellectual conservatism its proponents had envisioned would have a decisive influence on future German politics.

5 The Politics of Discontent: Right-Wing Radicalism in West Germany

SCHÖNHUBER'S RISE

In the late 1980s right-wing radicalism and right-wing extremism returned to West German politics. Right-wing extremist parties such as the NPD and the German People's Union (DVU) achieved gains in local elections, particularly in areas such as in Bremen where unemployment was high (see Betz, 1988, p. 153). However, it soon became clear that in terms of electoral support right-wing extremism was a thing of the past. If there was any chance for a right-wing party to succeed at the polls, this would be the representatives of right-wing radical populism who called themselves the Republikaner.

The Republikaner were founded at the end of 1983 by Ekkehart Voigt and Franz Handlos, two former Bundestag members of the CSU and Franz Schönhuber, the popular moderator of a monthly political talk show on the Bavarian television network, which gave ordinary citizens an opportunity to vent their anger and frustration over Bavarian politics (see Craig, 1989; Leinemann, 1989; Hirsch and Sarkowicz, 1989). The foundation was motivated primarily by resentment and revenge: Handlos and Voigt sought to get back at Franz Josef Strauss, the Bavarian minister president and chairman of the CSU, whom they considered to have been instrumental in brokering a West German loan of one billion deutschmarks to the East German regime. Franz Schönhuber, in turn, was motivated primarily by a personal desire for revenge for having been fired from his job with the Bavarian television network and dropped by his influential friends in the CSU after publishing a book in which he recounted his adventures during World War II as a member of Hitler's Waffen-SS. By forming a party on the right of the CSU with a strong nationalist and populist orientation, the troika sought to compete with

Strauss's popular party, first in Bavaria, and then throughout the Federal Republic.

After a series of open and sometimes violent internal conflicts between Schönhuber and the two ex-CSU members over questions of politics and personality, the latter soon turned their backs on the party, leaving Schönhuber as its undisputed leader. Concentrating its efforts primarily on Bavaria, the party had its first big success in the Bavarian state elections in October 1986. State-wide the Republikaner gained three, and in some districts even more than five per cent of the vote. Though this result was not enough to threaten the CSU's hegemonic position in Bavaria, the CSU was clearly concerned about the competitor arising on their right. In the election campaign for the 1987 *Bundestag* elections that immediately followed the Bavarian elections, an 'unabashedly patriotic Strauss' increasingly used Republikaner rhetoric in order to re-absorb disenchanted voters on the right (*The New York Times*, January 13, 1987).

Strauss's efforts were largely successful. Concluding that they were still too weak, the Republikaner decided not to enter the race, and the remaining right-wing parties came nowhere close to the five per cent necessary to send representatives to the *Bundestag*. If Franz Josef Strauss had succeeded in the past to appeal to right-wing conservatives, his untimely death in early October 1988 deprived the center right of the opportunity to persist in this strategy. His death did contribute to the subsequent successes of Schönhuber's Republikaner who declared themselves to be the rightful heirs to Strauss's legacy. However, despite Strauss's acknowledged ability to appeal to voters on the right fringes of the center right parties, there is good reason to doubt that Strauss would have been able to prevent the further rise of the Republikaner in Bavaria and elsewhere in the Federal Republic. After all, their first significant gains at the polls had come during Strauss's tenure as minister president. This suggests that there was already growing resentment on the part of the Bavarian population against Strauss and the overwhelming power of the CSU, which finally boiled over in the European elections.

The reimbursement for the Bavarian election campaign (more than one million deutschmarks) gave Schönhuber the opportunity to expand his party almost throughout the Federal Republic. By 1987, party organizations had been established in all but one state. Much of the organizational drive owed to Schönhuber's personal attraction as a speaker in numerous rallies in beer halls and beer tents all over the country, during which Schönhuber skilfully played on his audience's growing disenchantment with the politics of the governing center right parties and managed to gather conservatives, neo-nationalists, and former members of the NPD into the fold of his party. The success in the Berlin and the European elections proved to what degree it was possible to mobilize popular political resentment. As a result, the Republikaner established themselves as the dominant political force on the radical right of the German party spectrum. Between January and April 1989 alone, the party claimed that its membership had increased from 8600 to roughly 14 000 (Lepszy, 1989, p. 3).

THE DIALECTIC OF MODERNIZATION

As is the case in other West European countries, the rise of right-wing radicalism in West Germany cannot be reduced to one single cause. More than anything else, right-wing radicalism is symptomatic of a number of deficits becoming increasingly apparent in all advanced industrial societies. In West Germany, after the establishment of the left-libertarian Greens in the early 1980s, the gains of right-wing radical parties, both largely at the expense of the established catch-all-parties, reveal above all the declining ability of the large parties to bind their traditional electorate. As in other West European countries, during the past decade the number of floating voters has increased considerably: from 24 per cent in 1980 to 37 per cent in 1989 (Gluchowski, 1989, p. 67). This comes at a time when the overwhelming majority of the West German population is deeply dissatisfied with politicians, parties, and the political process alike. In 1989, for example, more than 80 per cent of the population felt that most politicians did not know what the average citizen wanted, 75 per cent thought that political parties cared only about getting votes, and more than two-thirds held that one could not understand politics because the most important decisions were made behind closed doors.[1]

However, these signs of discontent are merely the expression of deeper socio-structural changes underway in most advanced capitalist societies. They represent a response to the transformation, fragmentation, and reorganization of all major aspects of social reality. From this perspective, right-wing radicalism is a reaction to the accelerated pace of modernization which characterizes present-day Western Europe, and which has led to the deterioration of the social and economic situation of a considerable proportion of the Western European population, to status insecurity, and a number of associated fears (see Glotz, 1989; Castner and Castner, 1989, pp. 36–7). In this great transformation, West Germany appears to have been particularly affected. Or perhaps the West Germans, owing to their special situation in Europe, once again showed themselves to be particularly sensitive to these changes. The following quotation aptly expresses the essence of a mood widespread throughout West German society:

> We live in a time of profound change including revolutionary changes in technology and economics; a value change in society on the dimension of a cultural revolution with ever greater differences in values and lifestyles . . . and a society which enjoys its apparently secure prosperity, yet is less and less able to deal with the flip-side of this prosperity, or which increasingly discovers the flip-side of prosperity . . . . More and more people feel threatened by the rapid change, feel less and less at home in the modern world and increasingly lost. Never before was the tension between tradition and progress, pressure to modernize and preservation of what has been achieved, and old and new values so great [as today]. In no other society . . . is there such a decisive tension between the generations.[2]

The reaction has been a reaffirmation on the part of a variety of social groups of traditional values, emphasizing particularly law and order, discipline, and the values of industrial capitalism and the Protestant work ethic, while rejecting everything that is perceived as alien—from new technologies and postmaterialist values and lifestyles to the uncertainties and challenges of the future integrated European market, and the continued inflow of foreigners. From this perspective, right-wing radicalism looks very much like the authoritarian, materialist counterpart to left-libertarian postmaterialism on the new politics axis defined by a new political conflict over the question which values will ultimately prevail in the postindustrial age (Flanagan, 1987; Minkenberg and Inglehart, 1989; Inglehart, 1989, pp. 273–80). The resulting political climate might be characterized best as one dominated by resentment, which right-wing radical parties have been quick to exploit.

There is growing evidence that the economic upswing which has accompanied the accelerated modernization drive of the 1980s in West Germany was bought at the expense of a number of serious problems, especially those associated with unemployment. Particularly young people without complete education or formal qualification are increasingly confronted by the threat of unemployment. In addition, a growing number of young people who have completed professional training are no longer able to stay in their chosen career (Beck, 1986, p. 239; Castner and Castner, 1989). In 1987, for example, the unemployment rate among twenty to twenty-four-year-olds was at 16.5 per cent almost twice as high as that of the population in general. Less than 50 per cent of young workers with professional training enjoyed a secure work place in their chosen career six months after they had completed vocation training. In the same year, unemployment rates for workers without qualification reached 18.4 per cent (see R. Roth, 1989, p. 25; Heitmeyer, 1989a, p. 2; Tessaring, 1989, p. 19). In the immediate future unemployment among the latter group is expected to grow as a result of further reductions in the demand for unskilled labor. Middle-of-the road projections estimate that by the year 2000 demand for unskilled labor will have declined by 3.2 million while demand for formally qualified labor will have increased by 3.5 million (Hoffman *et al.*, 1986, p. 7; see also Klauderer, 1990).

Young and unskilled workers are the most prominent victims of the transformation of West Germany's economy, but they are far from being the only ones. The rationalization of the production process as well as the flexibilization of the workforce, both consequences of the introduction of new technologies, have split the labor market into a number of core industries complete with secure, full-time work places and a growing marginalized periphery with insecure, often part-time jobs. As two observers note, the backbone of new high tech production consists of skilled male West German employees age thirty to fifty 'with a solid education background and formal professional education.' Opposed to these 'well-situated employees in sunshine industries' are the 'poor, chronically unemployed, who are fired and denied access to the functioning centers of the economy' (Kern and Schumann, 1989, pp. 98–9).

These developments have led a number of sociologists and party strategists to describe the present situation in terms of a 'socio-political dilemma' stemming from a growing bifurcation of society into a 'two-thirds society' (*Zweidrittelgesellschaft*)—a society in which the acceleration of modernization has meant greater affluence for a large majority whereas a minority of young people, unskilled or semi-skilled low-income workers, elderly people drawing small pensions, farmers fearing economic and social downward mobility, and lower level employees and civil servants without promotional opportunities have found themselves increasingly relegated to the margins of West

German society (Castner and Castner, 1989). Empirical evidence suggests that it is particularly among these 'modernization losers' (*Modernisierungsverlierer*) that the Republikaner have found sympathizers and electoral support (see Glotz, 1989, pp. 41, 94).

Although it is too early to make definite statements as to the composition of right-wing support, it is possible to make some preliminary observations (see Table 5.1). The results from Berlin and the European election as well as other survey results indicate that the Republikaner appeal to a much larger degree to men than to women (Hofman-Göttig, 1989b, pp. 28–31). Consistently almost twice as many males as females support and cast their ballots for the Republikaner. Secondly, the majority of Republikaner supporters have primary education which in turn is reflected in their predominant occupational background: it is particularly among unskilled and semi-skilled workers and to a lesser degree lower-level employees and civil servants that the Republikaner find the largest support (see also Roth, 1989a, pp. 12–14; Veen, 1989, p. 58). In the European election the Republikaner gained the highest proportion of their votes in rural and small urban communities with a high proportion of blue-collar workers (10.4 per cent) or a high proportion of employees (9.5 per cent; Forschungsgruppe Wahlen, 1989, pp. 20, 22). Finally, the Republikaner have managed to mobilize a considerable proportion of young voters. Although the proportion of young Republikaner voters in the European election was considerably smaller than in the Berlin election, they still attained their relatively best result among voters age 18 to 24 (Veen, 1989, p. 57; Hofmann-Göttig, 1989; Hofmann-Göttig, 1989b, pp. 26–7). Evidence suggests that, at least in part, it is ambiguity and anxiety in the face of drastic socioeconomic changes affecting West German society which accounts for the support of these groups for the Republikaner (See Veen, 1989, pp. 64–5). In Berlin, for example, their gains—and the CDU's losses—were highest in those working class districts with a 'localized political climate . . . characterized by social insecurity and anxiety about status loss, to which the center parties . . ., according to those affected, have found no credible answers.'[3] A representative survey conducted in March 1989 found that a disproportionately large number of Republikaner supporters viewed themselves as belonging to the bottom third of society and assessed their economic situation as bad or very bad (see Table 5.2). This might account for the fact that particularly in the large metropolitan areas in the north and west of West Germany (particularly in the Ruhr area), the Republikaner found considerable support from former SPD voters.[4]

Table 5.1   Right-wing radical support: social and educational background (in per cent)

	Population	Rep. supporters
Age:		
16–29	27	30
30–44	25	25
45–59	23	23
60–	25	22
Men	47	65
Women	53	35
Education:		
Primary	55	66
Middle,		
Secondary, Graduate	45	34
Social background:		
workers:		
unskilled,		
semi-skilled	15	20
skilled	23	33
employees and		
civil servants:	17	13
lower, middle-level	36	31
higher-level	14	9
farmers	3	3
self-employed,		
free professions	9	4
N	12 559	609

Source: Allensbacher Archiv, IfD-Umfragen 5017/5019–23, March–August 1989.

Table 5.2   Individual perceptions of social location (in per cent)

Question: There is lots of talk about a two-thirds society. The majority of two-thirds of the citizens of the Federal Republic are doing very well or at least well, whereas one-third is not doing well. Where would you locate yourself?

	Total	*CDU/CSU*	*SPD*	*FDP*	*Greens*	*Rep*
Top two-thirds	77	85	73	81	71	71
Bottom one-third	22	14	26	19	28	26
N	2272	766	836	165	185	104

Source: EMNID, Spiegel-Umfrage, March 1989.

The analysis of the social structure of right-wing support suggests that one of the major reasons for the electoral success of the Republikaner lies with the structural changes which have affected a sizeable proportion of the West German population. As one commentator recently noted, social fragmentation and marginalization 'have caused enormous fear. It is the fear of a crisis of "meaning", the destruction of all institutions. This fear manifests itself not only on the right; however it is more widespread as well as panicky there' (Glotz, 1989, p. 95). The response has been a search for and new emphasis on traditional values, an exclusive 'German' national identity, and traditional German nationalism.

The differences in the value system become most clear when one compares the supporters of the Greens with those of the Republikaner (see Table 5.3). Among the issues and values the voters of the Republikaner consider most important are law and order, cleanliness, honesty, a sense of duty, a willingness to work hard *(Leistungsbereitschaft)*, and the preservation of traditions. On each of these issues and values the supporters of the Greens rank disproportionately low. However, the relationship is reversed when it comes to issues and values such as tolerance towards different opinions, working towards peace, and helping those in need. In addition, the fact that more than 50 per cent of Republikaner supporters consider prosperity an important goal supports the contention that the rise of right-wing radicalism can be explained at least in part as a materialist backlash to the growing spread of non-materialist concerns (Inglehart, 1990, p. 277).

Table 5.3   Percentage value preferences

Question: Could you say what you consider especially important?

| | Party preference | | | | | |
| | Age 39 and under | | | Age 40 and older | | |
	total	Greens	Rep.	total	Greens	Rep.
Honesty	71	58	75	75	75	75
Law and order	58	34	72	80	49	90
Working for peace	54	70	51	46	74	34
Tolerance	54	65	33	51	62	34
Sense of duty	51	32	64	67	46	78
Cleanliness	43	28	57	65	49	67
Hard work	35	20	46	45	30	50
Preservation of traditions	18	13	40	40	20	65
Prosperity	44	36	52	30	23	34
Social advancement	33	28	25	29	26	39
Progress	24	18	27	21	5	24
N	862	174	37	1185	38	41

Source: Allensbacher Archiv, IfD-Umfrage, 5019, April 1989.

The pronounced difference between left-libertarian Greens and authoritarian right-wing supporters illuminates the deep split which separates the two camps on the new politics axis. Whereas the Greens seek to redefine postmodern identity in terms of the fully emancipated individual, for right-wing supporters identity is defined in terms of national collectivism, subordination to hierarchy, the rejection of individual tolerance for disagreements, and an ahistorical German national identity complete with a catalogue of values/virtues tradition-ally associated with the Germans (hard work, sense of duty, support for law and order) which, however, in the West German consumer society have lost most of their meaning and appear strangely out of place and outdated (Koslowski, 1989, p. 24). Right-wing radicalism is thus at least in part firmly grounded in pre-modern ideologies which are mobilized against the onslaught of modernization and postmodern culture.

One of the most striking examples of these pre-modern tendencies is the way the Republikaner deal with the role of women in modern society. Women are said to have a special vocation and duty to create a 'climate of security' through 'warmth and devotion' in which family and children can thrive. Although acknowledging that women have a right to education and a qualified job training in order for women 'to gain more independence and self-esteem,' the Republikaner stress the necessity to give women the opportunity to fully develop their 'natural ability as mother and center of the family' (Die Republikaner, 1987, pp. 8–9). This example illustrates very pointedly the vast gulf which separates left-libertarian and authoritarian new politics. Whereas one of the primary objectives of the left-libertarian discourse consists in undermining the established image of women, the right-wing radical discourse seeks to validate and authorize it by presenting socially constructed roles as natural ones. The gulf which separates the two sides becomes also evident in regard to women's right to abortion. The Republikaner are vigorously opposed to any form of abortion, except if it has been established beyond any doubt that the lives of the mother or child are threatened (Die Republikaner, 1990, p. 21). Against these demands, which seek to reverse the growing assertiveness of women in German society, it is hardly a coincidence that the proportion of women supporting the Republikaner is considerably smaller than that of men.

THE POPULIST AGENDA

The Republikaner have been very adroit in exploiting the mixture of anxiety and popular resentment for political gains. Like their counterparts in other West European countries, the party pursues a primarily populist agenda. Central to this agenda is a strong emphasis on conservative issues such as law and order, traditional institutions like a strong state, the police, and the family, and traditional values like discipline and public spirit. However, this emphasis on a traditional value system hardly sets the Republikaner apart from the established center right parties. What distinguishes the Republikaner and makes for their right-wing radical character is their militant evocation of national identity and the preservation of national culture.

Over the past several years, the question of national identity has taken on a new urgency in West Germany. Emerging as a political and cultural issue during the controvery over the NATO decision in the early part of the 1980s to station new intermediate range nuclear missiles on West German soil it culminated in the well-publicized quarrel over the interpretation of German history in the second half of the decade (see Klönne, 1984; Honolka, 1987). Central to this renewed interest in German identity was the question to what degree Germany's past should and does impede the Germans from mastering the present (see Willms, 1982). For the far right the answer was clear: after the war the victorious powers, and particularly the United States, had emasculated the German people by indoctrinating them via a program of re-education devised by the United States that power was bad and dangerous, and that Germany must never again become a significant power (see, for example, Maschke, 1986, p. 172).

The Republikaner have adopted this reasoning making the struggle against what they regard the falsification of German history a primary objective of their political work. In the preamble to their program they complain that the 'war propaganda of the victorious powers' has been integrated into German history books and that young Germans have to 'believe their exaggerations and falsifications' because it is still impossible to write an objective interpretation of history (Die Republikaner, 1987, p. 1), which no longer reduces the whole of German history to Auschwitz. What the Republikaner want is an end to the stigmatization of the Germans, the 'decriminalization of German history,' and an acceptance of Germany as a 'normal nation' (Die Republikaner, 1987a, p. 1). Or as Franz Josef Schönhuber put it succinctly: 'We want to become a self-confident people again.'[5]

Recent events such as the controversy over President Reagan's Bitburg visit, the protracted *Historikerstreit*, and the controversy over Philipp Jenninger's unfortunate speech on the occasion of the fiftieth anniversary of the Nazi pogrom against the Jews on November 9, 1938 are evidence of the problems and difficulties West Germans still have in dealing with their past. (see Evans, 1989). They are on the one hand evidence of the growing desire on the part of West Germans to be rid of the past, on the other they show to what degree it is still necessary to confront the past at all. However, there appears to open a growing gap between these two processes, stemming from the fact that it was to a large degree the critical intelligentsia which confronted the past most uncompromisingly, whereas the majority of the population was rather annoyed by these attempts to force West German society to deal with the crimes of the past. This is supported by sporadic survey studies which indicate that a majority of West Germans, including the large majority of Republikaner supporters, feel that the debate about the Nazi past should be laid to rest.[6] This is not to say that right-wing radical thinking has reshaped mainstream political discourse in the Federal Republic; it appears rather that the opposite has happened.

With the growth of a new generation born after the end of World War II, direct memory of the past is being replaced by distance to it. Franz Josef Strauss was one of the first to sense the consequences of this process and the opportunities it presented to the far right when he astutely declared: 'We have to end the attempt to limit German history to the 12 years of Hitler—the representation of history as an endless path of German mistakes and crimes, criminalizing the Germans . . . We must emerge from the dismal Third Reich and become a normal nation again.'[7]

The question of national identity is closely connected to a broader issue which, with the recent events in East Germany and the prospect of an ever quicker movement towards reunification, has taken on central importance in German politics, namely the national question. Although the origins of the debate on the national question date back to the early 1980s, it was largely relegated to the margins of West German politics (see Klönne, 1984; Honolka, 1987). It was the Republikaner who seized the issue to present themselves as the main advocates of reunification. Appealing to a growing pacifist mood in West Germany in the wake of the controversy over the stationing of new intermediate missiles and particularly after the short-range missile debate, both of which raised questions amongst the West German public over West Germany's sovereignty, the Republikaner argued that as long as Germany was divided, there would be no peace in Europe. Since the main threat to European peace came from the stockpiling of nuclear weapons by the superpowers on German soil, only a united Germany no longer dominated by the superpowers could guarantee a 'durable continental peace order.'[8] In order to achieve this, the Republikaner proposed the initiation of negotiations for a comprehensive peace treaty between the German people and the World War II allies with the goal of a reunified Germany which would remain a member of NATO 'as long as this is compatible with the interests of the German people' (Die Republikaner, 1987, p. 3).

Though in the face of the dramatic events in East Germany it would appear that the emphasis of the Republikaner on national identity and reunification would have held great electoral promise, the reaction of the established parties to the situation in East Germany largely deprived the Republikaner of their advantage in regard to the national question. Although in late 1989 surveys indicated that a growing majority of the West German population both welcomed unification and believed it would inevitably come sooner rather than later, the Republikaner were largely unable to profit from the change in public mood. Chancellor Kohl's call for a confederation and a monetary union between the two German states dominated the political discussion on the question of unification. This left the Republikaner with only one issue—the growing problem of foreign immigrants.

Like their counterparts in other West European countries the Republikaner see the primary threat to the continued prosperity of the German people from the growing influx of foreigners. It is above all the growing wave of hostility towards foreigners *(Ausländerfeindlichkeit)* which explains the relative success of right-wing radicalism in the Federal Republic. These feelings of hostility might be deplorable, yet they are hardly surprising. In 1989, as a result of the East German revolution West Germany had to deal with a record number of East German emigrants *(Umsiedler)* in addition to the growing number of ethnic German resettlers *(Aussiedler)* from Eastern Europe and the Soviet Union and second and third world refugees. At the end of last year, more than 375 000 *Aussiedler*, almost 345 000 *Umsiedler*, and over 120 000 refugees had come to the Federal Republic. This was almost twice as many *Aussiedler* and more than eight times as many *Umsiedler* as in 1988.[9]

Confronted with this dramatic increase in the number of new arrivals the West German public turned increasingly hostile to them. In December 1988, almost 80 per cent of the West German population wished the government would adopt restrictions curbing the influx of refugees, and almost 70 per cent thought it should restrict the influx of *Aussiedler*.[10] Surveys showed to what degree these sentiments influence voter behavior. In Berlin, for example, for more than a third of the electorate the influx of foreigners represented a 'decisive motive' for their vote.[11]

The Republikaner were quick to make the campaign against the threatening 'foreignization' of West Germany their top political priority. Charging the established parties with having given into the trend towards a 'multicultural society' they demanded drastic restrictions on the right to asylum and measures to limit the possibility of foreign workers working in the country. Germany, one of the most densely populated countries in Europe, had to remain 'the land of the Germans' (Die Republikaner, 1987, p. 9). Although the vast majority of Republikaner supporters agreed with these views,[12] the question of how exactly to achieve such a country untainted by foreigners created growing difficulties for the party.

For increasingly West Germans refused to differentiate between ethnic Germans, refugees, even East German *Umsiedler*. Table 5.4 shows the development of public opinion towards these three groups. The results indicate that by the end of 1989, after initial enthusiasm about the opening of the Wall, the majority of the West German population, and a large majority of right-wing supporters, quickly began to favor a reduction in the number of all three groups. Although aversion against them decreased dramatically at the height of the East German revolution in October and November of 1989, the results from December indicated that the East German revolution could not change deep-seated aversions against anyone perceived to be a foreigner. By the early part of 1990, aversion was gradually turning into unconcealed hostility towards new arrivals from East Germany.[13] As a result the Republikaner were in a difficult situation. Their emphasis on German identity and German nationalism mandated that they explicitly welcomed and pronounced support for all ethnic Germans wanting to come to West Germany. As early as in their basic program of 1983 they had demanded better support for the integration of resettlers into West German society (Die Republikaner, 1983, p. 36). After sensing growing resentment against the new arrivals in the course of 1989, Schönhuber repeatedly underlined the party's commitment to East German emigrants and ethnic Germans resettling from the East warning against 'petty-bourgeois sentiments' *vis-à-vis* the new arrivals.[14] However, as Table 5.4 indicates, it was among his most loyal supporters that these very sentiments were most pronounced.

There is reason to believe that this aversion to immigrants is related to the socioeconomic basis of right-wing support. The majority of recent resettlers is under forty-five years of age with a disproportionately high number under eighteen (32.4 per cent of all resettlers in 1987–88 compared to 18.5 per cent for the whole population). Almost 50 per cent worked in industry or learnt a trade (compared to 37 per cent for the whole population).[15] This means that they compete with those occupational groups which represent the core of right-wing radical supporters and who are primarily motivated by anxiety, fear, and resentment. In fact, at the height of the inflow of East German emigrants into West Germany, a disproportionately large number of Republikaner supporters, as compared to the rest of the West German population, expected to be disadvantaged on the job market as well as in their search for housing as a result of the influx of East German emigrants into West Germany. In November 1989, for example, after

Table 5.4 Support for immigrant groups (in per cent)

	Total						Party preference Republikaner						Greens					
	Mar	Oct	Nov	Dec	Jan	Feb	Mar	Oct	Nov	Dec	Jan	Feb	Mar	Oct	Nov	Dec	Jan	Feb
East German emigrants																		
accept all	28	63	59	44	33	22	17	38	63	21	15	9	39	70	68	51	28	24
reduce somewhat	45	25	28	39	41	41	39	23	23	45	43	36	37	21	12	40	48	42
drastically reduce	26	11	12	16	25	36	44	39	15	35	42	55	24	7	18	9	24	33
Ethnic German resettlers																		
accept all	17	35	38	27	19	15	13	14	15	12	9	2	30	42	41	34	17	31
reduce somewhat	48	44	33	43	46	41	38	35	41	41	35	29	43	45	34	35	52	39
drastically reduce	34	21	26	29	35	43	49	51	45	47	56	69	26	12	22	29	31	30
N	2272	1935	1001	1927	1931	1923	104	78	23	69	67	51	185	153	52	141	125	124
Political refugees																		
accept all	32	26	48	26	24	23	14	18	34	5	3	8	65	61	79	60	49	58
reduce somewhat	38	41	24	36	33	30	28	23	14	25	23	25	25	26	16	28	30	25
drastically reduce	29	33	24	38	42	46	58	58	52	69	75	67	10	13	2	12	21	17
N	2272	960	1001	1927	978	1923	104	37	23	69	35	51	185	75	52	141	67	124

Source: EMNID, Spiegel-Umfrage March, October–February 1989.

the opening of the Wall, 41 per cent of right-wing supporters (compared to 16 per cent for the total population) feared the inflow of East German *Umsiedler* was going to lead to disadvantages on the job market, and 51 per cent (compared to 29 per cent) feared they would be disadvantaged on the housing market.[16]

The opening of the intra-German border in the closing months of 1989 followed by a rapidly paced movement towards unification thus confronted right-wing radicalism with a fundamental dilemma. On the one hand the Republikaner sought to establish themselves as a primarily middle class national-conservative political party on the right of the center right, a guardian of traditional conservative values and a strong German nation while largely failing to propose practical solutions to concrete economic and social issues. On the other hand, those social groups on whose support the Republikaner could count the most supported right-wing radicalism for social and economic rather than nationalist reasons, believing that the established parties were ignoring their grievances. For this group of core supporters, however, the question of unification was most likely going to entail as many new uncertainties and threats as it would fulfil nationalist aspirations. It was for this reason that the Republikaner remained curiously silent on the question of unification after the East German revolution and the opening of the Wall. It was Helmut Kohl who articulated the national question and presented it to the West German public, and played to the right wing within his party and to right-wing radical sympathizers outside by remaining vague on the inviolability of the German–Polish border, and thus adopted important elements of the right-wing radical agenda. All that was left for Schönhuber was to warn in early 1990 that unification, 'in which we are all keenly interested, must not come at the expense of the poorest of the poor, but those must help, who are capable of it, those circles must provide money that have it in abundance.'[17] This was nothing but a populist call for a tax on the rich to finance the project of German unification.

The Bavarian local elections in March 1990 showed that right-wing radicalism had, at least temporarily, run out of steam and lost much of its attraction. Despite the fact that the Republikaner received more than five per cent of the vote and managed to send more than 250 representatives into most city and county councils, this result was a far cry from their electoral triumph in Bavaria in the European elections. However, the vast majority of the votes for the Republikaner came from the CSU which lost more than 7 per cent of the vote. This could only add to the sense of panic in the CSU widespread after the

European elections. And thus, via the CSU, an important partner in the center right coalition, the impact of right-wing radicalism should not be discounted.[18]

FROM RIGHT-WING RADICALISM TO RIGHT-WING EXTREMISM?

In the longer run, the future of right-wing radicalism in a united Germany will depend on the question of whether right-wing radical parties, be they the Republikaner or any other right-wing party, will be able to reconcile the dialectic of unification. It can be expected that the process of unification will entail considerable economic as well as social costs for both parts of a unified Germany. For some time to come, for the affluent West German population it might entail higher taxes, inflation, higher interest rates, and with it higher unemployment in order to raise the funds necessary to rebuild the collapsed and largely obsolete East German economy and its decaying infrastructure, and to reverse the destruction of its environment. For at least some segments of the East German population a shift to a market economy will almost certainly mean the fear of redundancy and unemployment, economic hardship and insecurity. Under these circumstances, the proportion of those who consider themselves marginalized in a future united Germany can be expected to increase, thus opening up new opportunities for the radical right.

In order to appeal to these groups right-wing radicalism will have to move towards what one observer has called a 'social and Federal Republican[/German]-protectionist nationalism of the "ordinary people"' who feel threatened by the radical changes underway throughout Europe (Veen, 1989, p. 65). For this to succeed right-wing radical parties will most likely focus heavily on issues which already in the past appeared politically promising and which, under radically changed circumstances, can be expected to regain political urgency on the right of the political spectrum. The most important of these issues are Germany's membership in the European Community, the continued presence of foreign and particularly American troops if a unified Germany should remain part of NATO, and the question of the lost Eastern territories. Each one of these issues has been, or can at least be expected to become, a topic of growing public concern. This is not to suggest that right-wing radical thinking has reshaped mainstream political discourse in the Federal Republic; it appears rather that the opposite occurred. The radical right sensed the shift in public perceptions and opinion regarding these issues more quickly than other parties and were quick to take a position.

In those West European members of the European Community, where right-wing radical parties have achieved some success, they have appealed heavily to considerable sentiments of popular disaffection with the EC. West German surveys suggest that in 1989 about as many West Germans believed that EC membership had brought advantages to the Federal Republic as thought disadvantages outweighed advantages. In a similar vein, almost as many respondents approached 1992 with hopes as were afraid of the establishment of an integrated market. However, among right-wing sympathizers the overwhelming majority was opposed to both the European Community in general as well as the integration of the West European market.

Although proclaiming pan-European integration as one of their 'highest goals' besides national unfication (Die Republikaner, 1983, p. 34), in the past the Republikaner vigorously denounced West European integration and the European Community. In 1989, for example, opposition to the EC was the central issue of their campaign for the European elections. 'The Republikaner say no to a politics of one-sided Western integration, which will lead to a deepening of the German and the European division. Europe is larger than the EC!'[19] Arguing that the integrated market would only damage German interests, enhance the power of bureaucrats and corporations while destroying national diversity and cultural diversity, the Republikaner opposed to this image of a Europe of centralized bureaucracy and corporatist capitalism the vision of a Europe of free peoples, states, and citizens including Central Europe and the Soviet Union. Pointing out that West Germany had consistently paid more into the European Community than it received, they argued that confronted with mounting unemployment, environmental degradation, and new social problems German interests should take priority: 'We Germans need our hard earned money in our own country.' Faced with the costs of reviving a basically bankrupt East German economy and integrating a continued flood of resettlers from Central Europe and the Soviet Union, and confronted with the possibility of a mobile European workforce seeking employment in Germany, it is not difficult to imagine growing anti-EC sentiments in Germany.

If unification will create, at least in the short run, a host of economic problems for Germany, it is open to doubts whether it will solve the question of German sovereignty to the satisfaction of the nationalist right. As we have seen in the previous chapter, during the past decade, conservative writers increasingly declared West Germany's continued membership in NATO the primary impediment to full sovereignty. In their view, as long as NATO troops were stationed on German soil, Germany remained an occupied country. Although one should approach with caution surveys dealing with the question of German sovereignty because in the past such questions were largely presumed to be academic and irrelevant to concrete politics, there are indications of a growing support in the 1980s for a reunified, neutral Germany (see Neolle-Neumann, 1983, p. 89). In May 1987, for example, 80 per cent of the population said they preferred such a solution to the status quo.[20] At the same time, in response to Mikhail Gorbachev's foreign policy initiatives, West German perceptions of the military threat emanating from the East diminished dramatically. Whereas in 1981, 55 per cent of the population considered the Soviet Union a threat to West German security, in early 1989 that perception had declined to 20 per cent. At the same time, more West Germans trusted the East than mistrusted its intentions. For example, in October 1988, over four-fifths, and in May 1989, almost 90 per cent of the population said Gorbachev was a man one could trust.[21]

These sentiments reflected a significant change in West German public opinion. Its political impact was felt during the controversy over the modernization of American short-range nuclear missiles which was opposed by the vast majority of the people (Head, 1989) and the conciliatory stance of the 'new revisionists' within the Kohl government towards Soviet arms control initiatives (Joffe, 1989). Finally, it found expression in a growing resentment against the presence of American military forces, particularly in the wake of the air disasters at Ramstein and Remscheid which cost a number of German lives.

The far right was quick to exploit the shift in public perception. Although in their basic program the Republikaner represented themselves as faithful adherents to the Western community and to NATO, they made their commitment to both dependent on a solution to the German question. And even then their commitment was rather questionable. Thus in their 1987 program the party declared that a unified Germany would be a reliable partner within the Atlantic Alliance 'as long as this is compatible with the interests of the German people' (Die Republikaner, 1987, p. 3). In the meantime, West Germany should use the question of continued membership in NATO as a bargaining chip in future negotiations.[22] For the future the

Republikaner envisioned an armed neutral Germany able to defend itself,[23] a Germany between the blocs. West Germany should avoid being tied too closely to the United States, should slowly 'Europeanize' defense and develop initiatives that went beyond the 'stupid thinking in blocs.'[24] In one of his speeches in early 1990 Schönhuber said:

> We are anti-communists, without being cold warriors. We completely reject the Soviet system. However, we are and remain also skeptical in regard to the so-called American way of life, where riches are regarded as pleasing to God, and poverty is almost a sin. We are searching for a third way, determined by the traditional good European values. These are openness to the world, tolerance, a sense for beauty, the preservation of families, and patriotism.[25]

This pronounced anti-Americanism, fed in part by the traditional right-wing stereotype of American Coca-Cola culture, in part by resentment against the US role in the policy of re-education, stands in sharp contrast to the radical right's position on the Soviet Union. Following the musings of conservative and right-wing intellectuals about the possibility if not necessity of a German-Soviet rapprochment, the Republikaner increasingly came to suggest that the growing domestic crisis faced by the Soviet Union offered an opportunity to deal with the Soviet Union as equals. Thus Schönhuber suggested that the right should distinguish 'between the necessary ideological struggle against communism on the home front and foreign policy maneuverability *vis-à-vis* Moscow' (quoted in Craig, 1989, p. 24; translation slightly altered). Reminiscent of the Russophile sentiments of members of the conservative revolution some sixty years earlier, Schönhuber continued:

> The Soviet Union has remained Russia. And Russia is nearer to us than America, not merely geographically. Here I am a follower of Bismarck, who believed that the key to the fruitful development of our fatherland lay in a positive relationship with Russia.

In the far right's view Germany's past experience with Russia had largely proven beneficial to both countries. The Republikaner pointed particularly to the Prussian–Russian agreement of Tauroggen which 'laid the foundation for a German–Russian alliance against Western imperialism and initiated the wars of liberation' (Bauer, 1990, p. 12).

Implicit in this was the argument that once again a German–Russian rapprochement would lead to liberation of Germany from Western, particularly American, hegemony. It was thus hardly a coincidence that after his success in the European elections Schönhuber invited the right-wing historian Hellmut Diwald, a pronounced proponent of a German–Soviet rapprochement (see Diwald, 1988, pp. 41–2), to advise the Republikaner on foreign affairs and to write the introduction to the new party program.

What the radical right envisioned was a trade with the Soviet Union which would involve German reunification in exchange for West Germany's withdrawal from NATO and subsequent armed neutrality. If the Soviet Union were to agree to German reunification, the Republikaner vowed to be willing to contribute to the 'pacification of the common European house' and to lend economic support to the Soviet Union without, however, turning this co-operation against the United States.[26] However, with the acceleration of events in East Germany and once German unification appeared to be only a matter of time, it became increasingly clear that the far right had to make more militant demands if they wanted to continue to claim the national question for themselves. If in the past, the Republikaner had demanded *that* Germany be allowed to unify, in early 1990 they began to focus on the question *what* exactly unification entailed. This involved in particular the question of the lost territories in the East, and especially the common border with Poland.

An extensive survey conducted in March 1989 found that whereas two-thirds of the West German population was willing to accept the existing border between Poland and Germany and thus to resign themselves to the loss of the Eastern territories, a third (and 45 per cent of center right supporters) were not. This might be one major reason why despite domestic and international pressure the center right parties steadfastly refused to recognize formally the inviolability of the German–Polish border. Despite internal critique that the dream of a reconstructed Germany in the borders of 1937 was an 'unrealistic fantasy' (Bauer, 1990, p. 13) the Republikaner quickly demanded just that. In order to justify this demand they could point to the fact that the March survey had shown that almost two-thirds of their potential supporters had not resigned themselves to the Oder-Neisse border between Germany and Poland.

Arguing that Pomerania, East Prussia, Stettin, and Königsberg were occupied territories, the Republikaner demanded the reunification of Germany within the borders of 1937.[27] In order to halt the inflow of resettlers from the Soviet Union, Schönhuber suggested that Gorbachev resettle them in the Soviet-occupied parts of East Prussia and particularly in Kaliningrad.

> Historically East Prussia belongs to Germany, so does the Memel land. Here we strive for negotiations with the Soviet Union. Of course we exclude any idea of the use of violence. We further demand that the question of the German borders be held open. Until a peace treaty is ratified, Germany, with the exception of the Memel land, continues to exist within the borders of 1937.[28]

Under the present circumstances one should hardly expect that the Soviet Union would abandon its claim to the formally German territories under its control. However, this question might become less academic should it come to a gradual dissolution of the Soviet empire and, for example, the Baltic republics become independent. Under those circumstances German territorial claims on whatever would emerge from its ruins in exchange, for example, for economic and security co-operation might suddenly become much less fantastic.

The rise and political success of right-wing radicalism in West Germany is a result of a far-reaching social, cultural, and political transformation of West German society. If in the past, scholarly interest has focused predominantly on the impact of the shift from materialist to left-libertarian values on politics, the emergence of right-wing radicalism has drawn attention to a broad range of problems resulting from the accelerated pace of modernization. It is above all from among those groups in society which consider themselves marginalized by modernization and abandoned by the established parties that right-wing radical parties gain support at the polls.

Survey findings indicate that the potential level of support for right-wing radical parties in West Germany range from between 10 to 15 per cent (see, for example Inglehart and Rabier, 1986, p. 466). In addition, evidence cited above shows considerable agreement on the part of the West German public with right-wing radical demands. However, these results should not be taken as evidence that right-wing radicalism will grow much beyond the 7 to 10 per cent it attained so far in elections. The experience of the Greens shows that despite broad public concern for environmental issues, electoral support for the Greens stagnated after an initial upsurge in the early 1980s. The reason is first that only a minority of the West German electorate considered environmental issues *the* political priority overriding all other concerns, and second, that the Greens represent a variety of issues with which the majority of the population either fails to identify very strongly, or which it rejects altogether, and third, that the Greens appealed to a very closely circumscribed milieu. In a similar vein, right-wing radicalism will only continue to have a chance of success, if it continues to appeal to marginalized groups.

Similarly to the Greens, the right-wing agenda is largely influenced by the social basis of right-wing radical support. From the development of the core elements of the right-wing program sketched above emerge the contours of a political agenda with a dominant focus on a protectionist, neutralist, and perhaps revisionist and expansionist German nationalism. Whether or not the Republikaner, or any other right-wing radical or extremist party, will be able to appeal to a more than marginal proportion of the German population will depend above all on the question to what degree the double pressure of modernization and German unification will exacerbate already existing processes of social marginalization and to what degree the established parties will be willing and able to alleviate their consequences. In the past, the majority of those working in the insecure sector of the economy tended to support the Social Democrats, whereas core sector workers preferred the center right. Evidence presented above suggests that some of the former might have moved from the SPD to the Republikaner. From this one might conclude that the past strategy of all major parties to focus on the affluent two-thirds of West German society has hurt them politically while contributing to the rise of right-wing radicalism. Should they continue to fail to respond to their demands the disadvantaged of a future united German consumer society may well have found a permanent political home.

6 The Dialectics of Postmodern Politics

In the second half of 1989 two developments exerted growing influence on West German politics. In international relations, West Germany's situation suddenly and quite dramatically changed as a result of Mikhail Gorbachev's politics of non-interference in the internal affairs of Eastern Europe. His repudiation of the Brezhnev Doctrine led to a rapid liberalization process in Poland and Hungary, which in turn had a dramatic impact on East German politics culminating in the East German revolution and the opening of the Berlin Wall in the late fall of 1989. As a result, the German question assumed top priority on the German as well as European political agenda. In domestic politics, the electoral success of right-wing radicalism first in Berlin, then in the European elections, sent shock waves through the political establishment. At a time of rapid transformation in European international relations the rise of the Republikaner was symptomatic of the degree to which West German politics was in ferment.

As I have tried to show in the preceding chapters, the revival of German nationalism on the right reflected a slow process of transformation of the broader West German political culture. It can be attributed above all to the waning of 'the dual anti-totalitarian consensus' (Habermas, 1987, p. 176) which had shaped West German political culture well into the late 1960s. The attempts to relativize the monstrous crimes of the past, the yearning for normalcy forty years after the end of World War II, the appeal to the 'grace of late birth' by a new generation of politicians gradually taking over the commanding heights of West German politics, and finally the attempts somehow to exonerate the German people exemplified by the *Historikerstreit*, reflected the fact that West German society was trying to escape from the shadows of the Third Reich. At the same time perceptions, to which the West German public appeared to have become accustomed, started to change. The growing awareness of the crisis of the Soviet economy together with the experience of detente and *Ostpolitik* led to a more relaxed approach to the Soviet Union, reduced West German distrust of Soviet motives, and thus deprived anti-communism of much of its foundation (Honolka, 1987, p. 159; Joffe, 1989; Schlauch,

1989, pp. 3–4). At the same time there was a growing feeling, not only confined to the radical right, that the hegemonic position of both superpowers was on the decline, and that for the first time in postwar history it might be possible to challenge the postwar settlement.

Together these developments were deeply unsettling to West German political culture. If in fact it was true that the established *weltbilder* were losing their influence on West European and West German perceptions, how would the West Germans define their identity? As long as West Germany was formally integrated into the Western Alliance, the West Germans considered themselves part of the West. The erosion of the established anti-totalitarian consensus, however, was forcing the West Germans to clarify for themselves to what degree they were committed to the West. Had the West Germans merely accommodated themselves to the superior economic and military power of the West without being convinced of the intrinsic value of Western-style democracy and democratic values or did West German commitment to the West in fact represent 'an intellectual reorientation, grounded in convictions and guided by principles' (Habermas, 1987, p. 176) rather than a mere bowing to what one could not change anyway?

It would be presumptuous to believe that questions as far-reaching as the future direction of German national identity could be resolved within a short period of time. Tectonic changes tend to be slow, whether they occur in the deep layers of the earth's crust or in the realm of political culture. It is possible, however, to stake out the range of options available to a given political culture to define its identity. In the previous chapter we have seen the contours of one possible resolution of the German problem of national identity: an identity which is inward-looking, self-occupied, based on traditional values, pursuing a third road between East and West and hostile to the challenge of postmodernity. In this chapter I will focus on the left-libertarian conception of identity which in many ways represents the opposite mirror image of this right-wing radical, German nationalist conception outlined above. The purpose of the following discussion is not only to provide an anlysis of the evolution of Green politics towards questions central to the understanding of present and future German foreign policy, but also to suggest how the postmodern approach, which so far has focused almost exclusively on values related to domestic political concerns, might be extended to include ones related to international relations.

In their influential work on disorganized capitalism Scott Lash and John Urry (1987) argue that the rise of postmodern politics should be seen as a result of the growing disorganization of capitalism in the postmodern age. Disorganized capitalism is characterized by an extensive international division of ownership and production, the separation of financial and industrial capital, the decline of regional economic centers, and the growth of the service sector. This new 'world community of producers and consumers' (Jencks, 1986, p. 44) has accelerated the worldwide spread and diffusion of capitalism, which makes it increasingly difficult for the individual nation–state to control its own national economy. Disorganized capitalism is further characterized by the emergence of 'an integrated system of global communication' (Jencks, 1986, p. 44), which allows both for the accumulation, storage and rapid transmission of information world-wide as well as the electronic monitoring and surveillance of large populations, the gathering of information on everything from personal and political preferences, credit and health status to market behavior (Poster, 1989, p. 122).

As we have seen in earlier chapters, the emergence of new social movements and the Greens represented a direct challenge to the progressing commodification of everyday life and the growing power of the state in the 1970s and 1980s. To counter these developments the new social movements and Greens put great emphasis on individual autonomy and self-creation and a lifestyle which, however, is potentially highly compatible with the emerging postmodern consumer society. Similar tendencies can be found in the Green perspective on international relations. This perpective is very much informed by the cognitive model of disorganized capitalism outlined above and seeks to offer an alternative to the system of transnational capitalism dominated by multinational corporations and bureaucracies. Proceding from the recognition that the traditional nation-state is increasingly becoming obsolete, the Greens promote the vision of a peaceful, united Europe, an economically decentralized Europe of regions, and an individualized pro-Western identity. It is this alternative vision which largely explains Green policy towards German reunification, NATO, and European integration.

THE NATIONAL QUESTION

The early position of the Greens on the national question was strongly influenced by two groupings which had a long history of support for German nationalism. They were on the right the *Aktionsgemeinschaft Unabhängiger Deutscher* (AUD), and on the left several Maoist cadre parties, the most influential of which were the KPD and the KBW (see Chapters 2 and 3). In the late 1970s and early 1980s most of these groupings joined the emerging Green party and sought to determine its future political and ideological direction.

Although the AUD's stance towards the national question was discussed earlier, it might be useful to provide a short review of the party's position.[1] The AUD argued that as long as Germany was not free from external constraints, it could not develop a free domestic order. Thus reunification was intimately connected to social change. Only under these conditions would Germany be able to regain its lost identity, previously destroyed by ideologies imposed from outside and by the integration of the two parts of Germany into opposing camps. However, reunification would be impossible so long as there existed in both German states small but powerful elites who profited from the division of Germany and whose very survival depended on it. Therefore, social emancipation of the German population could only derive from an act of 'national liberation' which would destroy the established structures and their beneficiaries and lead to a new social order, a genuine alternative to Western private and Eastern state capitalism. With this act of national liberation and national reunification the Germans would not only overcome the division of their country but would render an invaluable service to all of Europe. Since the division of Europe was a direct function of the German division, and since within the existing bloc structure it was the two German states which represented the most immediate threat to peace, German unification would be a decisive step towards peace and security in Europe.

The Maoists' position on the national question resembled in many ways that of the AUD. Among the various Maoist groups espousing German nationalist tendencies the most important was the KPD.[2] For the KPD the division of Germany was the result of a combination of US imperialism, Soviet revisionism, and the reactionary politics of the Adenauer regime. Whereas Stalin's politics had aimed at unifying Germany into a neutral, democratic, and peace-loving state, the revisionist policies pursued by the Soviets after the twentieth party congress and supported by the East German socialists had done everything in their power to deepen the rift between the two German states. Suppressed by both East Germany's new bourgeoisie and West Germany's monopoly bourgeoisie and their supporters in both superpowers it depended on the revolutionary force of the working class to translate its dream of an independent, united, and socialist

Germany into reality. Therefore the struggle for reunification had to be directed above all against the hegemonic pretensions of both superpowers which in the KPD's view represented the main threat to peace. Reunification thus meant not only an end to the division of Germany but also a decisive step towards a peaceful new world.

The conceptions developed by the AUD and the nationalist wing of the Maoists informed the debates of the Greens and particularly the peace movement in the early part of the 1980s. Within the Green party it laid the theoretical and ideological basis for a national-neutralist wing which found support among a minority within the party.

Among the key documents of the national-neutralists was the book *Die Linke und die nationale Frage*, edited by Willy Brandt's son, Peter, and Herbert Ammon (1981), both members of the Alternative List in Berlin. The book's central premise was that in the past, the left had failed to develop a 'national-democratic identity' and had thus contributed to the national catastrophes of 1914 and 1933 as well as to the division of Germany in the post-World War II era. The authors clearly felt that the political situation in Germany was once again reaching a point where the national question would be put back on the political agenda. In this situation the left should not repeat their earlier mistake of abandoning the national question to the right. 'Whether the national question *will become* a rightist issue will depend—not for the first time in German history—to a large degree on the left' (Brandt and Minnerup, 1982, p. 112).

The national-neutralists' conception of an alternative peace plan started from a critique of *Ostpolitik*. They maintained that despite its positive results *Ostpolitik* had been seriously flawed. On one hand it had impeded the formation of grassroots opposition in both systems which might disturb the warming of superpower relations, on the other it had made the political situation in Europe dependent on the political climate informing the relations between the superpowers. As the Soviet invasion of Afghanistan and the so-called dual track decision had shown, the European influence on the superpowers was very limited at best. Under these circumstances it was up to the two German states, on whose division the architecture of the blocs was founded and which served as the central nuclear battlefield in case of a conflict between the two blocs, to take the initiative and secure European peace. They had to take steps to withdraw their respective territories from the superpowers' spheres of influence. Among the most important of these steps they considered the creation of a nuclear free zone in Central Europe, the withdrawal of both German states from their respective alliances, the conversion of both states' military forces into purely defensive forces, and finally the withdrawal of the forces of the victorious powers from German territory and the reduction of the allied forces in Berlin to a symbolic contingent. For the longer-term future the national-neutralists envisioned the creation of a German community in the form of a German confederation which would assure close political, economic, and cultural co-operation. Their ultimate goal was the conclusion of a peace treaty with Germany's former adversaries, guaranteeing non-alignment and the renunciation of intervention in Germany.

The national-neutralist conception owed much to the interpretation of Germany's political and military situation advanced by influential segments of the peace movement. According to this interpretation the superpowers still regarded—and treated—both German states as 'occupied countries' without full sovereignty, assigned to serve as firing ranges in case of nuclear conflict in Europe. Therefore any change in the European status quo, including German reunification, could only be effected against the superpowers, in an act of self-liberation. It was as a result of such thinking that the proponents of German reunification could claim that any attempt to overcome the confrontation of the blocs on German soil was far from 'being a nationalist rebellion against Europe,' but the only way to make 'peace, democracy, and national autonomy in East and West a single interlocking issue.'[3]

After the failure of the peace movement to prevent the installation of new American medium range missiles in West Germany, the national-neutralists soon lost all influence in the discussion within the left on the national question. Only a small group of predominantly ex-KPD members continued to carry on in a working group on Germany and Berlin of the Alternative List in Berlin until they were finally forced out of the party in late 1987.[4] By then Green politics towards the national question had decisively turned against unification.

For the majority of the Greens the German question was not one of unification but of how the Germans confronted their history and how they could arrange their affairs with their former adversaries and among each other in such a way as to definitely break with the past (see Schmierer 1985; Schnappertz 1985; Schneider 1985). Having been responsible for two world wars and the horrors associated with them it was the joint duty of the Germans in both East and West to preserve peace. This duty had to take precedence over all other values, hopes, and aspirations. Since the specter of a reunified Germany could only revive old fears of German hegemony over Europe and therefore only harden the existing bloc structure, the Germans should renounce reunification for the sake of preserving European peace.

Their acceptance of the territorial results of World War II did not, however, entail recognition of all existing realities. The Greens made a clear distinction between territorial realities, which they accepted, and sociopolitical realities, which they sought to change. If the postwar territorial reorganization of Europe had proven to be a stabilizing factor in European international relations, its sociopolitical reorganization was far from acceptable. However, until now it had been primarily the threat of territorial revisionism which had cemented the bloc structure and thus assured the preservation of the established sociopolitical conditions. Therefore only the renunciation of territorial revisionism and reunification on the part of all Germans could lay the foundation for a peaceful transformation of the European status quo.

Green *Deutschlandpolitik* had above all to serve peace. This meant that the Greens had to seek contacts on the societal as well as state level. Therefore the Greens advocated close co-operation with independent East German grassroots movements (for example peace groups) in order to exchange ideas and experiences as well as with the East German government in order to influence the relations between the two German states towards a common peace policy. This inclusion of the state level resulted primarily from the recognition 'that, within the foreseeable future neither the borders will fall nor the states will dissolve, and that a European peace order has to start from the existing state structure' (Schnappertz, 1985, p. 3).

The logic of this argumentation led the Greens increasingly to demand that the Federal Republic recognize the GDR. Already in their program for 1985 the Alternative List in Berlin stated that the majority of the AL no longer hoped for reunification but for European unity.[5] Only under these conditions could they imagine an end to allied control over Berlin. In the same vein the Greens' programmatic pronouncements for the 1987 elections recognized the existence of two German states and demanded West German 'self-recognition,' meaning that the Federal Republic abandoned the notion that it was only a provisional entity (Die Grünen, 1987, p. 14). The Federal Republic should stop deceiving itself about the continued existence of an all-German identity and instead advance the development of an independent, democratic identity as well as turn self-critically towards its own democratic constitution. The Federal

Republic should base its relations with the GDR on dialogue and measures that would create trust, and should use the relations between the two states as an instrument to widen the possibility of communication between the two societies and their people. However, the Greens warned that recognition also entailed continued criticism of the East German regime's repressive measures and demands both for their abandonment as well as support for the victims of that oppression.[6]

The Green position on the national question was thus informed by two factors: first, the attempt to learn from Germany's past and to eliminate those factors which they considered to have been decisive in taking Germany down the road of military aggression, territorial expansionism, and a war of racial extermination. 'Auschwitz and the victims of World War II are not forgotten.'[7] The revival of the German question would only evoke new fears about a *grossdeutsche* nation state in the center of Europe. Second, the concern for the preservation of peace at a time of heightened superpower confrontation together with the notion that only mutual security and trust could lay the foundation for broadly based sociopolitical changes in both German states and on both sides of divided Europe. Empirical evidence shows that the Green position reflected the attitudes of a majority of their supporters and voters. Polls taken in the spring of 1989 revealed that almost two thirds of the Green supporters considered the German question no longer open (see Table 6.1) Even at the height of nationalist euphoria in November 1989 less than 50 per cent of Green supporters said they were in favor of unification, compared to 70 per cent of the whole population. The rest was either opposed or said they did not care either way. Finally polls taken in December showed that the majority of Green supporters agreed with the party's emerging position on the future shape of Germany. Almost two thirds of Green supporters favored the continued existence of two German states over a unified Germany.

NATO

Among left-wing parties in Western Europe, the Greens have been among the most vociferous opponents of the Western Alliance. 'Wir müssen raus aus der NATO!' (We have to get out of NATO)—this slogan, adopted first in 1983 at the height of the INF controversy over the stationing of new American intermediate nuclear weapons on West German soil, has summed up the party's position on NATO ever

Table 6.1   Attitudes towards German unification (in per cent)

	Total	CDU/ CSU	SPD	FDP	Greens	Rep.
			Party preference			

Is the German question still open? (March 1989)

	Total	CDU/ CSU	SPD	FDP	Greens	Rep.
is no longer open	44	34	48	52	65	32
must remain goal of German foreign policy	56	66	51	45	34	68
N	2272	766	836	165	185	102

Support for unification (November 1989)

	Total	CDU/ CSU	SPD	FDP	Greens	Rep.
support	70	79	67	70	47	76
oppose	15	9	19	15	28	11
don't care	12	9	12	11	22	13
don't know	3	4	2	5	3	–
N	1017	312	374	59	72	50

In the future, should Germany be a united country or two independent countries?

December 1989:

	Total	CDU/ CSU	SPD	FDP	Greens	Rep.
united country	56	59	48	50	33	57
two countries	41	28	51	45	62	38
don't know	3	4	1	5	5	5
N	978	343	324	52	63	38

February 1990:

	Total	CDU/ CSU	SPD	FDP	Greens	Rep.
united country	65	74	62	68	44	64
two countries	34	25	37	30	56	35
N	1923	667	653	148	124	51

Source: EMNID, Spiegel-Umfrage, March 1989, February 1990; Forschungsgruppe Wahlen, ZDF-Politbarometer, November, December 1989.

since. However, the party's apparent consensus on this question, repeated in party platforms and election programs, is deceiving. In reality the party's stance towards NATO is highly ambiguous and has become even more so within the last few years. The primary reason for this ambiguity is that the question of West German membership in NATO goes beyond purely defense or military considerations. What lies at the heart of it is above all West Germany's integration into the West as a political and cultural system. If this question was largely ignored in the early years of the debate on NATO, it has forcefully come to the fore in response to the dramatic domestic as well as international changes discussed earlier.

The position of the Green party on NATO developed quite gradually. One of their first and most elaborate expositions on security matters, the 1981 'Peace Manifesto,' largely adopted the peace movement's line of reasoning that the threat to peace in Europe resulted primarily from the confrontation between the blocs. Because of West Germany's importance in the Western Alliance the gradual withdrawal of the Federal Republic from NATO was therefore considered a necessary precondition for a bloc-free Europe. The Greens declared that their goal was a nuclear-free, demilitarized Europe, independent of the superpowers and neutral (Die Grünen, 1981, p. 10). Similarly both the first and the second edition of the federal program called for the immediate dissolution of the military blocs as a first step towards the overcoming of the division of Europe and Germany (Die Grünen, 1980, p. 19). By way of initial practical steps the Greens proposed *inter alia* unilateral disarmament, the withdrawal of all foreign troops from foreign territories, and a reversal of the two-track decision.

It was not until November 1983, at a party congress held on the eve of the Bundestag vote on deployment of new American missiles, that the Greens spoke out against NATO without, however, having defined a clear position on the most important security issues or having developed concrete steps to implement it.[8] As one critical observer noted, on the question of how to translate 'strategic orientations (dissolution of the military blocs, withdrawal from NATO, bloc-transcending orientation of the peace movement, solidarity with the Third World) into *politics*,' the Greens were only prepared to make appeals (Fücks, 1983, p. 19). However, the vagueness of the program should not obscure the fact that by 1983 the party had become the most militant opponent not only of INF but also of West Germany's continued membership in NATO.

In the following years the Greens attempted to make their program more concrete by shifting their attention to unilateral disarmament as an important first step towards the realization of their vision of a bloc-free Europe. As a result of this debate the Greens introduced a new political strategy which centered around the call for 'unilateral independent disarmament' and led to a renewed call for West German disarmament and subsequent withdrawal from NATO. Since unilateral disarmament would inevitably lead to a conflict with NATO and particularly the United States, West Germany would have to withdraw from the alliance. In addition, the Greens asserted that NATO was structurally incapable of maintaining peace. Despite bitter controversies in the party between hardliners and moderates this line of reasoning became the official Green position for the 1987 federal elections. The election program stated:

> We understand a strategy of unilateral disarmament as a process of withdrawing the Federal Republic from NATO, which has consistently been the driving force behind the armament spiral. . . . We must get out of NATO, because NATO is incapable of maintaining peace, and because the weakening, disintegration, and final abolition of this alliance is essential for the creation of peace. NATO cannot be reformed. (Die Grünen, 1987, p. 14)

The Greens believed that a West German withdrawal from NATO would weaken NATO and the United States, minimize West Germany's ability to pursue an aggressive foreign policy and thus contribute considerably to the easing of the bloc confrontation and lessen the possibility of war in Europe. In addition, by withdrawing from NATO West Germany would very likely provoke the dissolution of NATO and, in response, of the Warsaw Pact. This would then lead to the dissolution of the European bloc system as a whole (Böge, 1987, p. 13). By the time of the 1987 federal elections the Greens had finally reached a consensus on national security and German politics. The core of this position included the promotion of unilateral disarmament, recognition of the GDR, West German self-recognition, withdrawal from NATO, and a European peace order. Although these propositions still left many questions unanswered, they at least provided a firm basis from which the majority within the party believed a comprehensive security policy could be developed.

Green policy towards German unification and the Western Alliance in the 1980s was informed by two motives: the fear of a revival of a strong Germany dictating its policies to a weakening East (a fear which is hardly unfounded if one considers the rather smug attitude of the Kohl government towards Poland and the GDR after the East German revolution) while dominating the European Community, and the hope that West German defection from NATO would undermine the rationale behind the continued existence of both military blocs to such a degree as to lead to their dissolution and to open up opportunities to overcome the social, economic and ideological division of Europe. For the Greens these two considerations were closely intertwined. For without a weakening of the German position in Europe the disintegration of the military alliances seemed hardly conceivable. It was rather to fear that a strong Germany would provoke a counter alliance designed to stifle any future German hegemonic pretensions in Europe, thus once again suppressing the possibility of a truly united Europe.

These fears found expression in occasional Green statements that betrayed a rather ambiguous position towards the Western Alliance. Although the Greens reaffirmed that they still thought that the main purpose of the Western Alliance was to secure Western spheres of influence, they conceded that there might have been a second equally important objective behind the formation of NATO, namely to protect Europe from a revival of German hegemonic ambitions. Although in the past West German governments might have regarded the Western Alliance as a prime instrument in their quest for national reunification, 'for the Western countries NATO was and is also an instrument to control the Federal Republic and thus to prevent reunification' (Damus and Wortmann, 1983, p. 37).

Although this positive view of the Western alliance never attained more than a minority status in the party, evidence suggests that this ambiguity towards the Western Alliance appears to have been widely shared among Green party supporters. Table 6.2 explores the attitudes of the West German electorate towards key national security issues. The results reveal that the majority of Green supporters differed quite dramatically from the supporters of the other West German parties. In 1989, the majority of Green supporters neither thought that NATO was necessary to preserve peace in Europe nor that Europe needed to rely on American forces to safeguard its security. However, although the proportion of Green supporters who thought that it was good West Germany was a member of NATO was considerably smaller than the proportion of supporters of the other parties, nevertheless the majority agreed with this statement. In the light of what was argued above one might suggest that this result was less a support for NATO as the best instrument to secure European peace, but for NATO's role in integrating West Germany into the Western value sphere and containing potential foreign policy ambitions. Despite harsh criticism particularly from the fundamentalist wing of the party this view found a number of influential supporters within the Green party (see Betz, 1989). Some of them even went so far as to suggest not only that

Table 6.2 Attitudes towards Western Alliance and the presence of American troops in Europe (in per cent)

	Total	CDU/ CSU	SPD	FDP	Greens	Rep.
			Party preference			

1. NATO is necessary for the preservation of peace in Europe

necessary	78	86	79	79	41	77
not necessary	19	11	18	21	54	21
don't know	4	4	3	–	5	1

2. Do you think it is good that the FRG is a member of NATO?

good	80	88	81	83	55	84
don't think so	7	2	6	9	33	11
don't care	10	8	12	4	12	6
don't know	2	2	2	4	–	–

3. To what extent do we need American forces to protect our security?

present extent	22	36	14	28	6	30
less	54	52	61	52	52	37
not at all	19	7	21	8	41	32
don't know	5	5	4	13	1	2
N	1002	266	394	41	67	49

Source: Forschungsgruppe Wahlen, ZDF-Politbarometer, May 1989.

NATO had been successful in controlling German ambitions but that West Germany's integration into the Western alliance had given West Germany the opportunity as the first state in German history 'to develop pluralist democracy and cosmopolitan tolerance.'[9] This was a powerful reminder that although the Greens vigorously oppose Western (and Eastern) military integration, they equally vigorously support European cultural integration (and continued German integration into the West) on the basis of Western values and the achievements of Western civilization.

EUROPEAN INTEGRATION

Underlying the Green view of the future course of European integration and of international relations in general is the recognition that the time of the sovereign nation state has past, that for better or for worse capitalism has developed into a global system and that for this reason the world has become interdependent. This opens up new opportunities for the individual to abandon his or her national identity and develop a new identity which might be characterized as that of the transnational *citoyen* inhabiting a multicultural society. However, the Greens caution that this project can only succeed if integration is developed from below, from the grassroots level, rather than being promoted and established by individual nation-states, transnational bureaucracies and multinational corporations. A peaceful Europe no longer susceptible to militarism and imperialist pretensions could only be achieved on the basis of universalist political and cultural values including formal, democratic parliamentarism, human rights and liberties, and the culture of the Enlightenment and openness to the world and via supranational rather than national forms of organization (Schnappertz, 1988a, pp. 34–5). For West Germany that meant to abandon the ideology of national identity and to bring the 'self-deception of a pan-German perspective' to an end.[10] Joscha Schmier-er, the editor of the influential left-libertarian journal *Kommune*, might have characterized the Green vision of an alternative European future best when he described it as a combination of 'multifarious individuality' and 'egalitarian democracy' in a 'postcolonialist, multiracial and multicultural Europe.'[11]

This alternative conception of a future united Europe attained new urgency with three developments which overshadowed the start of the 1990s: the coming of the internal single market planned for 1992, the spreading resentment and increasingly vocal opposition *vis-à-vis* foreigners and particularly Third World refugees and immigrants throughout Western Europe, and finally the realization that Europe would be faced with a fully united Germany, perhaps even before the Europeans could seek to harness its potentially enormous economic and political power within a unified Europe. Each one of these developments confronted the Greens with a decisive challenge to their vision of a united Europe forcing them to focus on the European Community and to clarify their position on European integration.

Despite the fact that the Greens gained their first electoral success on the federal level not in national elections but in the elections to the European parliament, Green policy towards the European Community has tended to be far less developed than the party's positions on other vital questions of German foreign policy. This failure to develop a coherent and consistent policy towards the arguably most important transnational organization in Europe stems from a variety of reasons.

These range from initial indifference to any international issue area not directly connected to either military questions or the problems of the Third World, to conflicts over the question who should work on the different political issue areas directly affected by the European Community.[12]

Primarily, however, the Green reluctance to confront the reality of European integration stemmed from the fact that their thinking on economic questions tended to concentrate on the domestic rather than on the international market. Green programs openly expressed their hostility to the international division of labor and foreign trade. This hostility stemmed largely from the Green analysis of the relationship between the rich northern countries and the poor south (see Die Grünen, 1980, p. 20). In the Greens' view this relationship was largely characterized by Third World dependency on the economic development and economic growth within the highly advanced industrial countries. Unable to compete with the industrial countries the weak countries of the Third World were systematically pushed out of the world market. That, together with the growing domination of international trade by multinational corporations, led to the increasing impoverishment of the Third World which threatened their ruin. Ruin could only be averted if the highly advanced industrial countries stopped economic expansion and drastically changed their relationship with the Third World from exploitation to partnership in order to allow the peoples of the Third World to recuperate the social and ecological foundations of life that are necessary for their prosperity.

In order to attain these goals and reverse West Germany's dependence on economic growth and its export orientation the Greens proposed that West Germany 'decouple' itself as much as possible from the external world by drastically decreasing and limiting the amount of imports and exports. Against the prospects of a fully integrated world market the Greens posed the vision of a decentralized domestic economy with the region rather than the nation-state as its point of departure. Only such a drastic reorientation would meet each of the basic Green demands: by no longer relying on economic growth and a constant increase in the amount of foreign trade it would satisfy central ecological demands; by renouncing and reversing the trend towards specialization and the further intensification of the division of labor it would satisfy the demand for a socially rather than technologically and profit oriented economy; and by decentralizing and integrating production on the regional and local level it would allow for a democratic control of production, exchange and consumption. In terms of Green concerns about West Germany's potential hegemonic position within the internal market, export limitations and a drastic economic reorientation would prevent West Germany from pursuing 'German great power politics' under the guise of the European Community (Die Grünen, 1989a). It was for these reasons that the Greens considered the 'region the point of departure and point of reference of Green economic and foreign trade policy' (Stratmann, 1985, p. 336).

From this perspective, the policies of the European Community violated and contradicted the very foundation of the Green economic, social and political program. The main charge of the Greens against the Community was that it had come to be dominated by politicians from the individual member governments in the Council of Ministers which had escaped from control by both the European Parliament and the electorate in the individual member states. As a result the large multinational economic powers had been allowed to act in a 'democratic vacuum: as far as people and nature are concerned, [these powers] pursue a politics of the lowest common denominator, however when it comes to advancing their concentrated economic power via research and the standardization of markets, they make a concerted effort' (Die Grünen, 1989, pp. 12–13).

Against this model of European integration, which in the Greens' view had already become the prevailing reality in Europe, the Greens proposed that the European Community shift its focus of attention from economic to non-economic issues. In the Greens' view a policy designed primarily if not exclusively to facilitate the movement of corporations was not the right way to solve transnational environmental problems, to achieve more equality between rich and poor regions, or to expand democracy within the Community. Therefore the Greens called on the European politicians to desist from further liberalizing economic relations within the Community and instead to concentrate on developing and enforcing social and ecological policies designed to prevent 'the further increase in the concentration of capital' and the growing disparities between regional economies while furthering small-scale, regionally oriented and energy efficient structures of production (Stratmann, 1985, p. 347; Die Grünen, 1989, p. 18).

However, despite all their reservations about the process of European integration, the Greens proved to be its staunchest supporters. As Table 6.3 shows, for the majority of Green suppporters the process of European unification was not going fast enough.

Table 6.3   Attitudes towards European integration (in per cent)

	Total	CDU/ CSU	SPD	FDP	Greens	Rep.
			Party preference			
1. The process of European unification:						
should go faster	33	34	34	46	52	18
should go slower	14	11	12	8	9	43
should continue the way it has	51	55	53	49	39	41
2. Attitude towards the internal market						
hopes	47	52	47	62	69	23
fears	48	43	49	32	29	73
3. Should problems be solved on a national or European basis?						
a) foreign and security policy						
national basis	44	47	41	39	30	58
European basis	55	53	59	61	70	42
b) fighting crime						
national	41	44	39	36	25	52
European	59	55	61	64	75	48
c) unemployment						
national	65	65	67	66	50	64
European	34	35	33	34	50	36
d) economic development						
national	52	55	52	47	42	55
European	47	44	47	53	58	45
e) refugee problem						
national	43	41	44	43	37	51
European	57	59	56	57	63	49

Source: Forschungsinstitut der Konrad-Adenauer-Stiftung, Archive-Nr. 8901, March 1989, about 2000 respondents (questions 1 and 2); Institut für praxisorientierte Sozialforschung Mannheim, March–April 1989, 2040 respondents (question 3).

The supporters of no other party were more willing to transfer responsibility for major political problems from the national to the European level. Even in their attitudes towards the prospect of an integrated market in 1992, Green supporters were considerably more positive than the rest of the population and the major two parties. These results indicate that the Greens are by far the most pro-European group in West German society. They also seem to suggest that support for European integration is an important aspect of left-libertarian postmodern politics if it is interpreted less in terms of economic rather than cultural and political integration.

The Greens' fear of and opposition to a future integrated Europe jointly administered and dominated by politicians and bureaucrats for the sole benefit of large corporations mirrored their resistance in domestic affairs to the growing power of the state as the privileged instrument to initiate and effect social change. As we have seen earlier, this aversion to the state stemmed from a profound and deep-seated suspicion of any large, hierarchically structured, bureaucratic organization that characterizes not only Green left-libertarian politics, but the politics of new social movements in general (Inglehart, 1989, pp. 302–5). They view these organizations not only as a potential source of oppression and exploitation, but as an impediment to the development of full individual autonomy and expression. Green politics towards the European Community thus follows the general logic of left-libertarian politics which seeks to shift the locus of political power from central, large organizations and structures in favor of an individual's greater control over his or her life and the decisions which affect it.

The demand for individual autonomy and unhampered expression of one's individuality informs the positive Green vision of a future united Europe. This vision was perhaps best expressed in the 'short program' to the European elections in 1989. These elections where overshadowed a great deal by the growing hostility towards political refugees and Third World immigrants throughout Western Europe. In this manifesto the Greens attempted to integrate different, sometimes seemingly contradictory strands of a left-libertarian approach to transnational integration which would further both individual self-determination and social equality without destroying distinct cultural identities. This manifesto thus represented a direct response to the challenge from the xenophobic right. The following excerpt represented the core of the Green vision for a future united Europe:

The Greens have a dream—the dream of a transformed world, in which non-violent, democratic self-determination from below has been realized across all borders and in which every people (*Volk*) finds a way to balance its way of work, its way of life, its culture and living conditions in a socially and ecologically acceptable fashion. In order to make this dream reality the peoples (*Völker*) of the world have to take their affairs finally into their own hands. . . . However, the dream, the real utopia of the Greens is also a dream of Europe, in which the new Soviet formula of a 'common European house' finds its historical meaning. . . . However we can only speak of a 'common European house' if its inhabitants determine themselves how they want to live in it without allowing potential 'architects' (Brecht), self-styled 'landlords'—or worst yet, custodians—to patronize them. Such as 'house' must have many rooms, must exist in harmony with its surroundings and must offer everyone a liveable space without ransacking one's neighbors for it. And its doors must be open for everyone who seeks help and refuge. (Die Grünen, 1989, pp. 6–7)

The last sentence represented a clear rejection of the possibility that a united Europe might lead to a 'fortress Europe' closing its extended borders to the rest of the world in order to safeguard affluence and prosperity within. In the face of growing resentment against non-European immigrants and the prospects of even more vocal, if not increasingly violent opposition to the continued influx of Third World refugees and immigrants throughout Western Europe in the late 1980s, the Green appeal to openness to the world meant above all the support for the right of non-Europeans to make Europe their home. It was for this reason that the Greens fought the election campaign for the 1989 European elections with the slogan 'Green—For a multicultural Europe.'

The growing focus of Green politics on the plight of immigrants and foreigners living in West Germany and the European Community in general found expression in a number of bills introduced in 1989 with the objective of extending the rights of foreigners in West Germany. Thus the Greens proposed that all foreigners older than eighteen who had resided in West Germany for more than five years be given the right to vote and, upon demand, the right to German citizenship; that wives of foreigners working in West Germany be given the right to join their husbands and to reside in West Germany independent of their husbands' right of residence; and that foreign residents be given the same access to social benefits and public education and the right to become public servants as Germans. Poll data show to what degree some of these Green demands clashed with the political preferences of the majority of the West German population (see Table 6.4). Whereas in March 1989 almost two thirds of Green supporters agreed that foreigners should be allowed to vote in local elections, this view was shared by only roughly a quarter of the population, while 85 per cent of center right and 100 per cent of far-right sympathizers were opposed. Against that two thirds of the population thought that

Table 6.4   Attitudes towards foreigners in West Germany (in per cent)

	Total	CDU/ CSU	SPD	FDP	Greens	Rep.
			Party preference			
1. Right to vote in local elections:						
favor	27	14	33	35	60	—
oppose	72	85	66	65	39	100
2. Foreign workers should only be allowed to enter West Germany for a few months or one year:						
favor	65	73	62	59	33	92
oppose	34	27	37	41	67	8
3. Foreign workers to leave after one year of unemployment:						
favor	67	76	63	68	32	94
oppose	32	23	36	32	67	6
4. Young foreigners born in the FRG should have right to German citizenship:						
favor	69	62	75	67	91	41
oppose	30	38	24	33	9	59
5. Wives of foreign workers should be allowed to join their husbands:						
favor	62	56	67	64	80	34
oppose	37	43	33	35	20	65
N	2272	766	836	165	185	104

Source: EMNID, Spiegel-Umfrage, March 1989.

foreign workers should only be allowed to enter West Germany for a few months and then sent back home. This was opposed by two thirds of Green supporters. Similarly two thirds of the population, but only one third of Green supporters thought foreign workers should have to leave the country if they had been unemployed for a year. However, there was a certain consensus (save for far-right sympathizers) that young foreigners born in the Federal Republic should have a right to become German citizens, that it should be made easier for foreigners who had lived in the Federal Republic for some time to become German citizens, and that wives of foreigners should be allowed to join their husbands in West Germany. In each case the supporters of the Greens came out most strongly for these policy proposals.

The support Green politics accorded the question of immigration and the future of European culture can be interpreted as a result of the general Green support for the rights of minorities which, as pointed out in earlier chapters, has been one of the main characteristics of postmodern left-libertarian politics in West Germany. However, the particular emphasis on foreigners might also be interpreted as a significant symbol of a much larger issue, namely the question of the future of the nation state. In the West German case, this question is intimately connected to the question of German unification and the future role of a unified Germany in the process of European integration. Ambiguity and anxiety over this question is hardly confined to the West German Greens. However, among the West German parties, only the Greens expressed these fears and anxieties once the possibility of a united Germany appeared to have turned into more than a distinct possibility.

It is only from this perspective that we can understand the perhaps perverse logic underlying the fact that in 1989 Green supporters were almost twice as willing to accept all political refugees (largely from the Third World) as they were willing to accept ethnic German resettlers from Eastern Europe and the Soviet Union (see Table 5.4). Underlying this ambiguity towards *Übersiedler* (who were often perceived as being the last true Germans), and to some degree also towards *Umsiedler* from the GDR, was the fear that their growing numbers would lead to the revival and spread of German nationalism (and with it the revival of the German question) throughout West German society and thus halt the further erosion of national identification and destroy the prospects of transnational integration (Schmierer, 1990). German unification, in turn, would only entail the return to a Europe oriented towards the nation state, a 'Europe of the fatherlands,' a potentially fatal constellation with the new German nation state as the new central European hegemonic power. This would not only impede the possibility of finding solutions for transnational problems (such as the ecological crisis affecting both parts of Europe), but would also mean the return of 'authoritarian, intolerant, and volkish orientations' in German culture, society and politics.[13]

It is for these reasons that after the successful East German revolution the Greens were less than enthusiastic about the prospects of a unified Germany. Although they supported the East German population's right to self-determination and welcomed the East German revolution and the fall of the repressive, authoritarian SED regime in East Berlin, they vigorously opposed the hasty move towards unification in both German states, but particularly in West Germany. Instead they demanded that West Germany respect the inner dynamics and autonomy of the developments in East Germany without interfering in East Germany's internal affairs in order to influence them in a direction favorable to West German plans. As far as the Greens were concerned, opting for reunification, like the flight of refugees from East Germany, represented a symbol of resignation, of 'the failure of the attempt to renew society from within.' East Germany needed self-determination, not reunification. 'The more there is self-determination for the people in the GDR, the more the question of the nation state loses its meaning.'[14]

Instead of joining in the growing chorus of supporters for quick unification within all established parties, the Greens renewed their demand that West Germany recognize the existence of two German states and the existing borders in Europe. In reponse to the government's ambiguous position on the inviolability of the German–Polish border the Greens argued that only by recognizing the territorial status quo could the Europeans achieve a transformation of the political situation in Europe.

> Borders have to be recognized in order to become permeable. The era of the nation state is over. Europe is on its way to act on a transnational basis. However, before we can achieve a European community, we first have to work off our deeply buried national past. The 'German question' must no longer be open, it must be closed to allow the GDR to open itself to European developments.[15]

However, although this position reflected longstanding Green policy towards the two German states, it very quickly threatened to become a rather empty and helpless response to the acceleration of political developments in East Germany. The quickening pace of political collapse, the fear of an imminent economic collapse and the growing and increasingly urgent popular demands in East Germany for rapid unification forced the Greens to confront the fact that it was no longer a question of whether unification would occur (and whether it could be prevented), but how and how quickly it would be accomplished.

The Green response was once again to emphasize the right to self-determination, however this time not of the East German population *vis-à-vis* West Germany, but of the population of both German states *vis-à-vis* a united front of politicians who sought to accomplish unification from above. The Greens vigorously rejected what they considered to be a mere *Anschluss* of East Germany (reminiscent of Hitler's forced incorporation of Austria into the German Reich in 1938) which would transform the economically backward, poor East German state into 'the Sicily of the Federal Republic.'[16] Instead they demanded that the population of both German states be given the opportunity to choose in a plebiscite between different options regarding the future of Germany. Although the Greens conceded the possibility of a united Germany comprising East and West Germany and Berlin, they put forward as an alternative option the idea of an 'ecological confederation of two radically democratic German republics in a pacifist Europe.'[17] A confederation would allow both German states to preserve their national particularities, it would allow the economically weak East German state to deal with the prosperous Federal Republic on an equal footing, and it would slow down the process of rapprochement between the two German states and thus alleviate the fears of Germany's neighbors while adjusting it to the pace of European integration. In addition, the mere existence of an autonomous East German state would weaken and perhaps even stop the processes of centralization within the European Community while strengthening forces of resistance against the destruction of national peculiarities.[18]

Behind these proposals stood the fear that a united Germany would not only disrupt the process of European integration but push it in a new and dangerous direction. A united Germany would only strengthen those tendencies within the Community which thought of the Community in terms of a Europe of the fatherlands, dominated by the European great powers. A united Germany might thus provide a new impetus towards a conception of European integration as a new concert system dominated by the great powers and thus further impede the development of a 'European polyphony' on a regional and federal basis. At its worst, a united Germany might assume the position of a new hegemonic power in Europe or, if checked by the other powers, provoke the revival of the old highly unstable power constellations and rivalries that had characterized the first half of the twentieth century (see Schmierer, 1990, esp. p. 6). It was for these reasons that the Greens advocated that the development of the relationship between the two German states be part of a larger European process of mutual understanding and peace.[19]

At the time of this writing the future of a unified Germany is far from clear. After the dust has settled somewhat and after the initial euphoria has given way to uncertainty and anxiety in both parts of Germany it does appear that the skepticism and often negative response on the part of the Greens and their supporters were perhaps justified. This response reflected as much the pro-modernist left-libertarian values of the postmodern left as it reflected the tensions and ambiguity inherent in Green postmodern politics. As had been the case with their domestic agenda, in their approach to West Germany's position in international relations the Greens illuminated central questions and problems. Among them were the questions of how to construct something of a national identity without threatening West Germany's neighbors, how to integrate an economically, militarily and increasingly politically powerful country into an evolving Europe without dominating it, and how to welcome East German refugees as refugees from a dictatorial regime without reviving German nationalism and raising the specter of German reunification. The Greens' response to each of these questions was a renewed emphasis on a European rather than national solution, a call for a multicultural Europe open to the world and a partner to the disadvantaged in which the German longing for national identity and unification could safely diffuse.

Underlying the Green debate about West Germany's position in NATO, the question of unification and European integration was once again an attempt to break with Germany's ill-fated past—not by forgetting and laying the past at rest, but by actively confronting the reality of German responsibility and drawing the proper conclusions from it. The main conclusion was that the German problem had largely stemmed from the attempt to create a centralized nation state. It was from this realization that the Greens regarded any attempt to reconstitute Germany as a unified state a first step towards a repetition of the past. From this perspective the Green policy towards the German question and the GDR represented a part of a larger project of moral rehabilitation which began with the student movement in the late 1960s.

However, this profound concern with an exclusively German problem, namely how to avoid a repetition of the past, should not distract from the fact that the Green emphasis on integration and transnational solutions to pressing political problems represents one important aspect of a new set of left-libertarian values which have emerged together with the transformation of international politics over the past few years. They are a response to the erosion of the central position of the nation-state caused and reflected by its diminished ability to exert power, influence and control not only over its own affairs but also over the behavior of other actors in international politics. Confronted with this reality, right-wing radical parties have sought to reassert the power of the state by promoting the virtues of hierarchical structures and traditional values; against that, left-libertarian parties such as the Greens have sought to base international relations on the same individualized, fragmentized basis that characterizes their domestic politics agenda. The two conceptualizations mark the boundaries within which the future of Europe will most likely be decided.

Conclusion: The Future of Postmodern Politics

More than a decade ago, Richard Löwenthal (1977, pp. 10–11) observed that the contemporary Western world was caught in a 'long-term process of loss of meaning' whose main characteristic was what he called a 'loss of world orientation.' What this involved was the collapse of faith in both a 'recognizable meaning of human life' as well as in social evolution. This loss of meaning, he argued, was a belated result of modernity's rejection of 'an effective faith in revealed, transcendent meaning' and its attempt to compensate for it with a secular belief in progress, which, in the aftermath of the Enlightenment and the industrial revolution, spread throughout the world.

Despite the fact that the shocks of two world wars, Nazism, and Stalinism seriously undermined faith in the notion of progress, the postwar success of the advanced industrial societies of the West in securing steady economic growth and a co-operative international regime that precluded a resort to violence appeared to be proof that a 'progressive' solution to humankind's most pressing problems 'might at least be *possible*.' What advocates of progress tended to forget or ignore, however, was the fact that more often than not these successes extracted a heavy price. Security entailed an increasingly senseless nuclear arms race, prosperity in the West hunger and starvation in the south, while development in both parts of the world led to a progressively rapid exploitation of natural resources and the gradual destruction of the natural environment.

The growing awareness of the destructiveness of instrumental rationality, scientific-technical progress, and economic growth contributed largely to the 'end of certainty of a value-oriented historical progress *per se*' visible today in most advanced industrial societies. The skepticism towards the notions of progress and the ideological and political programs construed around it represented a second 'disenchantment' of the world, confronting the individual with a world 'that has become increasingly incomprehensible and menacing in its complexity without the support of a simplifying worldview.' In short, the secular faith of the postmetaphysical era has gone the way of religious faith.

It seems that this analysis captures the experiences of a majority of those living in highly advanced industrial countries during the last two decades which have given rise to the postmodern condition. On this view postmodernism represents above all a response to two things: on one hand the fragmentation of contemporary society and the spread of a new 'eclectic and amorphous culture exhibiting plurality, mixed lifestyles and new attitudes based on immediate gratification, fantasy, novelty, play, hedonism, consumption and affluence' (Gibbins, 1989, p. 15) which has been furthered by new advances in communications, the invention of new technologies and the spread of flexible specialization; on the other the menacing reality of an increasingly overcomplex 'risk society' where progress and disaster are closely intertwined (Beck, 1986) and where the individual is increasingly at the mercy of a flourishing expertocracy.

The resulting cultural climate that characterizes much of contemporary advanced industrial societies is a mixture of anxiety and a sense of loss and betrayal, a yearning for solid ground when everything that has been solid is rapidly melting away, and a nostalgia for a past which is irretrievably lost. The postmodern condition is thus highly ambiguous. Exposing the decay of the established images without offering little in terms of alternatives it leads across a thin line that separates cynical despair from the giddy excitement over the emerging signs of pluralism, heterogeneity, and discontinuity. The postmodern mood thus goes in two directions: 'a romantic yearning for a world elsewhere, and a cynical reaction to this very yearning.' In short, 'the 'homeless' of history want a home while simultaneously protesting that you can't go home again' (Carroll, 1986, p. 14).

Confronted with a revolution of this extent politics has increasingly come to be seen as helpless and makebelieve, compensating for its inability to deal with the mounting problems with the appearance of busy-ness. In the face of a multiplying number of risks, politicians have found it increasingly difficult to continue pursuing the politics that marked the postwar welfare era which centered on the 'technical elimination of dysfunctions and the avoidance of risks that threaten the "system"' (Held, 1980, p. 251). As Bernd Guggenberger (1988, p. 23) has recently written, although makebelieve politics fails to solve the problem, 'it tranquilizes the emotions by disclosing itself as an activity engaged in the energetic preparation of activity.' This has led to a new form of telegenic simulational politics: where 'there is nothing one *can* do, but is *forced* by the audience's expectation to do something, there is only one way out: to act as if one did something.' The result has been a growing dissatisfaction with traditional politics, its sameness, predictability, and growing distance from the citizenry. The popular disenchantment has led to a new type of politics 'featuring difference, dealignment and realignment, unpredictability, freedom, delegitimization and distrust, power and spontaneity' (Gibbins, 1989, p. 16).

Although all West European political systems experienced extraordinary social, political, cultural, and economic changes in the 1970s and 1980s (Dalton, Flanagan, Beck, 1984; Lawson and Merkl, 1988), few seem to have been affected to the degree West Germany is. This can be partly explained by the fact that because of its status as only one part, though the larger, of a divided country West Germany's identity has been far more tenuous and fragile than that of other West European countries. The heated and prolonged debate about the nature of West Germany's identity which swept the country in the early 1980s was evidence of the influence this had on West Germany's political culture.

Partly it can be explained by contrasting what Jürgen Habermas (1985) has called the '*neue Unübersichtlichkeit*' (the new obscurity) characteristic of West German contemporary culture and politics to the exceptional stability of the postwar West German polity. Aware of Germany's fatal recent history, West Germany has made a conscious effort to gain and preserve political and economic stability. The postwar period witnessed a gradual consolidation of the political system by eliminating right- as well as left-wing extremes and, save for a brief period in the late 1960s which saw the brief emergence of a radical right, the evolution of a stable two-and-a-half party system. Economically West Germany's *Wirtschaftswunder* of the late 1950s and 1960s weathered the storm of the turbulent 1970s much better than most of the rest of the Western world. The combination of an expanded welfare state and a highly competitive export oriented economy on which rested the success of Helmut Schmidt's *Modell Deutschland* laid the foundation which allowed West Germany to take full advantage of the economic upswing of the 1980s. However this success story has not been without shadows.

The rise and spread of new social movements and citizen initiative groups in the 1970s, the vocal and sometimes violent mass demonstrations that marked the struggle against nuclear power plants in the 1970s and the introduction of new medium range nuclear weapons in the 1980s, the consolidation of extra-parliamentary protest in the Green party, the rising concern about a new kind of poverty amidst affluence and the emergence of a two-thirds society in the 1980s, and finally the growth of nationalism and xenophobia that led to the rise of right-wing radicalism in the late 1980s were both symptoms of and responses to a growing number of deficits and contradictory tendencies inherent in the *Modell Deutschland.*

On one hand they marked an awareness of the destructiveness and heightened risks associated with an economic growth model that increasingly relied on constant scientific-technological innovation and application in high-risk areas; on the other hand they responded to the effects of this model—the growing demands for flexibility and mobility, the fragmentation and decomposition of traditional milieux and social institutions, and the individualization of life chances and life's misfortunes. The result has been a full-blown assault on the West German model of modernity and with it, on the project of modernity in general. This assault has found expression in the left-libertarian politics of the Greens as well as in the right-wing radical politics of the Republikaner.

It is hardly a coincidence that the majority of those involved in new social movements as well as in the Greens (as compared to these merely expressing concern for the degradation of the environment) have come predominantly from among social and cultural specialists who see their task primarily in developing as fully as possible the emancipated, autonomous individual. Their engagement for the Greens rather than their traditional home, the Social Democrats, can largely be understood in the context of their rapidly deteriorating chances in the 1970s to affect the direction of West German society in their favor. Although there were different causes for the diminishing chances of the two generations of highly educated young West Germans who have predominated among Green party supporters, the result has turned out to be the same: both considered themselves deprived of the opportunity to push for greater emancipation and democratization.

The rise of left-libertarian postmodern politics in the Federal Republic thus lends empirical as well as theoretical support to Mike Featherstone's (1989, p. 125) suggestion that postmodern culture should be interpreted in terms of an attack by outsider intellectuals on the existing system of classification. In order to gain legitimacy for their views the social and cultural specialists had to downgrade the social democratic priorities of economic growth and material redistribution in favor of environmental issues and the promotion of further individual emancipation. By advancing these goals they not only sought to reconstitute the symbolic order in their own favor, they also found a way to represent their very own interests. As such, left-libertarian politics is thus very much both politics of a class as well as on behalf of a class.

What are the political prospects of such a position? The short history of the Green party has shown that the Greens have been very successful among younger, left-leaning cohorts just entering the political arena. This has led some observers to suggest that the Greens represent a new left 'milieu party' (Veen, 1987, pp. 60–9) reflecting the growth of a new sociocultural, moral, and political/ ideological milieu comparable to the classical conservative, Catholic or Social Democratic milieux of the late nineteenth century. On this view the Green party is embedded in a specific social structure with shared postmaterialist values, forms of and feelings about life, and a rather tightly-knit organizational network. This view is supported by the fact that the Greens have traditionally done exceptionally well at the polls in university towns.

Although in view of the social composition of the Greens such an interpretation is intriguing, it appears largely to be based on dated experience gained primarily from the alternative scene. If Mathias Horx's recent journeys through the 'wild eighties' (Horx, 1987, ch.3; 1989) are any indication, then this postmodern milieu has been affected by the same differentiation and fragmentation that character-izes West German society as a whole. Although in view of their 'chronic aversion' to the Social Democrats (Horx, 1989, p. 122) it is highly unlikely that the majority of the new class of alternative yuppies without regular jobs and non-materialist values would return to the SPD, there is reason to doubt that the Greens will continue to be able to attract young voters to the extent they did in the past (see Müller-Rommel, 1989, p. 117). Local as well as the European elections in 1989 showed a stagnation if not decline in support for the Greens among the youngest age cohort (ages eighteen to twenty-four). At the same time there was an increase in support from young women and those in the twenty-five to thirty-four and thirty-five to forty-four age cohorts (see Hofmann-Göttig, 1989c). This supports the contention that Green support is largely a cohort effect (see Inglehart 1990, pp. 79–82).

The future of left-libertarian postmodern politics might well depend on the question of whether the Greens will be able to broaden their electoral appeal among new segments of the new service class. It appears that the surfeit of graduates in the late 1980s has had unforeseen consequences. Forced to look for new career opportuni-ties, a number of disenchanted graduates have followed the strategy developed by what Bourdieu has called the new petite-bourgeoisie (Lash and Urry, 1987, p. 295). They have created new jobs in alternative newspapers, journals, and magazines, in journalism, the media, and advertising; they have made themselves independent as 'publicists,' consultants and counselors, or as owners of book stores and street cafés; or they have joined the '*genialen Versager*' (Horx, 1987)—the brilliant failures who somehow get through life and even manage to pay for dance lessons. A number of them finally have made a detour to land in the expanding human services sector, having become social and cultural specialists of their own making, whose ranks are increasingly dominated by graduates (Stamm, 1986).

Projections indicate that during the next twenty years and regardless of the form a united Germany can be expected to take there will be a dramatic increase in highly qualified occupations, particularly in the quartenary and quinary sectors of the economy (management, R & D, education, counseling, publishing etc.; see Klauder, 1990, pp. 29–35). According to one projection from the mid-1980s, if in 1982 roughly 70 per cent employed in teaching and welfare services were graduates, by the year 2000 that number was expected to have increased to more than 90 per cent. The same is true for law-related fields (from 38 per cent to 71 per cent), and writing and the arts (from 35 per cent to 62 per cent; Rothkirch and Weidig, 1986). Even with a unified Germany a reversal of this trend is not expected. It is among the growing ranks of this new service class that left-libertarian postmodern politics must find its supporters if it wants to remain a relevant political force in Germany.

The social and age composition of right-wing radical supporters provides indications of where segments of the younger age cohorts might go in the future. The rise of right-wing radicalism, initially concentrated in the right-wing radical populism of the Republikaner, can be attributed to a variety of factors. Prominent among them range a growing hostility to any kind of immigrants, be they Third World refugees, ethnic Germans from Eastern Europe or the Soviet Union, or even resettlers from East Germany; growing resentment against the politics of the established parties which in the past have only seemed to care about the affluent two thirds of West German society; and a diffuse nationalism which seeks to disavow the past and advocates and promotes a revival of German power from a position of newly-found strength. To this one must add the uncertainties of a united Germany.

Various studies have shown that these sentiments are especially pronounced among unskilled or semi-skilled workers, those living on small pensions, skilled workers, small self-employed persons, and farmers fearful of economic and social downward mobility, lower level employees and civil servants without promotional opportunities, and particularly among unqualified youth (Castner and Castner, 1989). This list suggests a much greater diversity among right-wing supporters than is the case with left-libertarianism. What is particularly important, however, is the appeal right-wing radicalism has mustered among the youngest cohorts. Wilhelm Heitmeyer, for instance, has shown that among sixteen-to-seventeen-year-old primary and middle-school students more than 16 per cent held authoritarian-nationalist views. These views found expression in items such as 'Germany for the Germans' and 'foreigners out' (Heitmeyer, 1989, p. 182, 187). Other studies have found that these authoritarian-nationalist tendencies are especially pronounced among those young people who are fearful of unemployment and pessimistic about their economic future (R. Roth, 1989, pp. 33–7).

The rise of right-wing radicalism in West German society reflects thus above all the disenchantment of a growing West German underclass which considers itself marginalized by the latest modernization bout sweeping through contemporary West Germany and is afraid of falling behind in the race for ever more affluence and prosperity characteristic of the West German *société de consommation.* Its response is marked by an attempt to return to what it considers traditional German values, a militant hostility to anything and anyone foreign, and a latent authoritarian nationalism that gathered steam after the prospects of a united Germany became increasingly realistic.

Despite significant differences between Green left-libertarianism and right-wing radicalism, the two representatives of West German postmodern politics also show surprising similarities. Most important of all, both reflect the negative experience of significant segments of the West German population with, and an articulate response to, a dramatic transformation of West German society and, beyond that, of Western societies in general. It is thus hardly surprising that an extensive study of West German attitudes conducted in the early part of 1989 found that almost the same proportion of Republikaner supporters as Green supporters situated themselves at the bottom third of West German society (26 per cent of Republikaner versus 28 per cent of Greens).[1] Where they diverged completely was in their response. Whereas the left-libertarians' embrace of a pro-modernist version of postmodern politics is at least partly embedded in a conscious effort to come to terms with the lessons from the German past, the right-wing radicals' support for tradition values is as much a

result of their attempt to escape the burdens imposed by the past as it represents a conscious effort to defeat the alleged cultural hegemony of the '68 generation.

Postmodern politics in West Germany has thus been embedded to a large degree in the divergent experiences of different generations. Although Featherstone's new middle class thesis goes a long way to explain the 68- and 78-generations' support for the Greens, it fails to explain the diversity of the support for the anti-modernist postmodern politics of right-wing radicalism. An alternative explanation, which takes into account the disproportionately large support for right-wing radicalism from younger cohorts, would focus on the rapid succession of generations and their divergent experiences. After the 68-generation whose idealism was shattered by the *Modell Deutschland* and the generation of 1978, whose expectations and prospects were destroyed by its crisis, a new generation has come of age. If we can believe Joachim Kutschke (1989), the 'consumer kids of '89,' at least those who come from affluent families, are cynical and fatalistic, and above all into consumption. Although it is still too early to tell where their political allegiance will lie in the future, it is probably fair to submit that a proportion of them might very well support right-wing radicalism.

The picture drawn so far suggests that postmodern politics in West Germany is as diverse and fragmentized as the groups that support it. Postmodern politics shares little of the giddy excitement expressed by so many commenting on the postmodern condition and the *société de consommation*. Postmodern politics reflects and responds above all to a larger crisis of Western society, a world increasingly gone topsy-turvy. Seen from this perspective, the rise of postmodern politics represents more than anything else a desperate attempt of resistance by an increasingly large part of society who find themselves beached on the postmodern shores.

One of the primary motivations behind the Green and right-wing radical assault on the West German version of modernity has been the attempt to reconstruct identity in the face of what is increasingly perceived as a rapidly progressing social decomposition. Both the left-libertarian pro-modernist embrace of total emancipation, pluralism and a multicultural, multiracial society integrated into a larger Europe without borders and the right-wing radical return to a static nationalism embedded in a new ideology of traditional values and ethnic diversity represent strategies to recover some sense of identity. Both are at the very least tenuous, for quite different reasons.

In their quest for differentiation the right-wing radicals appeal to allegedly German virtues which—if they ever existed—appear to have long since been lost. In the face of the massive social and cultural changes underway in all advanced industrial societies, and of a growing interdependence in international relations, an appeal to national identity, traditional values, and exclusion appears not only strangely quixotic but is ultimately incapable of halting the ever more rapid pace of technological change and commodification.

The left-libertarians, on the other hand, by laying claim solely to the Enlightenment's promise of full emancipation, are giving in to the social processes of fragmentation and individualization as well as the commodification of more and more aspects of life that mark the postmodern condition. Rather than attempting to stem the tide they in fact become the cheerleaders on the sidelines of the postmodern show. As Peter Koslowski (1989, p. 25) has remarked, at a time where there is much lament over the growing erosion of life worlds and the diminishing identity of ways of life and cultures, it is questionable whether more individual autonomy can fend off the increased colonization of the life world. One might wonder whether this aspect of the left-libertarian attempt to create identity by pushing modernity to its self-proclaimed limits might not falter in the face of the hyper-modern tendencies inherent in the postmodern condition.

Both approaches thus suffer from a major deficiency which stems directly from the dialectics of postmodern politics. Identity in the postmodern age will have to include both, a postmodern concern for the particular as well as a unifying system of values arrived at by consensus rather than dictate. Faced with the postmodern condition European culture has to find a way 'which allows for individual life forms while securing social cohesion and giving rise to a responsible, autonomous organization of one's own life' (Koslowski, 1989, p. 26). The left-libertarian emphasis on emancipation and the virtues of Enlightenment values fulfils the first demand while neglecting the second. This might be the ultimate result of the left-libertarians' failure to engage in a constructive dialogue with conservative Greens in the late 1970s. The right-wing radical emphasis on traditional values, on the other hand, recognizes the growing lack of social cohesion and seeks to remedy it. Its exclusive focus on national identity and individual subordination to that identity, however, not only precludes any possibility of individual emancipation, but also places right-wing radicalism squarely in the traditional anti-modernist authoritarian camp. The main reason for these deficiencies is, as previous chapters

have shown, that both the left-libertarians as well as the right-wing radicals are as much concerned with differentiating themselves from each other as they are in constructing an autonomous position.

It is for this reason that both sides fall short of their ultimate objective, namely to propose an alternative to the dominant project of modernity, commodification, and the *société de consommation*. Rather than offering a sweeping alternative they have come to represent the grievances and interests of a variegated clientele. As Ulrich Beck (1984, p. 497) has suggested, the social fragmentation and decomposition underway in all advanced Western societies makes traditional lines of conflict increasingly irrelevant. New lines of conflict emerge along 'assigned' characteristics, like race, gender, sexual preference, old age or ethnicity. To this one might add social and economic 'superfluity' in societies where individuals still define themselves largely by their position in the workforce, but where the availability of meaningful work is increasingly determined by forces beyond the individual's control (for example, economic crises and upswings, belonging to a baby boom or baby bust generation, long-term regional shifts from north to south or east to west, and so on). Increasingly, these new lines of conflict are becoming politicized.

So far the traditional parties, still to a large degree focused on welding together new core constituencies, have been largely unable, or unwilling, to engage these new lines of conflict. Here lies the continued opportunity for postmodern parties, not only in West Germany, but in all advanced societies whose electoral process allow minority parties to be represented. By focusing on a growing group of the newly marginalized, postmodern politics might not only have found its place in the rapidly changing political landscape of the postmodern *société de consommation*, it might represent the wave of the future, a future which would no longer be characterized by the dominance of mass and catch-all parties but by the heterogeneity and some might say chaos of fragmentized multiparty systems. This is an achievement, however a far cry from the sweeping alternative which both Greens as well as right-wing radicals claim to have found.

POSTSCRIPT: IS THERE POLITICS AFTER GERMAN UNIFICATION?

Part of the excitement but also penalty of writing on contemporary political affairs is that the subject matter of one's enquiry constantly changes. During the past year, this has posed considerable problems to all those writing on Eastern Europe and Soviet affairs, but particularly those writing on the two German states. Two years ago no one could or would have predicted the rapid collapse of the Honnecker regime and or the lack of Soviet resistance to German unification. Conventional wisdom held that even though reforms might occur in East Germany, the country was much too valuable strategically and economically for the Soviet Union to allow unification with West Germany. Polls taken merely two months apart at the end of 1989 showed both the extent to which this view was accepted by the West German public as well how quickly the West German public responded to dramatically changed circumstances after the opening of the Wall. Asked in September whether or not they believed Germany would be unified within the next ten years, almost two thirds of the population answered negatively. In December the situation had changed completely. More than three quarter of the population expected to see in the next ten years either a united German state or at least a confederation between the two German states; only one fifth expected to see two independent countries.[2]

The growing national preoccupation in West Germany with unification had a considerable impact not only on all political parties, but especially on the political priorities of the West German public, pushing less urgent problems into the background. In the months following the collapse of the communist regime and the growing uncertainty as to East Germany's political future the national question became the dominant issue in West German electoral politics, particularly in view of the upcoming federal elections in December 1990. The problems of marginalization, anxiety over the rapid pace of modernization, and the widespread discontent and resentment among a sizeable proportion of the electorate with the politics of the established parties were at least temporarily overshadowed by the enormous challenge of unification. As a result both the Greens as well as the representatives of right-wing radicalism appeared to lose support. This was quite evident in the Bavarian local elections, where in their homeland the Republikaner came nowhere close to the results they had gained in the European elections.

However, the prospects of rapid unification have not changed the structural problems underlying the politics of resentment. On the contrary. In the immediate future, unification might even compound these problems while creating new ones. It might very well be that the economic and political uncertainties associated with unification will create a new social base susceptible to right-wing populism in both parts of Germany. Already there is growing disenchantment among West German employers with resettlers from East Germany unaccustomed to the the standards demanded in West Germany's highly export oriented ecomomy. As a result, a considerable number of former East German workers were quickly dismissed, increasing the number of the unemployed and the number of the discontented. Moreover, no one can predict what unification will mean for the East German population. In the short run, disappointed expectations (as the demonstrations in East Germany in response to the West German wavering on the exchange rate between East and West German marks showed in the spring of 1990), but also 'the expectation of high unemployment, lost benefits and other hardships once the process of unification gets seriously under way could provide fertile soil for far-right politics.'[3]

The results of the March elections in East Germany indicated two things: the majority which voted for the conservative alliance did so because they expected quick improvements of their material circumstances through unification. Under these circumstances there is always the possibility of equally quick disappointment and disillusionment. On the other hand, the relatively strong support for the reconstructed communist party (PDS), which had heavily campaigned for preserving the achievements of the East German welfare system, was an indication of the anxiety of a sizeable minority of the population (even if they were merely the remaining members of the defunct communist party fearing for their jobs) about the economic and social uncertainties of unification. The future will tell whether right-wing populism will be able to benefit from this political climate.

Although our earlier analysis suggests that the negative response of the Greens to reunification should not hurt their electoral chances, unification poses a number of challenges to the party which are intimately connected with the very nature and composition of the Greens. The extent of the environmental catastrophe in East Germany should prove fertile ground for any party concerned with ecological issues. The same will probably hold true for the question of national identity. It can hardly be expected that a unified Germany would be less desirable a destination for political refugees and Third World immigrants than the Federal Republic has been. In addition, the East German population appears hardly less hostile to foreigners and particularly East Europeans than the West German population. Under these circumstances left-libertarian politics might become even more important than in the past. Finally, compared to the other parties the Greens can rely on a circumscribed clientele which shares common values and lifestyles and which will hardly disappear because of unification.

The problem and challenge for the Greens lies somewhere else. They stem from the plural nature of the left-libertarian project, which includes a large segment which still dreams of a genuinely leftist alternative to advanced consumer capitalism. The relative success of the PDS in East Germany has revived this dream, threatening the breakup of the party. If this should happen, left-libertarian non-materialist politics might quite likely disappear as an independent political force being absorbed on the one hand by social democracy, on the other by a new radical leftist socialist party. However, one should hardly expect that such an outcome of the current uncertain political situation in Germany will diminish the importance of postmodern politics in Germany. Quite on the contrary, it might make politics once more exciting.

Notes

Introduction: The Postmodern Challenge

1. *The Economist*, October 14–20, 1989, p. 106.
2. French opinion polls have shown, for example, that what differentiates National Front supporters from the supporters of the center right is their opposition to immigrants and their heightened sense of insecurity. See "Extrême droite: radioscopie d'un vote," *L'Express*, May 6, 1988, p. 14.

1 The Transformation of the New Left

1. For an excellent synopsis of this position see Löwenthal, 1981. The crucial sentence is: 'Social Democracy is a product of industrial society and a champion of democracy in state and society. With those, who consider the modern world a world-historical wrong way (*Irrweg*), it cannot make compromises' (p. 1087).
2. Dutschke, 1979. See also the discussion following Dutschke's article 'Und Vietnam und . . . ?' pp. 13–15; and the collection of essays *Der Mythos des Internationalismus*, Kursbuch 57 (October 1979), particularly Tilman Spengler, 'Wenn China nicht klappt,' pp. 9–32.
3. 'Und Vietnam und . . . ?' p. 15. The skepticism and suspicion towards liberation movements has not changed. A small article on a controversial 'dictionary of political philosophy,' distributed by the Sandinistas to the Nicaraguan population, is evidence of the depth of these feelings. The article appeared in *Pflasterstrand* (no. 237, 1988, p. 8), the bi-weekly journal of the Frankfurt new left. Above the article, there was a figure of a Sandinista soldier standing beside the figure of Stalin. The caption read: 'Stalino meets Sandino.'
4. A few select examples from their 1981 program: Konchok Dorje, *Marxismus und Meditation*; Yann Daniel, *Das Nebelpferd* (The Fog Horse); Harold A. Hansen, *Der Hexengarten* (The Witches' Garden); Sergius Golowin, *Magische Gegenwart* (Magical Present); *Die Rückkehr des Imaginären* (The Return of the Imaginary).
5. See for example the program of the 'Bunte Liste "Wehrt Euch!"' in Cologne (1979) which carries this slogan on the cover page.
6. Alberto Melucci (1980, p. 221) argued in a similar vein. He wrote: 'The body in its different significations becomes the cultural locus of resistance and of desire; it stands opposed to rationalization and it authorizes delirium.'
7. Invitation leaflet to the congress, in *Zwei Kulturen? Tunix, Mescalero und die Folgen*, p. 93.
8. This was one of the slogans of the French May 1968 Movement. The journal of the Frankfurt spontis, *Pflasterstrand*, and the journal *Unter*

dem Pflaster liegt der Strand, edited by Hans-Peter Dürr, allude to this slogan.

9. The social scientists Tilman Fichter and Siegward Lönnendonker quoted in a Spiegel report on the sponti movement, *Der Spiegel,* no.13, 1979, p. 62.
10. Ibid., pp. 65, 67.
11. Autorenkollektiv: Qinn der Eskimo, Frankie Lee und Judas Priest, '"Zum Tango gehören immer zwei, wenn ich komme, kommst du mit!" (Malcolm X),' in *Zwei Kulturen? TUNIX, Mescalero und die Folgen,* p. 131.

2 From Green to Red

1. 'Presseerklärung zur Monitor Sendung am 22. April 1980,' Bonn, April 28, 1980, p. 2.
2. 'Aus den "Dreissig Punkten,"' *Die Grünen,* April 26, 1980.
3. First proposal for the preamble to the basic program, in 'Die Grünen im Vorfeld der Gründung,' Die Grünen, Kreisverband Nürnberg, 1979, no page.
4. Ibid.
5. See also the declaration of the Hamburg Greens on the situation of the Greens after the Dortmund party congress, 'Presse-Information,' June 7, 1980, p. 2.

3 Postmodern Politics and the Greens

1. Petra Kelly, 'Wir sind die Antipartei-Partei,' *Der Spiegel,* no. 24, 1982, p. 47.
2. My classification of social and cultural specialists follows closely the definition given by Steven Brint (1984, pp. 45–6) save for minor changes regarding medical professions and lawyers which Brint includes in a variety of groups depending on whether they are employed in the private or public sector. The occupational groups are constructed according to the *International Classification of Occupations,* Geneva, 1968. They include managers (categories 201–219, 400, 500), professionals (011–013, 021–031, 041, 043, 061–067, 121, 122, 129), social and cultural specialists (071, 131–139, 141, 149 151–193, 195), and blue-collar workers (700–999).
3. Feist and Krieger (1987, p. 43) have graphically shown the split that goes through the Green constituency. In the 1987 *Bundestag* elections the Greens got the largest support from those employed in the extremely endangered full-time sector and the insecure segment of the labor market (9 and 12 per cent, respectively), and the most secure public service sector (10 per cent). In the most secure private sector segment they only gained two per cent of the vote.
4. Die Grünen im Bundestag, *Bulletin Sonderausgabe '89,* November 1989, p. 29.

4   Postmodern Anti-Modernism

1. A few days before the elections in Frankfurt, the voter potential for the *Republikaner* was twice as high as that for the NPD (see Roth, 1989, p. 5).
2. 'Gastarbeiterfrage als ökologisches Problem,' *Nation Europa* 31 (July–August 1981), pp. 67–9.
3. Barkholdt, 1981, p. 33. One of the initiative's fliers ('Ausländerstopp— Deutschland den Deutschen!' [Stop Foreigners—Germany for the Germans]) carries the slogan: 'An end to the policy of melting in. Foreigners too have a right to the preservation of their national and cultural particularities!' On the NPD's position see K. H. Vorsatz. 'Der Weg nach vorn!' *Profil*, Nationaldemokratische Schriftenreihe, no date (ca. 1984).
4. *Nation Europa* 31, no.7/8, pp. 71–2.
5. 'Warum Deutsche Gemeinschaft? Deutsche Sozialordnung—lebendige Demokratie—nationale Unabhängigkeit,' two-page leaflet, Munich, no date.
6. Lothar Penz, letter to the editor, *Neue Zeit*, no.2, 1987, p. 26.
7. Sache des Volkes, NATIONALREVOLUTIONÄRE AUFBAUORGA- NISATION, 'Vorwärts im nationalrevolutionären Befreiungskampf für die Neuschaffung Deutschlands! Unser Programm für Deutschland,' no date.
8. 'Kolonie Deutschland,' *Neue Zeit* 6, 4 (1977), p. 14.
9. 'Den Frieden retten—Deutschland vereinen!' *Frankfurter Rundschau* no.29, February 3, 1984. Among the co-signatories were the national revolutionaries Wolfgang Strauss and Wolfgang Venohr; the neo- conservative publicist Gerd-Klaus Kaltenbrunner; Wolfgang Seiffert; the left neo-nationalist Theodor Schweisfurth; and Wolf Schenke, together with Haussleiter a leading new nationalist and the editor of *Neue Politik*, a journal which in the late 1970s moved towards the Greens.
10. 'Erklärung des Deutschlandrats vom Dezember 1983,' *Nation Europa*, 34, January 1984, p. 81.
11. Interview with Sven Thomas Frank, Beilage zu *neue zeit*, 8, no.4 (1979), p. 3.

5   The Politics of Discontent: Right-Wing Radicalism in West Germany

1. EMNID/Spiegel poll, March 1989.
2. Alois Glück, 'Die gegenwärtige politische Situation—Probleme und Perspektiven,' CSU internal paper, Munich, July 1989; and interview with Alois Glück, *Münchner Merkur*, November 10 1989, p. 3.
3. Forschungsgruppe Wahlen in *Die Zeit*, February 10, 1989, p. 4.
4. Veen, 1989, pp. 56–7. According to one very controversial study by FORSA of former SPD voters in the north of Dortmund, a traditional SPD stronghold, who switched to the Republikaner, almost three times as many SPD voters who sympathized with the Republikaner considered themselves to belong to the bottom third of society as did SPD voters in

general. FORSA, 'Rechtswähler in einer SPD-Hochburg, dargestellt am Beispiel des Dortmunder Nordens,' Dortmund, 1989, p. 13. For a critique of this study see Glotz, 1989, pp. 163–4.

5. *Der Spiegel*, no. 43, 1986, p. 53.
6. See Renate Köcher, *Deutsche und Juden vier Jahrzehnte danach*, Institut für Demoskopie Allensbach, 1986. Excerpts appeared in *Stern*, no.16, 1986, pp. 32–5, 240; for 1989 data see *Der Spiegel*, no.15, 1989, p. 154.
7. *The New York Times*, January 13, 1987, p. A4.
8. Die Republikaner, 1987, p. 3; also 'Koblenzer Erklärung für Frieden und deutsche Einheit,' no date.
9. *Frankfurter Allgemeine Zeitung*, January 6, 1990, p. 2; *Der Spiegel*, no.8, 1990, p. 29.
10. *Der Spiegel*, no.52, 1988, p. 50. See also surveys in *Der Spiegel*, no.16, 1989, pp. 151–63, and the report on *Ausländerfeindlichkeit* in *Der Spiegel*, no.7, 1989, pp. 26–50.
11. *Der Spiegel*, no.7, 1989, p. 31.
12. According to a study from April–May 1989, almost 80 per cent of Republikaner supporters (compared to 50 per cent for the whole population) thought the number of foreign workers should be reduced, more than half (compared to a third for the whole population) did not like the fact that West Germany guaranteed the right to asylum, and more than a quarter (compared to 13 per cent) thought West Germany should not accept any refugees. See Institut für praxisorientierte Sozialforschung, *Einstellungen zu aktuellen Fragen der Innenpolitik 1989*, Mannheim, 1989, pp. 78–83.
13. On the situation of *Aussiedler* see Christian Wernicke, 'Erst gerufen, dann verachtet,' *Die Zeit*, no.27 (June 30, 1989): 3; and the 1989 *Spiegel* series on immigrants, particularly nos. 7 and 8, 1989. On the situation in early 1990 see the report '"Wieso kommen die noch?",' *Der Spiegel*, no.8, 1990, pp. 29–32, which culminated in the comment by one West German mayor of a small city: 'I hope they close the Wall soon.'
14. *Der Republikaner*, no.11, 1989, p. 1; *Der Republikaner*, no.12, 1989, pp. 3, 11.
15. Stefanie Wahl, 'Wer sind die Neuankömmlinge?' *Das Parlament*, no. 35 (August 25, 1989), p. 2.
16. Forschungsgruppe Wahlen, ZDF-Politbarometer, November 1989.
17. Franz Schönhuber, 'Angriff heisst die Parole!' *Der Republikaner*, no.2, 1990, p. 6.
18. See Hans Holzhaier, 'Fleisch vom Fleische der CSU,' *Süddeutsche Zeitung*, March 22, 1990.
19. 'Ja zu Europa—nein zu dieser EG!' leaflet for the European elections, 1989.
20. *Quick*, no.23, 1987, p. 28.
21. Forschungsgruppe Wahlen, *Meinungen der Bundesdeutschen und der Moskauer Bürger*, Mannheim, October 1988, and May 1989.
22. 'Deutsche Interessen haben Vorrang.' Die Dinkelsbühler Erklärung der REPUBLIKANER zur Europawahl, December 1988, no page.
23. Interview with Harald Neubauer, July 1989.
24. *Europa vorn*, no.2, 1989, p. 4.

25. *Der Republikaner*, no. 2, 1990, p. 6.
26. Interview with Harald Neubauer.
27. For a graphic example of the Republikaner view of Germany's claims see the map in the appendix to the 1990 party programme which includes among others East Prussia, the Sudetenland and the Memelland. Another Republikaner tactic has been to commit conscious errors. Thus, for example, Karl Richter, the editor of the party newspaper writes: 'German unity refers to both German states. Mecklenburg is part of it as is Bavaria, Stettin as well as Stuttgart. For 80 million Germans the Federal Republic is too small.' (Karl Richter, 'Ein Volk—eine Nation.' *Der Republikaner*, no.3, 1990, p. 2) Whereas Mecklenburg belongs to the GDR, Stettin is in Poland.
28. *Der Republikaner*, no. 12, 1989, pp. 3, 5.

6 The Dialectics of Postmodern Politics

1. *Die Deutschen und ihre Teilung*, Munich: AUD, no date.
2. The following discussion is based on the reports, 'Die Lage in Deutschland,' Rechenschaftsbericht des ZK der KPD an den II. Parteitag der KPD—verabschiedet am 31.1.77, Cologne, 1977 and 'Für ein unabhängiges, vereinigtes und sozialistisches Deutschland!' Erklärung des ZK der kommunistischen Partei Deutschlands, November 1975, Cologne, 1977.
3. E. P. Thompson, quoted in Ammon and Brandt, 1983, p. 96.
4. Franz Dormann, 'Zurück zur Revolutionierung des Bewusstseins,' *FAZ* May 5 1989, p. 9.
5. *Kurzprogramm der Alternativen Liste*, 1985, pp. 32–3.
6. Die Grünen im Bundestag, 'Wider die Mauern auch in den Köpfen,' no date.
7. Ibid.
8. 'Wir müssen raus aus der NATO,' Erklärung zur Friedenspolitik der GRÜNEN, verabschiedet von der 6. ordentlichen Bundesversammlung vom 18. bis 20. November 1983 in Duisburg.
9. Karitas Hensel in a speech in the German *Bundestag*. Deutscher Bundestag, 11. Wahlperiode, 158. Sitzung, September 14, 1989, p. 12041.
10. Jürgen Schnappertz, '"Ende der Idee und Wirklichkeit der deutschen Nation"' (Einleitungsbeitrag zur Podiumsdiskussion auf der Jahrestagung der Deutschen Burschenschaften am 3. Januar 1987), mimeo, p. 5.
11. *Kommune*, no.7, 1988, p. 3.
12. See Wolfgang von Nostitz, 'Blaue Augen und goldene Nase,' Die Grünen im Bundestag, *Bulletin*, March 1989, p. 8.
13. Die Grünen im Bundestag, *Bulletin*, special edition '89, Bonn, 1989, p. 41.
14. Ralf Fücks, 'Stolz auf die eigene Vortrefflichkeit und den Wohlstandkuchen,' *Frankfurter Rundschau*, November 17, 1989.
15. Die Grünen, 'Pressemitteilung Nr. 817/89,' Bonn, October 2, 1989.
16. Antje Vollmer, 'Ökologische Konföderation beider deutschen Staaten: Gemeinsamkeit in Autonomie,' mimeograph, Bonn, January 1990.

17. Antje Vollmer in a speech before the German Bundestag, January 18, 1990, in Die Grünen, *Deutschlandpolitische Pressemitteilungen und Reden der GRÜNEN im Bundestag*, Bonn, 1990, p. 160.
18. See Vollmer, 'Ökologische Konföderation.'
19. See for example Die Grünen, 'Pressemitteilung 144/90,' Bonn, November 2, 1989, in which the Greens expressed their support for integrating the future Germany into a new European peace order which would rest on the recognition of the postwar borders, the large-scale demilitarization of the two German states, the overcoming of the military blocs and the co-operation of all European countries on an equal basis.

Conclusion: The Future of Postmodern Politics

1. EMNID/Spiegel poll, March 1989.
2. Forschungsgruppe Wahlen, ZDF-Politbarometer, September, December 1989.
3. Serge Schmemann, 'Far-Right Party Loses Steam As Unity Enchants Germans,' *The New York Times*, March 30, 1090, p. A6.

Bibliography

ADELSON, L. (1983) 'Subjectivity Reconsidered: Botho Strauss and Contemporary West German Prose' *New German Critique* 28 (Winter) pp. 3–59.
AIGNER, D. (1987) 'Fetisch und Tabu' *Criticon* 104 (November–December) pp. 257–62.
ALBER, J. (1985) 'Modernisierung, neue Spannungslinien und die politischen Chancen der Grünen' *Politische Vierteljahresschrift* 26 (3) pp. 211–26.
AMMON, H. and SCHWEISFURTH, T. (1985) *Friedensvertrag, Deutsche Konföderation, Europäisches Sicherheitssystem* (Starnberg: ibf-Verlag).
AUGSTEIN, R. (1981) 'Ein Nietzsche für Grüne und Alternative?' *Der Spiegel*, no.24, pp. 156–84.
BACIA, J. and SCHERER, K.-J. (1981) *Passt bloss auf! Was will die neue Jugendbewegung?* (Berlin: Olle & Wolter).
BACKES, U. and JESSE, E. (1989) *Politischer Extremismus in der Bundesrepublik Deutschland*, Schriftenreihe 272 (Bonn: Bundeszentrale für politische Bildung).
BADHAM, R. (1984) 'The Sociology of Industrial Societies and Post-Industrial Societies', *Current Sociology* 32 (Spring).
BAHRO, R. (1982) *Socialism and Survival*, translated by David Ferbach (London: Heretic Books).
— (1982a) *Wahnsinn mit Methode* (Berlin: Olle & Wolter).
BARKHOLDT, B. (1981) 'Die Bürgerinitiative Ausländerstopp,' *Nation Europa* 31 (2) pp. 33–7.
BARTSCH, G. (1980) 'Ökologischer Humanismus—eine Stufe der Menschwerdung? pp. 77–91 in W. Heidt (ed) *Abschied vom Wachstum* (Achberg: Achberger Verlag).
BAUDRILLARD, J. (1983) *Simulations*, trans. by P. Foss, P. Patton and P. Beitchman (New York: Semiotext(e)).
— (1981) *For a Critique of the Political Economy of the Sign*, trans. by C. Levin (St Louis: Telos Press).
— (1975) *The Mirror of Production*, trans. by M. Poster (St Louis: Telos Press).
BAUER, M. (1990) ' "Freunde", "Feinde" und deutsche Interessen' *Europa vorn*, 3 (January) pp. 11–13.
BAUMANN, Z. (1987) *Legislators and Interpreters* (Ithaca and New York: Cornell University Press).
BECK, U. (1987) 'Beyond Status and Class: Will There Be an Individualized Class Society?' pp. 340–55 in V. Meja, D. Misgeld and N. Stehr (eds) *Modern German Sociology* (New York: Columbia University Press).
— (1986) *Risikogesellschaft* (Frankfurt: Suhrkamp).
— (1984) 'Jenseits von Stand und Klasse' *Merkur* 38 pp. 485–97.
BELL, D. (1989) 'The Third Technological Revolution and its Possible Socioeconomic Consequences' *Dissent* (Spring) pp. 164-176.
— (1976) *The Cultural Contradictions of Capitalism* (New York: Basic Books).

BERMAN, R. (1982) 'Opposition to Rearmament and West German Culture' *Telos* 51 (Spring) pp. 141–8.

BERTENS, H. (1986) 'The Postmodern Weltanschauung and its Relation with Modernism: An Introductory Survey,' pp. 9–51 in D. Fokkema and H. Bertens (eds) *Approaching Postmodernism* (Amsterdam, Philadelphia: John Benjamins Publishing Company).

BETZ, H.-G. (1989) 'Strange Love? How the Greens Began to Love NATO' *German Studies Review* 12 (3) pp. 487–505.

— (1988) '*Deutschlandpolitik* on the Margins: On the Evolution of Contemporary New Right Nationalism in the Federal Republic' *New German Critique* 44 (Spring–Summer) pp. 127–157.

BISCHOFF, J., LUEN, K. D. and MENARD, M. (1983). 'Grüne Radikalität oder: Die sanfte Alternative,' pp. 69–96 in *Nicht Links nicht Rechts?* (Hamburg: VSA-Verlag).

BODENHöFER, H.-J., OFNER, F., KAISER, M., OTTO, M. and v. LANDSBERG, G. (1986) *Ingenieure in der Wirtschaft* Beiträge zur Gesellschafts- und Berufspolitik, no. 122.

BÖGE, V. (1987) '"Tabubrecher" versus "Dogmatiker"? Grüne Friedenspolitik' *links* 212 (November) pp. 12–13.

BOPP, J. (1981) 'Trauer-Power' *Kursbuch* 65 (October) pp. 151–68.

BRACHER, K. D. (1985) *Zeit der Ideologien* (Munich: DTV).

BRAND, K.-W., BÜSSER, D. and RUCHT, D. (1983) *Aufbruch in eine andere Gesellschaft* (Frankfurt: Campus).

BRANDT, P. (1980) 'Reale Mythen des Marxismus—Einige Bedenken' *Befreiung* 19–20 pp. 9–19.

— and AMMON, H. (1981) *Die Linke und die nationale Frage.* Reinbeck bei Hamburg: Rowohlt.

— and MINNERUP, G. (1982) 'Die deutsche Frage—Problemskizze und Thesen,' *Prokla,* 47 pp. 91–118.

BRAUNTHAL, G. (1983) *The West German Social Democrats 1969–1982* (Boulder: Westview Press).

BRINKMANN, H. U. (1989) 'Neue Schicht—Neue Werte?' *Zeitschrift für Umweltpolitik & Umweltrecht* no.2, pp. 159–83.

— (1988) 'Wahlverhalten der "neuen Mittelschicht" in der Bundesrepublik Deutschland,' *Aus Politik und Zeitgeschichte* B30–31/88 pp. 19–32.

BRINT, S. (1985) 'The Political Attitudes of Professionals' *Annual Review of Sociology* 11 pp. 389–414.

BROCKMAN, S. (1989) 'After Nature: Postmodernism and the Greens' Paper presented at the 13th Annual Conference of the German Studies Association, Milwaukee, October 1989.

BRUHN, J. (1987) 'Winterpalais, Führerbunker, Meinungsbörse' *links* 19 (November) pp. 18–19.

BRUN, R., (ed) (1978) *Der grüne Protest. Herausforderung durch die Umweltparteien* (Frankfurt: Fischer).

BRUNKHORST, H. (1981) 'Marxismus und Alternativbewegung' *Neue Rundschau* pp. 101–15.

BUCHWALTER, A. (1984) 'Translator's Introduction,' pp. vii–xxxvii in J. Habermas (ed) *Observations on the "Spiritual Situation of the Ages"* (Cambridge, MA: MIT Press).

BÜRKLIN, W. P. (1987) 'Governing Left Parties Frustrating the Radical Non-Established Left: The Rise and Inevitable Decline of the Greens' *European Sociological Review* 3 (2) pp. 109–26.

— (1985) 'The German Greens. The Post-Industrial Non-Established and the Party System' *International Political Science Review* 6 (4) pp. 463–81.

— (1984) *Grüne Politik* (Opladen: Westdeutscher Verlag).

BURNS, R. and VAN DER WILL, W. (1988) *Protest and Democracy in West Germany* (New York: St Martin's Press).

CARROLL, N. (1986) 'Romanticism and Cynicism: Life in the Dead Zone,' pp. 14–23 in *Romanticism and Cynicism in Contemporary Art* (Publications of the Patrick and Beatrice Haggerty Museum of Art, Milwaukee: Marquette University).

CASTNER, H. and CASTNER, T. (1989) 'Rechtsextremismus und Jugend' *Aus Politik und Zeitgeschichte* B41–42/89 (October) pp. 32–9.

CONNOR, S. (1989) *Postmodern Culture* (Oxford: Basil Blackwell).

COTGROVE, S. and DUFF, A. (1980) 'Environmentalism, Middle-Class Radicalism and Politics' *The Sociological Review* 28 (2) pp. 333–51.

CRAIG, G. (1989) 'The Rising Star of the German Right' *The New York Review of Books* 36 (10) pp. 22–4.

DAHRENDORF, R. (1987) 'The Search for German Identity: An Illusory Endeavor?' pp. 135–146 in W. Pollak and D. Rutter (trans. and eds) *German Identity—Forty Years After Zero* 3rd. ed. (Sankt Augustin: COMDOC-Verlagsabteilung).

DALTON, R. J., FLANAGAN, S. C. and BECK, P. A. (eds.) (1984) *Electoral Change in Advanced Industrial Democracies* (Princeton: Princeton University Press).

DAMUS, R. and WORTMANN, R. (1983) 'Brauchen wir eine neue Deutschlandpolitik?' *Moderne Zeiten extra*, 3 (Sondernummer 11) pp. 36–37.

DAVIS, D. (1980) 'Post-Everything' *Art in America* 68 (February) pp. 11–14.

DEHOUST, P. (1985) 'Wann endet die Fremdherrschaft?' *Nation Europa* 35 (May–June) p. 3.

DEUTZ, M., KOLENBERGER, L., SCHROEDER, L. and SCHWARZ, H.-A. (1979) 'Alternativ oder konservativ?' *Ästhetik & Kommunikation* 36 pp. 29–42.

DIGGINS, J. (1977) 'Reification and the Cultural Hegemony of Capitalism: The Perspectives of Marx and Veblen' *Social Research* 44 (Summer) pp. 354–83.

DIWALD, H. (1978) *Die Geschichte der Deutschen*, (Frankfurt: Ullstein).

— (1988) 'Die Entscheidung von Tauroggen, II. Teil und Schluss,' *MUT* 245 (January) pp. 34–42.

— (1985) 'Deutschland—was ist es?' pp. 45–70 in W. Venohr (ed) *Ohne Deutschland geht es nicht* (Krefeld: Sinus).

DRÄGER, K. and HÜLSBERG, W. (1986) *Aus für Grün?* (Frankfurt: isp-pocket 17).

DUTSCHKE, R. (1979) 'Reale Kriege und realer Sozialismus' *links* 11 (April) pp. 10–12.

EBERT, W. (1985) 'Wir Wendekinder' *Die Zeit* (November 1) p. 65.

EICHBERG, Henning (1981) 'Balkanisierung für Jedermann?—Nation, Identität und Entfremdung in der Industriegesellschaft' *Befreiung* 19–20 pp. 46–69.

— (1978) *Nationale Identität* (Munich, Vienna: Langen-Müller).
ENZENSBERGER, H. M. (1978) 'Zwei Bemerkungen zum Weltuntergang' *Kursbuch* 52 (May) pp. 1–8.
ERLER, G., KIPPHARDT, H., SCHMID, T., SONNEMANN, U., WAGENBACH, K. (1978) 'Gespräch über die politische Kultur in Deutschland' pp. 93–116 in H. Brüggemann, H. Gerstenberger, W. Gottschalch, U. K. Preuss, G. Erler, H. Kipphardt, T. Schmid and U. Sonnemann *Über den Mangel an politischer Kultur in Deutschland* (Berlin: Wagenbach Verlag).
ESSER, J. (1987) 'Trouble in Kreuzberg. Von den Problemen grüner Politik mit der deklassierten Jugend' *Kommune* 5 (September) pp. 25–31.
EVANS, R. J. (1989) *In Hitler's Shadow: West German Historians and the Attempt to Escape From the Nazi Past* (New York: Pantheon Books).
FEATHERSTONE, M. (1989) 'Postmodernism, Cultural Change, and Social Practice,' pp. 117–138 in D. Kellner (ed) *Postmodernism Jameson Critique* (Washington, D.C.: Maisonneuve Press).
— (1989a) 'Towards a Sociology of Postmodern Culture." pp. 147–172 in H. Haferkamp (ed) *Social Structure and Culture* (Berlin, New York: Walter de Gruyter).
— (1987) 'Lifestyle and Consumer Culture' *Theory, Culture & Society* 4 (February) pp. 55–70.
FEHER, F. (1987) 'The Status of Postmodernity' *Philosophy & Social Criticism* 13 (2) pp. 195–206.
FEILER, O. (1984) *Moskau und die Deutsche Frage.* Edition d, no.8 (Krefeld: Sinus).
FEIST, U. and KRIEGER, H. (1987) 'Alte und neue Scheidelinien des politischen Verhaltens' *Aus Politik und Zeitgeschichte* B12/87 (March) pp. 33–47.
FEIT, M. (1987) *Die 'Neue Rechte' in der Bundesrepublik* (Frankfurt, New York: Campus).
FELDMEYER, K. (1988) 'Warum ist Deutschland seit mehr als vier Jahrzehnten geteilt?' *MUT* 248 (April) pp. 10–23.
FEND, H. and PRESTER, H.-G. (1985) 'Wie wird man Grünwähler?' *Schweizer Zeitschrift für Soziologie* 11 (2) pp. 373–90.
FICHTER, T. and LÖNNENDONKER, S. (1979) 'Von der APO nach TUNIX,' pp. 132–150 in C. Richter (ed) *Die überflüssige Generation* (Königstein: Athenäum Verlag).
FIEDLER, H.-M. (1987) '"Postmoderne". Negative und positive Signale eines Begriffs' *Nation Europa* 37 (July) pp. 5–14.
FISCHER, J. (1984) *Von grüner Kraft und Herrlichkeit* (Reinbek bei Hamburg: Rowohlt).
FLANAGAN, S. (1987) 'Value Change in Industrial Societies' *American Political Science Review* 81 (December) pp. 1303–19.
— (1982) 'Changing Values in Advanced Industrial Societies' *Comparative Political Studies* 14 (January) pp. 403–44.
FOGT, H. (1988) 'Wo die Helden von einst geblieben sind' *Rheinischer Merkur/Christ und Welt* 18 (April) p. 8.
— (1986) 'Die Mandatsträger der Grünen' *Aus Politik und Zeitgeschichte* B11/86 (March) pp. 16–33.

— (1983) 'Die Grünen in den Parlamenten der Bundesrepublik' *Zeitschrift für Parlamentsfragen* 14 (December) pp. 500–17.

— and UTTITZ, P. (1984) 'Die Wähler der Grünen 1980–1983: System-kritischer neuer Mittelstand' *Zeitschrift für Parlamentsfragen* 15 (June) pp. 210–26.

FORSCHUNGSGRUPPE WAHLEN (1989) *Europawahl—Eine Analyse der 3. Direktwahl zum Europaparlament*, Bericht der Forschungsgruppe Wahlen e.V., Mannheim, no.54.

FOSTER, H. (ed) (1987) *Postmodern Culture* 2nd. ed (London: Pluto Press).

— (1985) *Recodings* (Seattle: Bay Press).

FRACKMANN, M., KUHLS, H. and LÜHN, K.-D. (1981) *Null Bock oder Mut zur Zukunft? Jugendliche in der Bundesrepublik*. Hamburg: VSA Verlag).

FÜCKS, R. (1983) 'Grüne—Wohin des Wegs?' *Moderne Zeiten* 3 (December) pp. 18–19.

GIBBINS, J. R. (ed) (1989) *Contemporary Political Culture: Politics in the Postmodern Age*. Sage Modern Politics Series vol.23 (Newbury Park: Sage Publications).

GITLIN, T. (1989) 'Postmodernism Defined, at Last!' *Utne Reader* (July–August) pp. 52–61.

GLAESSNER, G.-J., HOLZ, J. and SCHLüTER, D. (eds.) (1984) *Die Bundesrepublik Deutschland in den siebziger Jahren* (Opladen: Budrich und Leske).

GLASER, H. A. (1987) 'Lasst alle Hoffnung fahren. Stumpfe Studenten, verzweifelte Professoren: Die deutsche Universität ist das Getto der Arbeitslosen' *Die Zeit* 16 (April) p. 55.

GLOTZ, P. (1989) *Die deutsche Rechte* (Stuttgart: DVA).

GLUCHOWSKI, P. (1989) 'Vom Milieu zum Lebensstil—Wandel der Wählwerschaft' *Eichholzbrief*, no.4, pp. 66–76.

GLUCKSMANN, A. (1984) *Philosophie der Abschreckung* T. Dobberkau and B. Hennings (trans.) (Stuttgart: Deutsche Verlags-Anstalt).

GROSS, D. (1989) 'Marxism and Resistance: Frederic Jameson and the Moment of Postmodernism,' pp. 96–116 in D. Kellner (ed) *Postmodernism Jameson Critique* (Washington, D.C.: Maisonneuve Press).

DIE GRÜNEN (1989) *Kurzprogramm der Grünen zur Europawahl '89*, Bonn.

— (1989a) *Grün—Für ein multikulturelles Europa*, Bonn.

— (1987) *Programm zur Bundestagswahl 1987* (Vorabdruck aus dem Protokoll der Bundesversammlung vom 16. bis 19. 5. 86 in Hannover), Bonn.

— (1986) *Umbau der Industriegesellschaft*, Bonn.

— (1983) *Sinnvoll arbeiten—solidarisch leben*, Bonn.

— (1981) *Friedensmanifest*, Bonn.

— (1980) *Das Bundesprogramm*, Bonn.

GRUHL, H. (1980) 'Der materielle Fortschritt und die Reduzierung der Menschlichkeit,' pp. 22–35 in H.-W. Lüdke and O. Dinne (eds) *Die Grünen*, (Stuttgart: Seewald).

— (1978) 'Die grüne Notwendigkeit,' pp. 117–121 in R. Brun (ed) *Der grüne Protest* (Frankfurt: Fischer).

— (1978a) *Ein Planet wird geplündert* (Frankfurt: Fischer).

GUGGENBERGER, B. (1988) *Sein oder Design* (Berlin: Rotbuch Verlag).

— (1980) *Bürgerinitiativen in der Parteiendemokratie* (Stuttgart, Berlin, Cologne, Mainz: Kohlhammer).

HABERMAS, J. (1987) *Eine Art Schadensabwicklung* (Frankfurt: Suhrkamp.

— (1986) *Autonomy and Solidarity*. Ed and intro. by P. Drews (London: Verso).

— (1985) *Die neue Unübersichtlichkeit* (Frankfurt: Suhrkamp).

— (1984) 'Introduction,' pp. 1–28 in *Observation on 'The Spiritual Situation of the Ages'*, ed by J. Habermas (Cambridge, MA: MIT Press).

— (1981) 'New Social Movements' *Telos* 49 (Fall) pp. 33–7.

HALLENSLEBEN, A. (1984) *Von der Grünen Liste zur Grünen Partei?* (Göttingen: Muster-Schmidt).

HANDY, C. (1985) *The Future of Work* (Oxford: Basil Blackwell).

HARTMANN, H. and FÜRST, A. S. (1986) 'Auf ewig machtlos?' *Criticon* 94 (March–April) pp. 72–5.

HARVEY, D. (1987) 'Flexible Accumulation Through Urbanization: Reflections on "Post-Modernism" in the American City' *Antipode* 19 (3) pp. 260–86.

HASENCLEVER, W.-D. and HASENCLEVER, C. (1982) *Grüne Zeiten* (Munich: Kösel).

HASSAN, I. (1987) *The Postmodern Turn*. Columbus: Ohio State University Press).

HASSE, J. (1989) 'Sozialgeographie an der Schwelle zur Postmoderne' *Zeitschrift für Wirtschaftsgeographie* 33 (1/2) pp. 20–9.

HAVERBECK-WETZEL, U. (1984–85) 'Brauchen die konservativen Kräfte eine eigene Partei?' *Junges Forum* (Winter) pp. 3–12.

HEAD, S. (1989) 'The Battle Inside NATO,' *The New York Review of Books* 36 (8) pp. 41–6.

HELD, D. (1980) *Introduction to Critical Theory* (Berkeley and Los Angeles: University of California Press).

HEPP, C. (1987) *Avantgarde* (Munich: DTV).

HEITMEYER, W. (1989) *Rechtsextremistische Orientierungen bei Jugendlichen*. 3rd. ed. (Weinheim, Munich: Juventa).

— (1989a) 'Jugend und rechtsextremistische Wahlerfolge,' mimeo, Fakultät für Pädagogik, University Bielefeld.

HILDEBRANDT, K. and DALTON, R. J. (1977) 'Die neue Politik: Politischer Wandel oder Schönwetterpolitik?' *Politische Vierteljahresschrift* 13 (November) pp. 230–56.

HILGENBERG, D. (1986) 'Hase, Eule und Lysistrate' *Die Zeit* no.45, p. 61.

HIPPLER, J. and MAIER, J. (eds.) (1988) *Sind die Grünen noch zu retten?* (Cologne: Förtner & Kroemer).

HIRSCH, K. and SARKOWICZ, H. (1989) *Schönhuber: Der Politiker und seine Kreise* (Frankfurt: Eichborn).

HIRSCH, J. (1985) 'Fordismus und Postfordismus' *Politische Vierteljahresschrift* 26 (2) pp. 160–82.

— (1982) 'The West German Peace Movement' *Telos* 51 pp. 135–41.

HOFMANN-GÖTTIG, J. (1989) 'Die fünfte Kraft,' pp. 64–74 in K. Hirsch and W. Metz (eds) *Die Republikaner—die falschen Patrioten*, Schriftenreihe der bayerischen SPD.

— (1989a) 'Selbst die NPD is jugendattraktiv—Von Jungen und Alten, Frauen und Männern bei der Kommunalwahl in Hessen vom 12. März 1989,' Bonn, mimeo.

— (1989b) 'Die neue Rechte: Die Männerpartei' *Aus Politik und Zeigeschichte* B41–42/89 (October) pp. 21–31.

HOFFMANN, E, P. Schnur, F. Stooss and M. Tessaring (1986) 'Die Zukunft der Arbeitslandschaft' *Materialien aus der Arbeits- und Berufsforschung* 6/1986.

HONOLKA, H. (1987) *Schwarzrotgrün* (Munich: C. H. Beck).

HOPLITSCHEK, E. (1982) 'Partei, Avantgarde, Heimat oder was?' pp. 82–100 in J. Mettke (ed) *Die Grünen—Regierungsparter von morgen?* (Reinbeck bei Hamburg: Rowohlt).

HORKHEIMER, M. and ADORNO, T. (1986) *Dialectic of Enlightenment* (New York: Continuum).

HORX, M. (1989) *Aufstand im Schlaraffenland* (Munich: Hanser Verlag).

— (1987) *Die wilden Achziger* (Munich: Hanser Verlag).

HUBER, J. (1980) *Wer soll das alles ändern?* (Berlin: Rotbuch Verlag).

HÜBSCH, H. (1980) *Alternative Öffentlichkeit* (Frankfurt: Fischer).

HÜLSBERG, W. (1988) *The German Greens* (London: Verso).

HUTCHEON, L. (1989) *The Politics of Postmodernism* (New York: Routledge).

— (1988) *A Poetics of Postmodernism* (New York: Routledge).

HUYSSEN, A. (1987) 'Foreword: The Return of Diogenes as Postmodern Intellectual,' pp. ix-xxv in P. Sloterdijk, *Critique of Cynical Reason* (Minneapolis: University of Minneapolis Press).

— (1984) 'Mapping the Postmodern' *New German Critique* 33 (Fall) pp. 5–52.

INFRATEST WIRTSCHAFTSFORSCHUNG GMBH (1980) *Politischer Protest in der Bundesrepublik Deutschland* (Stuttgart, Berlin, Cologne, Mainz: Kohlhammer).

INGLEHART, R. (1990) *Culture Shift in Advanced Industrial Society* (Princeton: Princeton University Press).

— and RABIER, J.-R. (1986) 'Political Realignment in Advanced Industrial Society: From Class-Based Politics to Quality-of-Life Politics,' *Government and Opposition* 21 (4) pp. 456–79.

JÄCKEL, G. (1984) 'Umerziehung des deutschen Volkes' *Nation Europa* 34 (September) pp. 22–26.

JAGER, M. (1986) 'Class Definition and the Esthetics of Gentrification: Victoriana in Melbourne,'in N. Smith and P. Williams (eds) *Gentrification of the City* (Boston: Allan & Unwin).

JAMESON, F. (1984) 'Postmoderism or The Cultural Logic of Late Capitalism' *New Left Review* 146 pp. 52–92.

JANSEN, M. (1987) '"Motherhood is Beautiful"' *Kommune* 5 (June) pp. 66–70.

JAY, M. (1984) *Marxism & Totality* (Berkeley and Los Angeles: University of California Press).

JENCKS, C. (1987) *What is Postmodernism?* 2nd ed. (New York: St Martin's Press).

JOFFE, J. (1989) 'The Revisionists' *The National Interest* (Fall) pp. 41–54.

JONES, B. (1982) *Sleepers, Wake! Technology and the Future of Work* (Melbourne: Oxford University Press).

JUNGK, R. (1979) *Der Atomstaat* (Reinbek bei Hamburg: Rowhohlt).
JURTSCHITSCH, E. and RIECKMANN, P. (1987) 'Rau macht flau—oder der Vernichtungsfeldzug der SPD gegen die GRÜNEN,' pp. 57–70 in E. Jurtschitsch, A. Rudnick and F. Otto Wolf (eds.) *Grünes & Alternatives Jahrbuch 1986–87* (Berlin: Verlag für Ausbildung u. Studium in der Elefanten Press).
KAES, A. (1989) *From Hitler to Heimat. The Return of History as Film* (Cambridge: Harvard University Press).
KAISER, M. (1981) "Berufliche Situation von Jungakademikern." *Materialien aus der Arbeitsmarkt- und Berufsforschung* 6/1981.
KATZENSTEIN, P. J. (1987) *Policy and Politics in West Germany* (Philadelphia: Temple University Press).
— (1982) 'West Germany as Number Two: Reflections on the German Model,' pp. 199–213 in A. Markovits (ed) *The Political Economy of West Germany* (New York: Praeger).
KELLNER, D. (1988) 'Postmodernism as Social Theory: Some Challenges and Problems' *Theory, Culture & Society* 5 pp. 239–69.
KELLNER, H. and HEUBERGER, F. (1988) 'Zur Rationalität der "Postmoderne" und ihrer Träger,' pp. 325–37 in *Soziale Welt* Sonderband 6: Kultur und Alltag.
KELLY, P. (1983) *Um Hoffnung kämpfen* (Bornheim-Merten: Lamuv).
KERN, H. and SCHUMANN, M. (1989) 'New Concepts of Production in West German Plants,' pp. 87–110 in P. Katzenstein (ed) *Industry and Politics in West Germany* (Ithaca and London: Cornell University Press).
KIRFEL, M. AND OSWALT, W. (eds.) (1989) *Die Rückkehr der Führer* (Vienna, Zurich: EuropaVerlag).
KITSCHELT, H. (1989) *The Logics of Party Formation* (Ithaca, London: Cornell University Press).
KLÖNNE, A. (1987) 'Bundestagswahl, Historiker-Debatte und 'Kulturrevolution von rechts" *Blätter für deutsche und internationale Politik* 32 (March) pp. 285–295.
— (1984) *Zurück zur Nation?* (Cologne: Diederichs).
KLAUDERER, W. (1990) 'Längerfristige Arbeitsmarktperspektiven' *Aus Politik und Zeitgeschichte* B3/90 (January) pp. 21–36.
KLOTZSCH, L. and STöSS, R. (1984) 'Die Grünen,' pp. 1509–1598 in R. Stöss (ed) *Parteienhandbuch der Bundesrepublik Deutschland 1945–1980*, 2 vols. (Opladen: Westdeutscher Verlag).
KÖRFGEN, P. (1978) 'Warum sie sich verweigern' *Merkur* 32 (10) pp. 993–1009.
KOLINSKY, E. (1989) 'Women in the Green Party,' pp. 189–221 in E. Kolinsky (ed) *The Greens in West Germany: Organisation and Policy Making* (Oxford: Berg Publishers).
KOSLOWSKI, P. (1989) 'Risikogesellschaft als Grenzerfahrung der Moderne. Für eine post-moderne Kultur' *Aus Politik und Zeitgeschichte* B36/89 (September) pp. 14–30.
KRAIS, B. (1980) 'Der deutsche Akademiker und die Bildugsexpansion oder Auflösung einer Kaste' *Soziale Welt* 31 (1) pp. 68–87.
KRAUS, H.-C. (1986) 'Habermas in der Defensive,' *Criticon* 98 (November/December) pp. 268–70.

KRAUSE, C., DETLEF, L. and SCHERER, K.-J. (1980) *Zwischen Revolution und Resignation?* (Bonn: Verlag Neue Gesellschaft).

KREBS, P. (1987) 'Die erste Partei des Geistes' *elemente* 2 (January/February) p. 2.

— (1982) *Die europäische Wiedergeburt.* Thule-Forum, no. 2 (Tübingen: Grabert).

— (1981) 'Aufruf zur europäischen Selbstbesinnung' *Nation Europa* 31 (November) pp. 3–12.

KREUTZ, H. and FRöHLICH, G. (1986) 'Von der alternativen Bewegung zum selbstverwalteten Betrieb' *Mitteilungen aus der Arbeits- und Berufsforschung* 19 (4) pp. 553–64.

KRIESI, H. (1989) 'New Social Movements and the New Class in the Netherlands' *American Journal of Sociology* 94 (5) pp. 1078–116.

KROKER, A. and COOK, D. (1986) *The Postmodern Scene* (New York: St Martin's Press).

KROKER, A. and KROKER, M. (eds.) (1987) *Body Invaders. Panic Sex in America* (New York: St Martin's Press).

KÜCK, M. (1985) 'Alternative Ökonomie in der Bundesrepublik' *Aus Politik und Zeitgeschichte* B32/85 (August) pp. 26–38.

KÜNAST, R. (1983) *Umweltzerstörung und Ideologie* (Tübingen: Grabert).

KUTSCHKE, J. (1989) 'Sie leiden nicht und haben kein Mitleid' *Der Spiegel* no.13, pp. 72–75.

LAFFERTY, W. M. and KNUTSEN, O. (1984) 'Leftist and Rightist Ideology in a Social Democratic State: An Analysis of Norway in the Midst of the Conservative Resurgence' *British Journal of Political Science* 14 (3) pp. 345–67.

LANGGUTH, G. (1984) *Protestbewegung* 2nd ed. (Cologne: Verlag Wissenschaft und Politik).

LANGNER, M. (ed) (1987) *Die Grünen auf dem Prüfstand.* (Bergisch Gladbach: Lübbe).

LASCH, C. (1984) *The Minimal Self: Psychic Survival in Troubled Times* (New York: Norton).

LASH, S. and URRY, J. (1987) *The End of Organized Capitalism* (Cambridge: Polity Press).

LAUBENHEIMER, R. (1979) 'Sozialismus, Ökologie und Nationalismus— Grundelemente menschlicher Selbstbefreiung' *wir selbst* (December), no page.

LAWSON, K. and MERKL, P. H. (eds) (1988) *When Parties Fail* (Princeton: Princeton University Press).

LEGGEWIE, C. (1989) *Die Republikaner* (Berlin: Rotbuch Verlag).

— (1987) 'Kulturelle Hegemonie—Gramsci und die Folgen' *Leviathan* 15 (2) pp. 285–304.

— (1987a) *Der Geist steht rechts*, Berlin: Rotbuch Verlag.

LEINEMANN, J. (1989) 'Biedermann und Brandstifter' *Der Spiegel*, no.22, pp. 45–56.

LEPSZY, N. (1989) 'Die Republikaner' *Aus Politik und Zeitgeschichte* B41–42 (October) pp. 3–9.

LIEBAU, E. (1984) 'Academic Study and Prospects for Life: Observations and Reflections on the Contemporary Situation of West German Students' *European Journal of Education* 19 (3) pp. 269–82.

LINSE, U. (1986) *Ökopax und Anarchie* (Munich: DTV).

LÖWENTHAL, R. (1981) 'Identität und Zukunft der SPD' *Die neue Gesellschaft/Frankfurter Hefte* 28 (12) pp. 1085–9.

— (1977) 'On the Disaffection of Western Intellectuals' *Encounter* 49 (July) pp. 6–13.

LOHMAN, H.-M. (1979–1980) 'Society Versus the State,' trans. by J. Daniel. *Telos* 42 (Winter) pp. 124–9.

LYOTARD, F. (1984) *The Postmodern Condition: A Report on Knowledge*, trans. by G. Bennington and B. Massumi (Minneapolis: University of Minnesota Press).

MAIER, C. (ed) (1987) *Changing Boundaries of the Political* (Cambridge: Cambridge University Press).

MAREN-GRISEBACH, M. (1982) *Die Philosophie der Grünen* (Munich: Olzog).

MARMORA, L. (1985) 'Die Grün-Alternativen zwischen "altem" Internationalismus und "neuem" Patriotismus—oder was ist "nationale Identität" ,' pp. 106–13 in Günter Hopfenmüller (ed) *Reader zum 1. Internationalismus-Kongress der Grünen, Kassel, 4./5./6. Oktober 1985* (Bonn: Die Grünen).

MARTIN, B. (1989) 'Symbolic Knowledge and Market Forces: Qualitative Market Researcher and Social Workers at the Frontiers of Post-Modernism' (Unpublished Manuscript).

MASCHKE, G. (1987) *Der Tod des Carl Schmitt* (Vienna: Karolinger Verlag).

— (1987a) 'Sterbender Konservatismus und Wiedergeburt der Nation,' pp. 359–371 in *Der Pfahl. Jahrbuch aus dem Niemandsland zwischen Kunst und Wissenschaft*, no. 1 (Munich: Matthes & Seitz).

— (1986) 'Die Verschwörung der Flakhelfer,' pp. 152–176 in J. Baudrillard, *Die göttliche Linke* (Munich: Matthes & Seitz).

MAYER, M. (1978) 'The German October of 1977' *New German Critique*. 13 (Winter) pp. 155–63.

MAYER-TASCH, P. C. (1976) *Die Bürgerinitiativbewegung* (Reinbek bei Hamburg: Rowohlt).

MEGILL, A. (1987) *Prophets of Extremity* (Berkeley, Los Angeles, London: University of California Press).

MEINRAD, M. (1973) 'Das Prinzip Nationalismus' *Junge Kritik* 3 pp. 7–16.

MELUCCI, A. (1980) 'The New Social Movements: A Theoretical Approach' *Social Science Information* 19 (2) pp. 199–226.

MILLS, C.A. (1988) '"Life on the Upslope" : The Postmodern Landscape of Gentrificaton' *Environment and Planning D: Society and Space* 6 pp. 169–89.

MINKENBERG, M. and INGLEHART, R. 'Neoconservatism and Value Change in the USA: Tendencies in the Mass Public of a Postindustrial Society,' in J. R. Gibbins (ed) *Contemporary Political Culture* (Newbury Park: Sage).

MINKS, K.-H. and REISSERT, R. (1985) *Der Übergang vom Studium in den Beruf*. HIS Kurzinformationen A 1/85 (Hannover: Hoschschul-Informations-System GmbH).

MOHLER, A. (1988) 'Entsorgung der Postmoderne,' *Criticon* 106 (March/April) pp. 81–3.
— (1987) 'Nachlese zur "Postmoderne"' *Criticon* 99 (January/February) pp. 38–9.
— (1986) 'Was ist "postmodern"?' *Criticon* 96 (July/August) pp. 157–61.
— (1982) 'Deutsche Aussenpolitik,' pp. 37–101 in *Deutsche Identität.* edition d, no. 5. (Krefeld: Sinus).
— (1981) 'Die nominalistische Wende; ein Credo' pp. 53–74 in P. Krebs (ed) *Das unvergängliche Erbe* (Tübingen: Grabert).
— (1981a) *Wider die All-Gemeinheiten oder das Besondere ist das Wirkliche.* Edition d, no. 1 (Krefeld: Sinus).
MÜLLER-ROMMEL, F. (1989) 'The West German Greens in the 1980s: Short-Term Cyclical Protest or Indicator of Transformation?' *Political Studies* (37 (March) pp. 114–22.
— (1985) 'Social Movements and the Greens: New Internal Politics in Germany' *European Journal of Political Research* 13 (March) pp. 53–67.
MURPHY, D. (1986) 'Realos und Fundis, Ökosozialisten und Ökolibertäre. Politische Strömungen und innerparteilicher Konflikt bei den GRÜNEN' *Gegenwartskunde*, no.1, pp. 99–107.
MUSHABEN, J. (1985–86) 'Innocence Lost: Environmental Images and Political Experiences Among the West German Greens' *New Political Science* 14 (Winter) pp. 39–66.
NARR, W.-D. (1987) 'Ausnahmezustand und Normalität' *links* 19 (November) pp. 14–17.
NATH, C. (1986) 'Wider die Eindimensionalität. Aktualität und Perspektiven oppositioneller Bewegungen in der Bundesrepublik,' pp. 73–91 in *Wege des Ungehorsams.* Jahrbuch II für libertäre & gewaltfreie Aktion, Politik & Kultur 1986 (Kassel-Bettenhausen: Weber, Zucht & Co).
NOELLE-NEUMANN, E. (1989) *Die Republikaner.* Dokumentation des Beitrags in der Frankfurter Allgemeinen Zeitung Nr. 210 vom 11, September 1989 (Allensbach: Institut für Demoskopie).
— (1983) *Eine demoskopische Deutschstunde* (Osnabrück: Fromm).
— and PIEL, E. (eds.) (1983) *Allensbacher Jahrbuch der Demoskopie 1978–1983* (Munich: Saur).
NOWAK, J. (1979) ' "Alternative Liste" in Berlin' *Die Neue Gesellschaft* 26 (11) pp. 1032–5.
OBST, W. (1987) 'Bonn vor der nationalen Frage' *Criticon* 102 (July/August) pp. 149–52.
OECD (1972) *Review of National Policies for Education: Germany* (Paris: OECD).
ÖSER, K. (1978) 'Politische Strömungen in der "Ökologie-Bewegung",' pp. 92–104 in R. Brun (ed) *Der grüne Protest* (Frankfurt: Fischer).
OFFE, C. (1987) 'Challenging the Boundaries of Institutional Politics: Social Movements Since the 1960s,' pp. 63–105 in C. Maier (ed) *Changing Boundaries of the Political* (Cambridge: Cambridge University Press).
— (1985) *Disorganized Capitalism* (Cambridge, MA: MIT Press).
OPIELKA, M. and ZANDER, M. (1988) *Freiheit von Armut* (Essen: Klartext).

PAPADAKIS, E. (1984) *The Green Movement in West Germany* (New York: St Martin's Press).

PATERSON, W. E. and THOMAS, A. H. (eds.) (1986) *The Future of Social Democracy* (Oxford: Clarendon Press).

PATERSON, W. E. (1986) 'The German Social Democratic Party,' pp. 127–152 in W. E. Paterson and A. H. Thomas (eds.) *The Future of Social Democracy* (Oxford: Clarendon Press).

PIORE, M. and SABEL, C. (1984) *The Second Industrial Divide* (New York: Basic Books).

POSTER, M. (1989) *Critical Theory and Poststructuralism* (Ithaca: Cornell University Press).

RASCHKE, J. (1985) 'Soziale Konflikte und Parteiensystem in der Bundesrepublik' *Aus Politik und Zeitgeschichte* B49/85 pp. 22–39.

REICHEL, P. (1981) *Politische Kultur der Bundesrepublik* (Opladen: Leske und Budrich).

DIE REPUBLIKANER (1990) *Parteiprogramm 1990*. Draft, Bonn.

— (1987) *Programm der Republikaner 1987* Munich.

— (1987a) 'Das Siegburger Manifest, verabschiedet auf dem Bundesparteitag am 16. Juni 1987' Bonn.

— (1983) *Grundsatzprogramm der Republikaner*, Bonn.

RICHTER, C. (ed) (1979) *Die überflüssige Generation* (Königstein: Athenäum Verlag).

ROCHE, R. (1984) 'Graffiti—Sprachliche Wirkungsmuster und Aktionsziele einer Kontrakultur' *Aus Politik und Zeitgeschichte* B21/84 (May) pp. 29–44.

RÖNSCH, H -D. (1983) 'Die Grünen: Wählerbasis, politische Entwicklung, Programmatik' *Gewerkschaftliche Monatshefte* 34 (February) pp. 98–111.

— (1980) 'Die Grünen: einmaliges Wahlrisiko oder soziale Bewegung?' *Gewerkschaftliche Monatshefte* 31 (August) pp. 500–10.

— (1980a) 'Grüne Listen—Vorläufer oder Katalysatoren einer neuen Protestbewegung?' pp. 375–434 in O. Rammstedt (ed) *Bürgerinitiativen in der Gesellschaft* Argumente in der Energiediskussion, vol. 9 (Villingen, Neckar-Verlag).

ROTH, R. and RUCHT, D. (eds.) (1987) *Neue soziale Bewegungen in der Bundesrepublik Deutschland* (Bonn: Bundeszentrale für politische Bildung).

RÖTTGEN, H. and RABE, F. (1981) *Vulkantänze*. 3rd. ed. (Munich: Trikont).

ROHRMOSER, G. (1987) 'Genügt Optimismus? Konservatismus in der Kulturkrise,' *MUT* 239 (July) pp. 24–37.

— (1987a) 'Ist der politische Konservatismus in Deutschland am Ende?' *MUT* 241 (September) pp. 31–9.

ROTH, D. (1989) 'What is Happening to the German Party System? Interpretations of the Results of Right Wing Parties in Germany's Recent Elections' Paper presented at the Fourth Pacific Workshop on German Affairs, California State University, Long Beach.

— (1989a) 'Sind die Republikaner die fünfte Partei?' *Aus Politik und Zeitgeschichte*, B41–42 (October) pp. 10–20.

— (1986) 'Der Einfluss ökonomischer Faktoren auf die Wahlentscheidung' *Politische Bildung* 19 (2) pp. 59–75.

ROTH, R. A. (1989) 'Dispositionen politischen Verhaltens bei arbeitslosen Jugendlichen,' *Aus Politik und Zeitgeschichte* B29/89 (July 14 1989) pp. 25–38.

ROTHKIRCH, C. v. and WEIDIG, I. (1986) *Zum Arbeitskräftebedarf nach Qualifikationen bis zum Jahr 2000*. Beiträge zur Arbeitsmarkt- und Berufsforschung 95, (Nürnberg: Bundesanstalt für Arbeit).

RÜDIG, W. (1985–86) 'Eco-Socialism: Left Environmentalism in West Germany' *New Political Science* 14 (Winter) pp. 3–37.

SANDBERG, J.-U. (1983) 'Zwischen Legitimation und Kritik. Vorstellungen von Akademikern, Studenten und Bevölkerung zur sozialen Ungleichheit' *Zeitschrift für Soziologie* 12 (July) pp. 181–202.

SARKAR, S. (1986) 'The Green Movement in West Germany' *Alternatives* 11 (April) pp. 220–54.

SCHLAUCH, W. (1989) 'West Germany, the United States and the Dismantling of the East-West Conflict in Europe' Paper delivered at the 30th Annual Convention of the International Studies Association, London, March/April.

SCHLICHT, U. (1980) *Vom Burschenschafter bis zum Sponti* (Berlin: Colloquium Verlag).

SCHMID, T. (ed) (1986) *Befreiung von falscher Arbeit* (Berlin: Wagenbach Verlag).

— (1983) 'Über die Schwierigkeiten der Grünen, in Gesellschaft zu leben und zu denken' *Freibeuter* 15 pp. 44–55.

SCHMIERER, J. (1990) 'Kurz-Schlüsse' *Kommune* 8 (March) pp. 6–9.

— (1985) 'Das deutsche Weltmachtsprojekt gründlich zerschlagen' *Kommune* 3 (May) pp. 5–7.

SCHNÄDELBACH, H. (1984) *Philosophy in Germany 1831–1933*, translated by Eric Matthews (Cambridge: Cambridge University Press).

SCHNAPPERTZ, J. (1988) 'NATO-Austritt oder Auflösung der Militärbündnisse—Wie die NATO-Austrittsforderung populär wurde,' *Kommune* 6 (January) pp. 59–62.

— (1988a) 'Statt Nationalismus kosmo-politische Integration,' *Kommune* 6 (March) pp. 33–6.

— (1985) 'Von Blockaden, Blockierungen und Blockübergreifendem' *Grüne Rheinland/Pfälzer* no.4, pp. 3–4.

SCHNEIDER, D. (1985) 'Das Anerkennen der Grenzen und der Zweistaatlichkeit ist die Voraussetzung um friedenspolitisch in Europa weiterarbeiten zu können' *European Mobilisation for Survival Bulletin* no.17, pp. 15–23.

SCHNEIDER, P. (1973) *Lenz* (Berlin: Rotbuch Verlag).

SCHNEIDER, M. (1977) 'Von der alten Radikalität zur neuen Sensibilität' *Kursbuch* 49 (October) pp. 174–187.

SCHÖNHUBER, Franz (1989) 'Kein Mut zu neuen Wegen,' *wir selbst* (December/January) p. 14.

SCHRENCK-NOTZING, Caspar von (1985) 'Editorial' *Criticon* 90 (July/August) p. 143.

SCHÜLEIN, J. A. (1983) 'Normalität und Opposition. Über Ursachen und gesellschaftliche Funktionen der "Alternativbewegung"' *Leviathan* 11 (2) pp. 252–74.

— (1979) 'Von der Studentenrevolte zur Tendenzwende oder der Rückzug ins Private,' pp. 265–76 in H. Glaser (ed) *Fluchtpunkt Jahrhundertwende. Ursprünge und Aspekte einer zukünftigen Gesellschaft* (Bonn: Hohwacht).

SCHULTZE, R. O. (1987) 'Die Bundestagswahl 1987—eine Bestätigung des Wandels' *Aus Politik und Zeitgeschichte* B12/87 (March) pp. 3–17.

SCHWAB, G. (1969) *Der Tanz mit dem Teufel* (Hameln, Hannover: Sponholtz).

SEIFFERT, W. (1986) *Das ganze Deutschland* (Munich: Piper).

— (1984) 'Der deutsche "Faktor". Bilanz und Perspektiven der deutschen Teilung' *Information für die Truppe*, no.10, pp. 13–28.

SIEFERLE, R. P. (1984) *Fortschrittsfeinde?* Munich: C.H. Beck.

SIEGERT, J., ULRICH, B., HIRSCH, J. and KÜHLE, M. (1986) *Wenn das Spielbein dem Standbein ein Bein stellt* ... (Kassel-Bettenhausen: Weber, Zucht & Co).

SINGER, H. (1971) 'Basis für eine neue Politik?' *Nation Europa* 21 (June) pp. 35–8.

SINUS-INSTITUT (1983) *Die verunsicherte Generation* (Opladen: Leske und Budrich).

SLOTERDIJK, P. (1987) *Critique of Cynical Reason*, trans. by M. Eldred (Minneapolis: University of Minnesota Press).

SMITH, N. (1987) 'Of Yuppies and Housing: Gentrification, Social Structuring, and the Urban Dream' *Environment and Planning D: Society and Space* 5 pp. 151–72.

SONTHEIMER, K. (1976) *Das Elend unserer Intellektuellen* (Hamburg: Hoffman und Campe).

SONTHEIMER, M. (1988) 'Rebellion ist gerechtfertigt' *Aus Politik und Zeitgeschichte* B 20/88 pp. 36–46.

STAMM, K.-H. (1988) *Alternative Öffentlichkeit* (Frankfurt, New York: Campus).

STEIN, T. (1988) 'Sind die Grünen postmodern? Ist die Postmoderne grün?' *Kommune* 6 (June) p. 12.

STEVICK, P. (1985) 'Literature,' pp. 135–156 in S. Trachtenberg (ed) *The Postmodern Moment* (Westport: Greenwood Press).

STÖSS, R. (1988) 'The Problem of Right-Wing Extremism in West Germany' *West European Politics* 11 (April) pp. 34–46.

— (1980) *Vom Nationalismus zum Umweltschutz* (Opladen: Westdeutscher Verlag).

— (1978) 'Väter und Enkel: Alter und Neuer Nationalismus in der Bundesrepublik' *Ästhetik & Kommunikation* 9 (June) pp. 35–57.

STORR, R. (1984) 'Desperate Pleasures' *Art in America* 72 (10) pp. 124–30.

STRATMANN, E. (1985) 'Made in Germany: Vom Weltmarkt zum Binnenmarkt,' pp. 327–349 in F. Beckenbach, J. Müller, R. Pfriem and E. Stratmann, *Grüne Wirtschaftspolitik* (Cologne: Kiepenheuer & Witsch).

STRAUSS, B. (1982) *Paare Passanten* 6th ed (Munich: Hanser).

STRAUSS, W. (1984) 'Nihilismus in Grün—Lieblingsprodukt der Systemmedien' *Nation Europa* 9 (September) pp. 41–49.

STROHM, Holger (1978) 'Warum die Bunten bunt sind,' pp. 126–138 in R. Brun (ed) *Der Grüne Protest* (Frankfurt: Fischer).

TEICHLER, U. (1982) 'Recent Developments in Higher Education in the Federal Republic of Germany' *European Journal of Education* 17 (2) pp. 161–76.

TESSARING, M. (1989) 'Beschäftigungssituation und -perspektiven für Hochschulabsolventen' *Aus Politik und Zeitgeschichte* B50/89 pp. 14–24.

TÜRK, H. J. (1988) 'Zeitenwende in der Philosophie? Aufklärung, Postmoderne und New Age' *Stimmen der Zeit* 113 (March) pp. 147–63.

UHLITZ, O. (1987) 'Deutsches Volk oder "multikulturelle Gesellschaft"?' pp. 51–110 in H. Fischer (ed) *Aspekte der Souveränität* (Kiel: Arndt Verlag).

ULLRICH, O. (1984) 'Abschied vom Mythos der Grossen Maschine,' pp. 54–60 in W. Dirks, G. Erb, E. Kogon and F. W. Menne (eds.) *Nach 1984: Die Krise der Zivilisation und unsere Zukunft* (Frankfurter Hefte-extra 6, Frankfurt).

— (1983) 'Vom leichtfertigen Umgang mit wichtigen Themen' *Politische Vierteljahresschrift* 24 (December) pp. 445–9.

— (1979) *Weltniveau* (Berlin: Rotbuch Verlag).

ULRICH, Bernd (1988) 'Too Old to Rock'n'Roll Too Young to Die—Die 68er Generation oder Wie eine Generation anfing mir auf den Geist zu gehen' *Kommune* 6 (4) pp. 28–35.

VEEN, H.-J. (1989) '"Programm" und "Wähler" der Republikaner— Etablierung noch offen' *Eichholzbrief*, no.4, pp. 53–65.

— (1987) 'Die Anhänger der GRÜNEN—Ausprägungen einer neuen linken Milieupartei,' pp. 60–127 in M. Langner (ed) *Die Grünen auf dem Prüfstand* (Bergisch Gladbach: Lübbe).

— (1985) 'Die Wähler und Repräsentanten der Grünen: Zwischen aktuellem Protest und einer ganz anderen Republik' *Eichholzbrief* no.1, pp. 9–22.

— (1984) 'Wer wählt grün?' *Aus Politik und Zeitgeschichte* B35–36/84 (September) pp. 3–17.

VENOHR, W. (1982) *Die deutsche Einheit Kommt Bestimmt* (Bergisch Gladback: Lübbe).

— (ed) (1985) *Ohne Deutschland geht es nicht.* edition d, no. 10 (Krefeld: Sinus).

— (1982) 'Die Herrschenden und der neue Patriotismus' *Die Neue Gesellschaft* 28 (August) pp. 725–7.

VESTER, M. (1983) 'Die "Neuen Plebejer",' pp. 213–224 in H.-H. Hartwich (ed) *Gesellschaftliche Probleme als Anstoss und Folge von Politik* (Opladen: Westdeutscher Verlag).

VINCENT, J.-M. (1985) 'Pourquois L'Extreme-Droite?' *Les Temps Modernes* 41 (April 1985) pp. 1773–9.

VOIGT, K. (1986) 'Der Mythos des politischen Kontinuität' *Die neue Gesellschaft/Frankfurter Hefte* 33 (June) pp. 484–9.

VON BERG, H. (1987) 'Deutschland braucht einen Friedensvertrag,' pp. 129–152 in H. Fischer (ed) *Aspekte der Souveränität* (Kield: Arndt Verlag).

— (1986) *Marxismus-Leninismus* (Cologne: Bund-Verlag).

VON HELLFELD, M. (ed) (1989) *Dem Hass keine Chance* (Cologne: Pahl-Rugenstein).

VON KLIPSTEIN, M. and STRÜMPEL, B. (1985) 'Wertewandel und Wirtschaftsbild der Deutschen' *Aus Politik und Zeitgeschichte* B42/85 (October) pp. 19–38.

— (1984) *Der Überdruss am Überfluss* (Munich: Olzog).

WEINBERGER, M.-L. (1984) *Aufbruch zu neuen Ufern? Grün-Alternative zwischen Anspruch und Wirklichkeit* (Bonn: Neue Gesellschaft).

WEISSMANN, K. (1988) 'Die Achtundsechziger/ II. Teil' *MUT* 250 (June) pp. 47–51.

— (1986) 'Neo-Konservatismus in der Bundesrepublik?' *Criticon* 96 (July/ August) pp. 176–9.

WELLBERY, D. E. (1985) 'Postmodernism in Europe: On Recent German Writing,' pp. 229–49 in S. Trachtenberg (ed) *The Postmodern Moment* (Westport: Greenwood Press).

WELLMER, A. (1985) *Zur Dialektik von Moderne und Postmoderne* (Frankfurt: Surkamp).

— (1981) 'Terrorism and Social Criticism,' trans. by D. J. Parent, *Telos* 48 (Summer) pp. 65–89.

WILLMS, B. (1986) *Idealismus und Nation* (Paderborn: Schoeningh).

— (1984) 'Kampf um Selbstbehauptung' *Nation Europa* 34 (October/ November) pp. 7–19.

— (1984a) 'Politische Ideengeschichte, Politikwissenschaft und Philosophie,' pp. 33–64 in Udo Bermbach (ed) *Politische Theoriengeschichte*, Politische Vierteljahresschrift, Sonderheft 15/1984 (Opladen: Westdeutscher Verlag).

— (1982) *Die Deutsche Nation* (Cologne-Lövenich: 'Hohenheim').

WOLIN, R. (1984–85) 'Modernism vs. Postmodernism' *Telos* 62 (Winter) pp. 9–29.

Zwei Kulturen? Tunix, Mescalero und die Folgen (no date) (Berlin: Ästhetik und Kommunikation Verlag).

Index

Abortion 62, 85
  Republikaner view on 119
Achberg Circle 47
Action Unity of Independent
  Germans (AUD) 44, 48
  and APO 49, 50
  and Green position on German
    question 136
  membership 51
  and new nationalism 98
  and SPV 53–4
Alternative lists 56–61
Alternative movement 38–40
  size of 40
Ammon, Herbert 137
Anti-Americanism, and the new
  right 102, 129
Authoritarian materialism 113

Bahro, Rudolf
  and Green party 60, 81
  and holistic thinking 84
  and Marxism 28
Baudrillard, Jean 5–7
Bunte lists 56–61
Beck, Ulrich 17, 159, 167
Beuys, Joseph 48
Body, and resistance 32–3
Bourdieu, Pierre 13
Brandt, Peter 137
Brandt, Willy 19

Christian Social Union (CSU)
  and Republikaner 89, 110–11,
    125
Citizen initiatives 56
Cohn-Bendit, Daniel 35, 58
Communist Federation (KB) 58
Culture 10–11
  and anthroposophy 47

Disorganized capitalism 135
Dissatisfaction with parties 112

Diwald, Hellmut 103, 130
Dutschke, Rudi 25

East German emigrants 122
  general attitude towards 123–4
  Green attitudes towards 153
East German revolution 133, 143
  Green response to 154
Eastern territories 126
  views on loss 130
Eibl-Eibesfeldt 94, 95
Eichberg, Henning 99, 102
  and national identity 100
Enzensberger, Hans Magnus 27
Ethnic German resettlers 122
  general attitude towards 122–5
  Green attitudes towards 153
European Community
  attitudes towards 148–50
  Green view on 146–8
  Republikaner view on 126–7
European integration 18
  Republikaner view on 127
  Green view on 145–8, 155

Featherstone, Mike 7, 12, 161
Fischer, Joschka 23, 25, 59
Flexible specialization 11, 14, 159
Foreign workers, attitudes
  towards 152–3

German Communist Party
  (DKP) 20
German Community (DG) 49, 98
German confederation 101–2, 168
  Green conception of 155
  national–neutralist conception
    of 138
German Fall 20, 37, 56
German–Polish border
  attitude towards 130
  Green view on 154

German unification   18, 107, 168
  attitudes towards   125, 140–1,
    144–5
  dialectic of   126
  in exchange for neutrality   130
  views on   128
  Green opposition to   144, 153–5,
    169
Germany as occupied country   102
Glucksman, André   100
Gorbachev, Mikhail   131, 133
  attitudes towards   128
Green Action Future (GAZ)   44–5
  membership   45
  and SPV   53–4
Green List for the Protection of the
    Environment (GLU)   44–5, 53
Green postmodern politics
  definition   81
  goals   82–83
  and nature of work   86–7
Greens, Green party   4, 10, 16, 18,
    42–88 *passim*
  and new politics   15
  and postmodern politics   42, 64
  and 78-generation   80
  and 68-generation   79–80
Gruhl, Herbert   44–7, 52, 62
  and SPV   53–61
Guaranteed minimum
    income   86–87

Habermas, Jürgen   3, 15–16, 34,
    133, 134, 160
  new right attacks on   108
Haussleiter, August   44, 48–51
  and CSU   48, 50
  and National Socialism   49–50
  and SPV   53–54
Haverbeck, Werner   44
  and National Socialism   52
'Heidelberger Manifesto'   96
Historikerstreit   120, 133
Hostility towards foreigners   122
Hutcheon, Linda   5, 10, 59

Identity
  contextualized   10
  crisis of   97

German   107, 123, 134, 139, 160
  left-libertarian conception of   134,
    135, 165
  national   4, 91–2, 94, 96, 98, 102,
    103, 118–19, 121, 134, 146,
    156, 169
  national-democratic   137
  and new left   24–6, 33
  personal   30,
INF decision   97, 103, 121, 128
  Green response to   137, 140–5
Inglehart, Ronald   15, 65–7, 69–70,
    113, 150
Irrationalism   31–32

Jameson, Fredric   5–7, 12
  on commodification   6
  on Marxism   7
Jungk, Robert   48, 56

Kampuchea   25–6
Kohl, Helmut   107, 122, 125, 128,
    143
Krebs, Pierre   93–94, 102–3

Left-libertarian politics
  and the Greens   55–6, 60–2, 150,
    153, 163
  and unification   169
Left-libertarian values
  and postmaterialism   69–70
  and international politics   157
Löwenthal, Richard   63, 158
Lyotard, Jean-François   8–9, 84, 92

Maoism   22, 57
Maoist parties   23, 58
  and German question   136–7
Marginalization   17, 65
  and support for the Greens   71–7,
    80
  and alternative movement   75
Marginalized groups, Green appeal
    to   82, 83
Marxism
  and disillusionment   21, 24, 26
  and emancipation   9
  and Greens   81

and new left 23, 27
and new right 92
Medium range missiles 61
Melucci, Alberto 33
Minority rights 15, 153
Modernity 3, 5, 28, 41, 166
  attack on 28, 161
  end of 8–9
  Green oposition to 80–1, 87
  and right-wing radicalism 91, 108
Modernization losers 115, 131
Mohler, Armin 92–3
Multicultural Europe 146, 151, 156
Multicultural society
  and left-libertarian politics 165
  and new right 91, 97
  Republikaner attacks on 122
Mysticism, and new left 32

National Democratic Party
  (NPD) 20, 89–90, 96, 98, 110,
  112
National question 121
  Green views on 135–140
National revolutionaries 95, 99
National Socialism, Nazism 31,
  49–50, 52, 63, 91, 120, 158
NATO 18, 97
  demand for dissolution of 61
  and German sovereignty 128
  Green view on 140–5
  Republikaner view on 121, 126,
  128
New left 9, 18, 21
  and Green party 43, 56, 59, 63
  and identity 25, 31
  and internationalism 24–6
  and mysticism 32
  and state 33–4, 56
  and subjectivity 29, 32, 34
New middle class
  and CDU 107
  definition 66
  and postmaterialism 66–7
New nationalists 98
New politics 4, 10, 15
  and Green party 59, 80, 82
  and right-wing radicalism 118

New right
  French 3
  German 3, 4, 97, 108
  parties 18
  radicalism 18
New sensibility 3, 30
New service class
  definition 12, 16–17
  and left-libertarian values 70–1,
  87
  and new social movements 161
  and non-materialist values 70–1
  and postmaterialism 65–71
  and postmodern politics 64, 71
  and postmodernism 12–14
  and support for the Greens 67,
  80, 162
  and the welfare state 70
New social movements 3, 4, 10, 18
  and commodification 34
  goals of 16
  and Green politics 66
  and new politics 15
  supporters of 16
Nominalism 92–3
Non-materialist values 65, 67
  definition 69–70
  and work 69–70
Nuclear energy
  changing views on 64–5
  struggle against 56
Nuclear state 56
Nietzsche, Friedrich 29, 31

Offe, Claus 10, 16, 69, 80
Other Political Union The Greens
  (SPV) 44, 53–5, 59

Party of Democratic Socialism
  (PDS) 169, 170
Pluralism 10, 43
  and new right's conception of
  postmodernism 92
Political resentment 4
Postindustrial society 4, 5, 11, 13,
  17
  criteria for 11–12
  and importance of work 69

Postmaterialism   18, 65
  definition   65, 66
  and new middle class   66
Postmodernism
  ambiguity of   159
  as corrective force   9–11
  as cultural system   1–5
  definition   5–6
  and Jameson   5–7
  and politics   3, 8, 10–12
  and resistance   15, 87, 165
Postmodernity   5
Progress   8, 28
  changing views of   64, 158

Re-education
  new right attack on   102–3
Republikaner attack on   120, 129
Refugees   122
  attitude towards   122–4
  Green support for   150–4
  new right oposition to   90, 93
  and unification   169
Republikaner   4, 89–90, 110–32
    passim, 168
  self-placement of supporters
    of   164
  support for   115–17, 163–4
  value system of supporters   117
Resentment
  politics of   4
  and right-wing radical
    support   113, 123, 168
Right-wing anti-modernism,
  definition   91–2
Right-wing radicalism
  and international politics   157
  potential support for   131
Rüddenklau, Harald   102

Schmid, Thomas   31
Schmidt, Helmut   20, 78, 160
Schmierer, Joscha   146, 153
Schneider, Peter   29
Schönhuber, Franz   110–32 *passim*
  views on Russia   129
Schwab, Günther   51–2
Seiffert, Wolfgang   104, 105–6
Services   11–12

78-generation, and the Greens   77–9
68-generation   19
  and Greens   77–9
  and SPD   21, 78
Sloterdijk, Peter   33
Société de consommation   2, 13
  alternative to   167
  Green attack on   81
Social Democratic Party (SPD)
  and grand coalition   21
  and *Radikalenerlass*   20
Social movements   *see* New social
  movements
Socialist League of German Students
  (SDS)   21, 23
Spirituality   47–48
Soviet Union, new right's view
  of   105–6
Spontis   35–8
  and Green party   58–9
  and Nietzsche   32
Strauss, Botho   26
Strauss, Franz-Josef   110–11, 121
Symbolic specialists, *see* New service
  class

Tendenzwende   29–30
Trikont publishing house   30–1
Tunix congress   36–7
Two-thirds society   114, 161

Ulrich, Bernd   79, 80
Ullrich, Otto   27–8, 31
Unemployment   64
  as a result of unification   126, 169
  and support for the Greens   74–7
  and support for right-wing
    radicalism   114

Values   4
  left-libertarian   15, 18
  new politics   43
  non-materialist   15, 16, 113
  and new right   107
  traditional   113, 118–19, 125
Venohr, Wolfgang   101, 102, 105

Willms, Bernard 103–4
Winkler, Max 54
Women
  foreign women 85, 151, 153
  and Green left-libertarian
    politics 86
  Green politics towards 84–6

and right-wing radical
  politics 118–19
World Federation for the Protection
  of Life (WSL) 44, 51–2, 95

Xenophobia 106